Inclusive Education

Studies in Inclusive Education Series

Series Editor: Roger Slee, Dean of the Graduate School of Education,
University of Western Australia

Actively Seeking Inclusion: Pupils with special needs in mainstream schools
Julie Allan

Inclusive Education: International Voices on Disability and Justice
Edited by Keith Ballard

Inclusive Education:
International Voices on Disability and Justice

Edited by

Keith Ballard

UK   Falmer Press, 1 Gunpowder Square, London, EC4A 3DE
USA   Falmer Press, Taylor & Francis Inc., 325 Chestnut Street, 8th Floor,
        Philadelphia, PA 19106

First published in 1999

A catalogue record for this book is available from the British Library

ISBN 0 7507 0935 9 cased
ISBN 0 7507 0934 0 paper

**Library of Congress Cataloging-in-Publication Data are available on
request**

Jacket design by Caroline Archer

Typeset in 10/12pt Times by
Graphicraft Limited, Hong Kong

*Printed in Great Britain by Biddles Ltd, Guildford and King's Lynn on
paper which has a specified pH value on final paper manufacture of not
less than 7.5 and is therefore 'acid free'.*

Contents

Contents

List of Tables

Series Editor's Preface

Deep into this text Linda Ware, reporting on her research with parents of disabled students experience of inclusion and exclusion, declares:

> 'Among these parents, inclusion was fraught with as much complexity as when it is discussed among educators. Curriculum considerations were core to the debate, the preservation of services as hard-won entitlement, and the unyielding issue of interrupting authority in a functionalist organisation.'

As Keith Ballard makes clear in his introduction to this collection, inclusion is variously understood and theorised. Indeed, I live in the Australian State of Western Australia where the Minister for Education made great fanfare of that State Education Department's inclusion programme. The programme consists of a *bold experiment* of including ten children with intellectual disabilities in regular schools. I am extremely uncomfortable with referring to such policy as inclusive education, given its incremental and conditional quality. What is also clear is the editor's signalling that inclusion and, of course, exclusion is not a realm for the isolated professional consideration of expert educators who can then profess ways ahead based on new models of special educational delivery in new settings. Inclusive education is intensely political. It is about who is in and who is out, about which students are in the educational mainstream and who is consigned to the status of 'others'.

   This collection of chapters has its origins in an initiative of the Special Needs Research Centre at Newcastle University in England. Alan Dyson, Catherine Clark and David Skidmore invited a group of researchers from the United Kingdom, North America, the Netherlands, Norway, New Zealand and Australia to spend an uninterrupted few days (quite a luxury for some of us) discussing each others' position papers on the issue of inclusive education. The gathering has travelled since that time. As a participant in two of the meetings it impresses me in its provocation. Participants frame inclusive education within their different worlds of experience — cultural, professional and personal. The diversity of positions is manifest within these chapters.

   With '*voice*' as the organizing theme, we move from traditional research approaches and reportage of teachers' decision-making processes, to the politics of advocacy and the position of parents in processes of exclusion and inclusion. 'Partisan' research surfaces in the interplay between the author as researcher — parent. Both chapters on parents' voices introduce us, albeit through different approaches to similar questions, to the cultural politics of disablement and inclusion. The book also considers students' and disabled adults' accounts of their educational experiences. Again the theoretical positions and cultural locations of the authors contrast sharply. Though tempted, my purpose here is not to reproduce the editor's introduction to the chapters. Rather I am particularly interested in the way that *Inclusive Education* takes up the central purpose of this book series. This book hosts a continuing conversation which puts a number of counterpoints to challenge, cast doubt over and consequently make the field of inclusive educational theory and practice more robust.

Striking throughout this work is its sense of grounding. In their quest to host a range of voices, the researchers move directly into the field. There is a complex sense of urgency about the work. This urgency is present in the politics of the issues where we share outrage at injustices of exclusion and feel our impatience for social justice. The focus of others on schools; curriculum and teaching approaches, hospitals and service delivery programmes reinforces Ballard's reminder that this is not an 'experiment'.

Roger Slee
Series Editor

research group, that an emphasis on inclusion for disabled students occurs because the people researching and writing about inclusion often come from a background in special education. Yet, as Booth and Ainscow so cogently remind us, the idea of inclusion cannot refer to just some students and not others. To be inclusive requires that we strive to identify and remove all barriers to learning for all children. This means that we must attend to increasing participation not just for disabled students but for all those experiencing disadvantage, whether this results from poverty, sexuality, minority ethnic status, or other characteristics assigned significance by the dominant culture in their society. To achieve this, say Booth and Ainscow, while working to understand inclusion we must give equal attention to understanding and removing the pressures for *exclusion* that exist within the cultures of our schools and society.

Booth and Ainscow (1998) refer to the difficulty of redefining the field from within. In editing the second collection of studies by the group they reported finding that the perspectives of the different researchers and research teams differed even more than might have been anticipated from the discussions at our meetings. Our own professional interests and paradigm commitments get in the way of achieving a common position. The same has proven true for this, the third project by the group, and it is clear that this research cannot be amalgamated in any cumulative, positivist way. What a diversity of work can achieve is to confront us with unfamiliar situations and ideas, and challenge us with interpretations that differ from our own. A lack of certainty is seen as one of the outcomes of creating diverse contexts, and as a stimulant to creativity and collaborative problem solving in inclusive schools (Skrtic, 1995). So too, perhaps, in the research arena (Reinharz, 1990). In any case, the fact that there is no easy summary or resolution may be no bad thing, given the potential importance of the issues involved in inclusive education. As Clark, Dyson and Millward (1995) suggested, to end discriminatory practices and to teach all children well would seem to require that we do not disengage from alternative positions that may help to clarify our purpose and how we are to proceed. The present text, then, offers further material for ongoing debate.

In the meantime, children who are excluded should not have to wait for more discussion or research to determine their fate, and we might elect to see inclusion as a 'value to be followed' rather than as an 'experiment to be tested' (Ferguson and Asch, 1989, p. 137). I think that we should proceed from this position because injustice, in this case state funded public education designed for some of the children in a society but excluding others, is inconsistent with human rights and democratic society. We might proceed with the understanding that, in any case, research may not offer clear evidence of a knowledge base for 'best practice' that could apply across settings, and that such a goal may be neither achievable nor desirable. Teaching is a complex process located within culture, place and the interactions of particular teachers and students. It is not a fixed, static enterprise, and specifying how to proceed may hide the messy reality of classrooms and limit the flexibility needed for ongoing problem solving.

We might also proceed to support efforts towards inclusive education from the position that, although not offering detailed guidelines, research has shown inclusive practice to be supported in schools where there is a culture and philosophy of inclusion (Booth and Ainscow, 1998). In part this seems to involve teachers believing that 'the education of each student is equally important' (Biklen, 1987, p. i; Giangreco, 1997), and understanding that seeing students such as the disabled as 'other' creates the discrimination of 'them' and 'us', valued and not so valued, that is a basis for exclusion. It is also evident that inclusion is enacted within wider social and ideological contexts. This means for many of us that we may need to be explicit about our motives and goals where there is pressure to trade off equity and justice for disabled and other minority students against teacher comfort and school rankings on standardized tests.

The Present Study

The present study set out to further explore these and related issues, and to do so by listening to the voices of those who have direct experience of inclusion and exclusion. Some of these voices, we believed, were rarely evident in the literature, and yet may have much to say on what happens to them at present and what they would wish for the future. In part we were motivated by an awareness that the voice of disabled people was largely excluded from discussion on education, and that disabled students and adults have been defined and categorized by professionals (such as ourselves) whose labels have dominated their lives, hiding their history and identity (Clough and Barton, 1995). Some chapters in this book include the voice of disabled people. Others record the experiences of parents of disabled children, while in other chapters teachers, students and researchers talk of what inclusion and exclusion mean to them in the context of schools that do not cater well for diversity and that, therefore, help create and sustain social and cultural divisions. From this work inclusive education is about confronting all forms of discrimination as part of a concern to develop an inclusive society based on 'social justice, equity and democratic participation' (Barton, 1997, p. 233).

In setting up this, the third project we had collaborated on as a research group, the 16 researchers from seven countries — Scotland, England, America, Norway, the Netherlands, Australia and New Zealand — agreed on a general goal, to attend to 'voices from the inside', focusing on 'the lived experience of people involved in and affected by inclusion'. (It will be evident that, as the person who wrote that statement, I had not, at the time we began this work early in 1996, seen the significance of explicitly attending to the issue of exclusion.) As in our previous collaboration we agreed that people should interpret the research task in their own way. We expected that this might result in a diverse range of studies, given the open-ended option regarding who might be included as participants and that people held different views on the kind of research method that should be applied.

Most of us met together in Auckland, New Zealand, in September 1996 to present our work for group discussion and critique (a report of the meeting was sent to those unable to attend).[2] We asked questions and made suggestions that we thought might help each study communicate its findings and interpretations to a wider audience through our intended publication of this book. Although we meet infrequently, from our previous work and through correspondence we have some idea of our various beliefs and preferences. Nevertheless, as Tony Booth and Mel Ainscow (1998) recorded from our second project, our different and strongly held views on the field of study and on the research methods most appropriate for its investigation meant that in our writing we would continue to represent a diversity of work rather than achieve a more closely coordinated set of chapters, easily related, one to another. I think this is a strength rather than a weakness. Our beliefs and convictions mean that we may not always hear what is being said by others, at least not at the time. Hence my own advocacy-oriented focus on inclusion and disability did not let me see the point that Tony and Mel made at our meeting in Auckland about the importance of attending to pressures for exclusion. But even if we had tried for conformity in approach, it is still yet another person, the person using the research, the listener or reader, who interprets and transforms what we present through the lens of their own experiences, passions and preferences, and may see or not see what the writers intended (Wolcott, 1994). What we might have thought of as being coordinated and interrelated, another may read as material that has been forced to conform to predetermined parameters of study and to conventions of research writing that some of it, at least, does not fit.

A further challenge was that of context. Would the reader need to know about the cultural, political, legislative and organizational arrangements of the people who speak in these studies? If so, in how much detail, and what of the local and even individual translations and transformations of policies and practices? I agree that context is important to understanding, and the reader will find in each chapter a country's social and political circumstances presented either in an outline of legislation, structures and belief systems or indirectly through the comments of participants. But I take responsibility for not requiring more detailed information for the present studies. People might include it if they wished, but it seemed to me that the additional material could extend the length of a report unreasonably and test the reader's attention. I wanted the focus to be on people in schools and other settings talking about the reality for them of inclusion and exclusion. To the extent that we make their voices dominant in this text, we might decrease our construction of them as the objects of research (Fulcher, 1995). If readers want information on the school systems in our various countries then, where this is absent, I must refer them to our group's two earlier publications, or they might consult other literature on such issues.

For these reasons the reader will find in this book chapters that vary in approach and style. For some of the researchers, to understand people's experiences of inclusion and exclusion meant the use of statistical procedures in support of a belief that objective information on the phenomena under study was reported. For others, a case study approach provided material to be analysed from theoretical positions that might expose underlying assumptions and suggest alternative meanings and implications. The reader is even more central in a third type of study. Here, some experiences of inclusion and exclusion are presented and what they mean is largely for the reader to determine. These accounts invite a personal, emotional engagement with lives affected by powerful attitudes and structures within their respective societies. They require the reader to ask if they recognize these in themselves and in their own culture and communities, and what that might imply.

The Notion of Voice

We acknowledge in this work that the notion of 'voice' is problematic. Our underlying concern is with power and politics in education, yet the ability to scrutinize, to gaze on another, is itself premised on power (Shakespeare, 1994), and it is the researcher's voice that is dominant in the present accounts. There is the problem that recording the individual voice and experiences of participants might reduce attention to the wider economic and other material circumstances that are the basis of disablism and other forms of oppression (Shakespeare, 1994). There is also the problem that some voices might be heard in ways that assert their authority and interests over those who cannot easily access a position to be heard. This might be the case for those who lack a clearly identifiable disability or group membership, or those whose voice is deemed to be outside the range that is considered to be authentic or valid (Barnes and Mercer, 1996; Dyson, 1996). In addition, a research text might silence a voice, or at least some of what is said. This might be done to protect a contributor's identity or because the researcher was not aware of the meaning or significance of what they were told (Clandinin and Connelly, 1994). Although we undertook our work with such challenges in mind, the reader is encouraged to look critically at what we have achieved in terms of our relationships with the people we worked with and how we have addressed political issues in our education systems and societies.

The idea of an 'authentic' voice also warrants a critical perspective. 'Insider' accounts are not necessarily 'true' or 'valid' in a realist or absolute sense. In reporting their experiences, people reconstruct what happened to them and what this meant. They may need to translate events and contextual frameworks into terms that will be understood by researchers and others who have not lived the experiences that they talk of. Although clearly open to critical analysis, such voices are, nevertheless, seen by Guba and Lincoln (1994, p. 114) to have 'educative authenticity' where they enhance our understanding of another person and what happens to them, and 'catalytic authenticity' should they stimulate the reader to action.

Our studies present a diversity of voices contributing to an ongoing international debate on inclusion and related concerns. As part of this project we decided to make explicit the voice of the researcher. This acknowledges that the account of each interview and the writing of each study is a reflection of the researchers' beliefs, preferred investigative strategies, and the concepts and constructions that they bring to the interpretation of their data. Both the researchers and those they study with, or focus on, have various motivations and understandings about what it is they set out to do in the name of research. The complexity and ambiguity of language and communication between researcher and participant are not in some final way brought under control by procedures such as statistical summaries, triangulation or collaboration (Scheurich, 1995). What we present, therefore, is made by us, and so we thought it important for the reader to know something about who we are, to include ourselves in our text. In each case, how to do that was left over to the writers, and it will be seen that people have various ideas about how they are part of their work.

Introducing the Chapters

The chapters involve a focus on different units of study, from the experiences of teachers, parents and students, to investigation of how a particular school works and what happens beyond school in the provision of services for young people. I have presented the chapters in this order. The reader may start by listening to some teachers, providing an insight into the kinds of issues that parents, students and others, influenced by what goes on in classrooms, also address, but the sequence is not an essential one.

Ysbrand Pijl, Sip Pijl and Kees van den Bos present in Chapter 2 an analysis of interviews in which teachers in the Netherlands were asked why they referred children for placement out of the regular classroom and into the separate special school system. Once placed in special schools, children rarely return to the mainstream, and Ysbrand and his colleagues record that in their country there is growing public concern that segregation in education may have gone too far. Because it is usually the regular school teachers who initiate referral, understanding their assumptions and motives is seen in this research as central to the task of making education more responsive to students experiencing difficulties in learning and behaviour.

The next two chapters focus on the interactions of parents with teachers and other professionals in their respective school systems. In Chapter 3, Colleen Brown examines the role of parents as advocates for their children in the New Zealand education system in which there is legislation supportive of inclusion, but many schools that exclude disabled children. As both a researcher and participant in these experiences Colleen examines why advocacy is necessary and the cost to parents and families of this unsought-for role. In her study from America presented in Chapter 4, Linda Ware also includes herself as one of a group of parents of children with disabilities who engage in four critical dialogues that examine inclusion experiences, struggles, meanings, implications and possibilities. The research strategy involves using parent knowledge to inform and extend the discourse on inclusion.

Talking to students was the basis for the next two chapters. In Chapter 5, Julie Allan draws on the tools of Foucault to examine how four disabled students shaped their own identities by transgressing the norms and limits imposed on them by teachers, peers and the organizational arrangements of their school and education system. Two of these Scottish students resisted the implications of being labelled special or disabled, whereas, in contrast, two acted to persuade others of their special status, often against pressures to the contrary. The idea of being included is shown to be a complex issue, and in this context greater attention to student wishes and desires, rather than needs, is suggested. In their study reported in Chapter 6, Jeff

Bailey and Belinda Barton examine the effect of chronic illness on the school experiences of two young Australians. Illness is seen as a neglected area in educational and inclusion research, yet it may involve issues similar to those identified for other minority students, together with social and emotional factors related to being unwell, unable to complete school work, or unable to attend school, that teachers need to know about.

Talking with disabled adults formed the basis of the next three studies. For the project reported in Chapter 7, Trevor McDonald and I worked with three people to record their experiences and interpretations of inclusion and exclusion in the New Zealand education system. Issues of labelling, impairment, and the complex interactions of these in school and tertiary settings are shown to be embedded in the social and political origins of disability manifest in the personal lives of these participants. The following two Norwegian studies also capture aspects of the socio-cultural origins of exclusion and inclusion in individual experiences. For Chapter 8, Kari Nes talked with three people about their lives at school and into the adult years. Questions are raised about how much teachers and other professionals know of children's experiences in special education, and what we mean by community integration for people with intellectual disabilities. In Chapter 9, the story of how one mother ensured that her daughter grew into adulthood in her local community is recorded by Marit Strømstad. Marit challenges her own attitudes to disability in telling of her personal thoughts as she met with her participants. By implication, she asks readers to reflect on their beliefs and actions on disability in their own communities.

Two English studies complete this research account. Both attend to voices on inclusion and exclusion and analyse these with reference to school and community contexts. In Chapter 10, Mel Ainscow, Tony Booth and Alan Dyson report on their interviews with 62 students at Richard Lovell secondary school. The students' views on issues such as streaming, teacher methods of classroom control, students with disabilities, and the presence of support staff are used to suggest the understandings and possible transformations that might be achieved from attending to student ideas on school organization and classroom practice. Examining complex relationships in this school, for example, shows that there are students not categorized by disability labels who may, nevertheless, be vulnerable to exclusion. In Chapter 11, Alan Dyson and Alan Millward use a Health Authority commissioned study that they undertook on the service needs of young disabled adults to contrast the inclusion that might be achieved in schools with the exclusion young people may subsequently experience in the adult world. Here they find fragmented and targeted services designed to ameliorate individual difficulties, but not to challenge the social structures that limit participation by disabled and other people in the economic and social life of their society. The insider voices in this chapter are those of the researchers themselves, and they challenge all of us working in the field of inclusive education to relinquish an exclusive focus on the familiar settings and discourses of education in order to develop ideas of inclusion that encompass the wider social and political contexts of our societies. This is one of the themes that I address in some concluding thoughts in the final chapter of the book.

Notes

1   In using the terminology 'disabled people' I acknowledge that others prefer the language of 'people with disabilities' and I do not mean to exclude or offend them. In New Zealand the latter terminology is preferred by the national Assembly of People with Disabilities and by people with intellectual disabilities, and so I also use that in my writing.
2   The research meeting in Auckland was supported by funding from the Ministry of Education and the Humanities Division, University of Otago. Grateful acknowledgment is extended to those agencies.

References

BARNES, C. and MERCER, G. (1996) 'Introduction: Exploring the divide', in BARNES, C. and MERCER, G. (Eds) *Exploring the Divide: Illness and Disability*, Leeds, The Disability Press, pp. 1–16.

BARTON, L. (1997) 'Inclusive education: Romantic, subversive or realistic?', *International Journal of Inclusive Education*, **1**, 3, pp. 231–42.

BIKLEN, D. (1987) 'Introduction', in FOREST, M. (Ed.) *More Education/Integration*, Downsview, Ontario, The G. Allan Roeher Institute, pp. i–ii.

BOOTH, T. and AINSCOW, M. (1998) 'From them to us: Setting up the study', in BOOTH, T. and AINSCOW, M. (Eds) *From Them to Us: An International Study of Inclusion in Education*, London, Routledge, pp. 1–20.

CLANDININ, D.J. and CONNELLY, F.M. (1994) 'Personal experience methods', in DENZIN, N.K. and LINCOLN, Y.S. (Eds) *Handbook of Qualitative Research*, Thousand Oaks, Sage, pp. 413–27.

CLARK, C., DYSON, A. and MILLWARD, A. (1995) 'Towards inclusive schools: Mapping the field', in CLARK, C., DYSON, A. and MILLWARD, A. (Eds) *Towards Inclusive Schools*, London, David Fulton, pp. 164–77.

CLOUGH, P. and BARTON, L. (1995) 'Introduction: Self and the research act', in CLOUGH, P. and BARTON, L. (Eds) *Making Difficulties: Research and the Construction of Special Educational Needs*, London, Paul Chapman, pp. 1–5.

DYSON, A. (1996) 'Review of "Making difficulties: Research and the construction of SEN, CLOUGH, P. and BARTON, L. (Eds)"', *Cambridge Journal of Education*, **26**, 1, pp. 124–8.

FERGUSON, P. and ASCH, A. (1989) 'Lessons from life: Personal and parental perspectives on school, childhood and disability', in BIKLEN, D., FERGUSON, D. and FORD, A. (Eds) *Schooling and Disability*, Chicago, National Society for the Study of Education, pp. 108–40.

FULCHER, G. (1995) 'Excommunicating the severely disabled: Struggles, policy and researching', in CLOUGH, P. and BARTON, L. (Eds) *Making Difficulties: Research and the Construction of Special Educational Needs*, London, Paul Chapman, pp. 6–24.

GIANGRECO, M.F. (1997) 'Key lessons learned about inclusive education: Summary of the 1996 Schonell Memorial Lecture', *International Journal of Disability, Development and Education*, **44**, 3, pp. 193–206.

GUBA, E.G. and LINCOLN, Y.S. (1994) 'Competing paradigms in qualitative research', in DENZIN, N.K. and LINCOLN, Y.S. (Eds) *Handbook of Qualitative Research*, Thousand Oaks, Sage, pp. 105–17.

REGER, R. (1972) 'The medical model in special education', *Psychology in the Schools*, **9**, pp. 8–12.

REINHARZ, S. (1990) 'So-called training in the so-called alternative paradigm', in GUBA, E.G. (Ed.) *The Paradigm Dialog*, Newbury Park, Sage, pp. 290–302.

SCHEURICH, J.J. (1995) 'A postmodernist critique of research interviewing', *Qualitative Studies in Education*, **8**, 3, pp. 239–52.

SHAKESPEARE, T. (1994) 'Cultural representation of disabled people: Dustbins for disavowal?', *Disability and Society*, **9**, 3, pp. 283–99.

SKRTIC, T.M. (1995) 'Special education and student disability as organizational pathologies: Toward a metatheory of school organization and change', in SKRTIC, T.M. (Ed.) *Disability and Democracy: Reconstructing (Special) Education for Postmodernity*, New York: Teachers College Press, pp. 190–232.

SONNTAG, E. (1994) 'Women of action: Caring at home for a daughter or son with an intellectual disability', in BALLARD, K. (Ed.) *Disability, Family, Whanau and Society*, Palmerston North, New Zealand, Dunmore Press, pp. 185–204.

WOLCOTT, H.F. (1994) *Transforming Qualitative Data: Description, Analysis, and Interpretation*, Thousand Oaks, Sage.

Chapter 2

Teachers' Motives for Referring Students to Special Education

Ysbrand J. Pijl, Sip Jan Pijl and Kees P. van den Bos

The educational system in the Netherlands consists of regular schools and special schools. Compared with many other European countries, the Dutch special education system is extensive, differentiated, and segregated. Since the 1960s, Dutch special education has developed into a wide-ranging system for students who cannot keep up in regular schools. In 1972, the total population enrolled in the 14 special education school types was 2.2 per cent of all pupils between 4 and 11 years of age (Dutch primary school age). In 1995, this percentage had increased to 4.3 per cent (Pijl, 1997; Pijl and Pijl, 1995). This increase was caused primarily by the growth of two of the system's major school types: schools for children with learning disabilities (LD) — in the Netherlands referred to as 'LOM' schools, and schools for children with mild mental retardation (MMR) — in the Netherlands referred to as 'MLK' schools. The 'LD' and 'MMR' labels cover a wide range of pupils and pupil needs. These labels are not defined very clearly, either by law, by teachers, or by experts in psychological and educational assessment who are involved in special education placements. Hence, circular characterizations of these groups ('pupils are learning disabled or mildly mentally retarded *because they are eligible* for placement in schools for children with LD or MMR') are rather common.

The separation between regular and special education is maintained through legislation, regulations and funding. The mechanism of funding means that the amount of money that regular schools have available to meet pupils' special needs (thereby preventing referral to special education) is considerably smaller than the amount of money that can be spent on pupils in special education. The average costs for learning disabled and mildly mentally retarded pupils in special education are twice as high as the costs for regular education (Meijer, 1994). So, funding itself acts as a powerful incentive to refer pupils to special schools.

For several decades, this highly differentiated, extensive and separated system of special education was considered to be the best form of expressing concern for pupils with special learning needs. However, more recently this point of view has become the subject of much debate. Various reviewers have pointed out that separated special education placement does not diminish the problems and academic difficulties of the pupils referred. Other criticisms involved the conflict with widely accepted human rights, the social undesirability, and the possibility of a separated special school system merely functioning as a 'safety valve' for regular schools (Tomlinson, 1982). This safety valve can be considered as an improper way of relieving regular education of pupils who are difficult to handle or 'time consuming' (Pijl, 1989).

Recently, a growing group of policy makers, educators and parents became convinced that segregation in education had gone too far. In 1990, the central government issued a document 'Together to school again' which intended to make a fresh start in integrating special needs pupils (Ministerie van Onderwijs and Wetenschappen, 1990). As a result, regular and special schools began working together, special needs coordinators were appointed in every regular school, teacher training programmes were launched, new legislation was passed, and new regulations for funding regular and special schools were proposed. All these measures were intended to act as a push towards integration.

The inclusion policy in the Netherlands has a financial goal as well. The goal is not to spend less money on education or to decrease budgets, but to stop the expected growth of the number of pupils in special education while at the same time improving the instructional quality for all pupils and the willingness of the regular schools to educate them all. This should result in a more stable pattern of expenditure (Meijer, Meijnen and Scheerens, 1993).

A gradually increasing number of parents want their child with special needs to attend a regular school, that is, the same neighbourhood school as his or her siblings, and they want their child to be educated together with other non-special needs children. They want their child to receive a schooling as normal as possible.

Of course, there is also scepticism about and opposition to these new developments. Although they do not principally reject the movement towards more integration, substantial numbers of both regular and special education teachers as well as parents of pupils now in special education still strongly believe that pupils with learning difficulties and/or mental retardation are just 'better off' in segregated special school environments with their highly differentiated, individual-focused teaching and counselling approaches. In accordance with this view of the specialness of special education they consider LD or MMR pupils to have profound and special problems that make a regular school placement inappropriate. They regard these pupils as 'different' from those in regular education: after all, why would they have been referred in the first place?

Although it is formally the parents who refer pupils to special schools, referrals are usually *initiated* by classroom teachers. The regular school teacher (in consultation with the school principal, the school support service, and the parents) takes the initiative to refer a pupil to a special school. On the basis of written information about the pupil and the documented actions of the referring regular school, a regional referral board evaluates the whole process and decides on the appropriateness of the referral. If considered appropriate, the admission board of the special school (a psychologist, a physician, a social worker and the school principal) performs an extensive assessment in order to decide whether the pupil is eligible for special education and decides on actual placement (Meijer, 1994). By legislation, admission boards are free to decide on placement, but in practice, over 90 per cent of the decisions are positive, that is, once a child is referred for placement, actual placement in a special school almost invariably follows (Meijer, 1988; Pijl, 1989).

Obviously, the initiating role of the regular school teacher has far-reaching consequences because it turns out that this initiative almost always leads to a placement decision. Currently, the procedures for referral and the role of admission boards are increasingly criticized. After admittance, only a very small minority (less than 1 per cent) of special needs pupils in schools for children with learning disabilities or mild mental retardation are annually replaced into regular primary education again (Central Bureau for Statistics, CBS, 1996). This once more emphasizes the importance of rational, well considered decision making on referring a student.

Research Question

Teachers initiating the process of referring a student make an implicit statement about the limits of their ability to adapt their instructional and educational skills to that particular student. From the teacher's perspective, the needs of the student can no longer be met in the existing situation and/or the teacher is unable to solve the problems the student causes. In documenting the referral and placement procedure, a lot of attention is usually given to describing the student's abilities, problems and needs, but accounts of the teacher's perspective are scant. Research in which the files of referred students were analysed has shown that they contained little or no information about the pupil's original problems that gave rise to the referral process (Pijl, 1989). Additionally, hardly any scientific studies focus in detail on the problems that are established by the referring teacher (in collaboration with parents and colleagues) and on the question of why these problems cannot be solved in the regular school setting.

As mentioned earlier, teachers can be considered as key persons in the referral of special needs students to special education in the Netherlands. The impact of that decision, both for students and parents, urges research on the motives and decision making of the referring teacher. The central questions in the research described in this chapter are: What grounds do teachers have for referring a student to a special school, and how does decision making proceed?

Method: The Open Interview

The goal of this study was not to interview all persons possibly concerned with referral processes, but rather to focus on teachers. The teacher could either still be the child's teacher (referral is in progress) or be the child's most recent or last *regular* school teacher ('outplacement' of the pupil has recently been completed). We assumed that the teacher had the most recent information about the pupil's development and the best insight into the referral motives, even though the placement decision was not theirs. Secondly, we were not so much interested in letting the teacher generate a list of learner characteristics, but rather in his or her analysis of the pupil's problems, and in their comments on alternative scenarios. Hence, we had planned *open* interviews. A more closed way of interviewing would have left too little room for the teachers' ideas and reasonings about the problems of students and the role of teachers in clarifying and solving these problems in the school.

A key question in the interview was why the referred student could not stay in the particular regular elementary school. This meant that not only were the student's problems discussed, but also the teacher's instructional and managerial difficulties related to that student were considered. Additionally, we wanted the interview to stimulate discussion on why the student was referred and why other pupils with similar problems had not been referred. In this context it was important whether or not the teacher had considered alternative possibilities, such as repeating the grade or providing extra help while keeping the child in the school. Which of these considerations were decisive in still proceeding with the referral?

The interview attempted to employ operational terms for such categories as definition of the pupil's problems and the instruction provided. Characterizations such as 'failure anxiety' were specified in terms of the behaviours observed, their frequencies, their correlation with times of the day and certain events, and the negative effects of the child's behaviour for the pupils themselves, their teacher, and peers. If learning problems were part of the teacher's problem description, these learning problems were described in terms of the teacher's measurement methods. Finally, it should be mentioned that the teachers were interviewed by one (male) interviewer.

Sample

The target population of teachers had to consist of teachers who had recent experience with referring one of their own pupils. 'Recent' meant that the last referral or admission session had occurred no more than half a year ago. The pupil could still be in the class, pending the admission decision, or have very recently been admitted to a special school.

In order to approach the 40 teachers we planned to interview, 89 primary schools had to be sampled. The sample was weighted according to the number of teachers in each school. Because within each school only one teacher was selected, this sampling procedure guaranteed equal probabilities for all Dutch teachers to enter the sample. An unweighted sample would have led to a large proportion of teachers from small schools in the country.

In contacting the schools, nine appeared not to exist any more. Another three school principals refused cooperation, and four school principals were too difficult to contact. Of the remaining 73 schools, 30 had referred students more than half a year ago. Of the remaining 43 schools, 43 teachers were approached for an interview appointment. With three teachers the appointment failed. One teacher was involved in an emigration procedure, another teacher refused cooperation after his initial consent, and the third teacher was unable to plan a short-term appointment.

Table 2.1   Interview structure

Biographical information
Gender of student
Type of special school where the student was enrolled or referred to
Birth date of student
Date of assessment session (admission board) and date of placement
Grade in 95/96
Previous school career
Problem description
Frequency of problem behaviour
Seriousness of behaviour disturbance and/or problems with academic performance. Indicate
    relative position among classmates on these dimensions
In what way can one speak of a problem? Who is affected by the problem?
How are the consequences of the student's problems dealt with in the regular school?
Analysis of the problems
How did the problems come into existence?
Were there possibilities or ideas about appropriate actions that might reduce or eliminate the
    problem?
Why referral to a school for special education?
Was the referral goal reducing the problems of the student and/or the teacher's problem with
    the student?
Were any statements produced by the special school about their ability to effectively treat the
    problem of the student?
Are there any negative consequences of referral and placement for the child, like feelings of
    rejection by his teacher and school or loss of friends?
If a special school would not be able to solve or considerably reduce the student's problem
    would it, then, be possible to have the student perform at a lower level in his (regular)
    school, and to give up the 'normal' learning goals of regular education?
Remaining practical considerations that have played a role in the referral procedure, such as
    the geographical distance to the special school, or the fact that one or more siblings already
    were pupils of this special school.
Evaluation of referral procedure
Is there feedback from the special school (after or during admission procedures) about the
    educational plans concerning the particular student?
Once placed, is there feedback from the special school, or did the regular school enquire
    about the results of the placement and the treatment in special education?
Did this information lead to reconsidering the earlier decision to start the referral process?

Instruments

Table 2.1 contains a schema that guided the interviews as well as the reports
thereof. From this schema it should be clear that it was not our intention to do the
assessment and decision making all over again. Nor did we want to reconstruct the
whole admission procedure or the student's course of life in great detail. Instead,
we wanted the interviews to focus on the question as to which children teachers
find their instructional skills and educational intentions no longer adequate to deal
with, and why not. All interviews were audiotaped for later analysis and as a means
to enhance the quality of the notes that the interviewer made during the interview.
In order to minimize costs and time, the interviews were not literally transcribed.
Summaries comprised two to five text pages per interview.

Table 2.2   Mean interrater agreement (Hubert) and majority interrater agreement (three out of four) per variable (N = 40)

Variable	kappa	
	Hubert	majority
Referral initiative	.35	.79
Social-emotional problem	.71	.91
Learning problem	.43	.93
Negative consequences for:		
The student	.58	.86
The teacher	.37	.66
Classmates	.47	.82
Referral aim:		
Relieved performance pressure for student	.40	.82
Treatment	.52	.94
Relieved work pressure for teacher	.47	.79
Less frustration in the job (teacher)	.36	.97
Improvement of class atmosphere/functioning	.65	.97
Necessity of placement in special school	.69	.97

Analysis

Open interviews provide extensive information, but, on the other hand, this information is relatively unstructured and hard to integrate. In order to draw conclusions about the 40 reports, a system of categories was developed that covered a number of important theoretical and practical dimensions. Initially, for each of the 40 interviews the categories were independently rated by the first two authors of this article. However, interrater agreement (the similarity of the two ratings) appeared to be poor (Cohen's kappa ranged from .30 to .77). In order to investigate whether this result was caused by the specific combination of the two raters or by a fundamental interrater variance due to the combination of cases and the proposed system of categories, two more persons were asked to perform the ratings.

Table 2.2 contains two indexes for interrater agreement on the categories used in the analysis of the interviews. The first kappa (Hubert) represents the mean agreement of all rater pairs. The second kappa reflects the agreement of the majority of raters (three out of four raters).

The results show that the average rater (Hubert) was not doing very well. In general, majority ratings by a group of raters are more reliable and the kappas in the second column of Table 2.2 are therefore much higher. These kappas are quite satisfactory for all dimensions. For that reason the core of the descriptions of the 40 cases of recent referrals is based on these majority ratings. The results of this study should therefore be interpreted as a reliable estimation of what all samples of four raters from all experts in referral and admission procedures would find in their analysis of all Dutch referral cases. The reason for this is that the distribution of majority ratings may differ systematically from the distribution of the original ratings without integrating them into a majority rating. A final remark on the use of

Table 2.3 Distribution of majority ratings of 40 interviews for the variables referral initiative and nature of major problem

Referral initiative
1 Regular school or teacher	28
2 Parents took initiative	4
3 Shared initiative of parents and school	1
No agreement	7

Nature of major problem area
Learning results/functioning in one or more academic subjects
1 No problem in this category	3
2 Problem exists	35
No agreement	2

Social behaviour and/or socio-emotional development
1 No problem in this category	11
2 Problem exists	26
No agreement	3

majority ratings concerns the fact that the distribution of the 40 cases across the categories of each dimension will always show some cases on which no three out of four judges could agree. In the tables we record these as 'no agreement'. However, these 'missing' ratings can also be considered as contributing to realistic data description because the uncertainties of the four raters are directly reflected in distributions and tables.

Referral Initiative and Characterization of the Problems

Although pupils' problems were often elaborately described in the interviews, they are only briefly mentioned here. The reason is that learner characterizations are not the primary aim of the present research study. Moreover, there are plenty of Dutch studies on this question (Meijer, 1988; Pijl, 1989; van IJzendoorn, 1990). The major objective of the present study was to investigate the teachers' reasons for referral. This also explains why in the present account the 'history' of the referral process is reduced to the issue of who took the initiative.

As shown in Table 2.3, in 28 of the 40 cases, teachers (schools) took the referral initiative. It is surprising that in 10 per cent of the cases parents took this initiative. Within this group of parents there were some who already had experience with a school for special education (another child of their family had been placed). These parents were often afraid that the regular school would wait too long before referral. They were also confident that the special school would be able to provide more help for their child than the regular school. In the remaining cases, raters were unable to conclude from the interview which party had taken the referral initiative.

Learning problems were assumed for the majority of the students (35 out of 40 cases), and for 26 students deviant social behaviour and/or problems in socio-emotional development were assumed. In 22 cases combinations of these categories were found that often seemed causally related. School failure and the resulting special position in the class may lead to feelings of inferiority and anxiety. The reverse was sometimes true as well. The following case can serve as an example of the former situation.

Case no. 11: ... arithmetic performance deteriorated fast. Next, the student got trapped in a vicious circle of frustration, anxiety failure, and further impoverished performance. The student constantly compared herself with other classmates who performed well. The problem of failure anxiety became central and generalized to other performance areas such as spelling. At home she developed crying fits and physical complaints (stomach aches), and at the sports club her performance deteriorated as well because she felt clumsy and insecure. The parents attributed the behaviour problems to the school problems.

In only two cases raters decided that the teachers indicated 'pure' behaviour problems. In one case the teacher was unable to indicate any abnormality. This case concerned a boy who — in the course of late kindergarten — had been referred to a school for children with learning disabilities. However, due to a waiting list for that particular school, the child had remained in the regular school for the next year (grade 1). The following text was sampled from the interview report:

Case no. 98: The teacher indicates that, considering the child's present performance and behaviour, he would not have referred this boy. The teacher also doubts the validity of the referral at that time. The precise motives for the referral have escaped the teacher, except that the boy had 'language difficulties'. The teacher does not doubt the integrity of his colleagues, but still mentions the frequent absences through illness of the kindergarten colleagues in the previous year as a possible explanation for the doubtful referral. With regard to the role of the admission committee, the teacher supposes that chances are high that poor learning students who were referred will also be admitted into special education.

Consequences of Learning and/or Behaviour Problems

The mere hypothesis of a learning or behaviour problem in a student does not necessarily lead to referral. When learning or behaviour difficulties do not have negative consequences for the pupil, the teacher or classmates, nobody seems to benefit from referral. Hence, we considered it essential to know if the student was perceived as having a problem that harmed either themselves or others. From the ratings of the teacher responses it can be concluded that in many cases the problems were minor.

As indicated in Table 2.4, there were, at the moment of referral, no negative consequences for the student in 21 cases. For seven students negative consequences were expected in the future, but for the remaining 14 students even this did not apply. The extent to which *teachers* were bothered by the students' problems remains vague, as judged by the relatively large number of cases (12) about which the raters could not decide. Of the remaining 28 cases, 19 did not involve negative consequences for the teachers.

Eight cases did pose a problem for the teachers, which meant that they experienced a greater work pressure because extra attention, guidance, and a special programme had to be provided. In only seven cases did the teachers indicate that other

Table 2.4 Distribution of majority ratings of 40 interviews for the variables negative consequences for student, teacher and classmates

Negative consequences of student's problem for student	
(Feelings of anxiety, depression, inferiority)	
1 No negative consequences	14
2 Negative consequences	14
3 At present no consequences, but they are predicted for the future	7
No agreement	5
Negative consequences of student's problem for teacher	
(Problems with class, time, task management)	
1 No negative consequences	19
2 Negative consequences	8
3 At present no consequences, but they are predicted for the future	1
No agreement	12
Negative consequences of student's problem for classmates	
(Atmosphere in class, too little attention for everybody)	
1 No negative consequences	27
2 Negative consequences	7
3 At present no consequences, but they are predicted for the future	0
No agreement	6

students in the class 'suffered' from the presence of the student with a learning or behaviour problem. In all these cases the problem was primarily a behavioural one (severe aggressiveness and acting out). An example:

> Case no. 52: . . . the teacher found his hypothesis about the boy's negative influence on his classmates' behaviour confirmed after expelling this 'leader' from the classroom for an indefinite period. Almost immediate and positive effects on the other students' disruptive behaviour and the class atmosphere resulted from this disciplinary measure. The improved atmosphere was noticed by the class as well as their parents.

Cross tabulation of the data presented in Table 2.4 revealed that in eight out of the 40 interview reports, raters were unable to find evidence for negative consequences in the present or near future for the student, the teacher or the class. One of these was the previously presented case (no. 98) for whom the teacher was unable to observe any learning or behaviour problem. The remaining seven teachers thought that the referred students had a learning problem, although this did not mean that they could indicate that somebody was actually bothered by this problem.

Besides this group, there appeared to be a fairly substantial group of 10 cases for whom at present no 'real' problems could be indicated, but who were considered to be 'at risk' in the future, or for whom the raters were unable to find unambiguous evidence for serious problems with negative consequences.

Aims of Referral and Placement

The teachers' arguments for referral and placement can be divided into two groups. First, there are arguments directed at getting the student treatment for their problems.

Table 2.5   Distribution of majority ratings of 40 interviews for the variable arguments for referral

Special school placement would result in lower performance pressure on student	
1 Argument was not used	26
2 Argument was part of referral aim	8
No agreement	6
A special school is better equipped for treating the student's problem and its consequences than the regular school	
1 Argument was not used	9
2 Argument was used in the context of judgement of quality and facilities of special schools	29
3 Argument was used in the context of judgement of predictions, claims, and treatment plan provided by the special school	0
No agreement	2
Referral would relieve teacher's task pressure	
1 Argument was not used	21
2 Argument was part of referral aim	12
No agreement	7
Referral serves as a means to get rid of negative feelings by the teacher, such as powerlessness, not being able to reach certain goals with the student	
1 Argument was not used	37
2 Argument was part of referral aim	2
No agreement	1
Referral means that negative consequences for the class can be avoided	
1 Argument was not used	33
2 Argument was part of referral aim	6
No agreement	1

The second group of arguments pertains to ideas about how referral contributes to avoiding negative consequences for the regular school. See Table 2.5.

In the arguments pertaining to treatment, two types could be distinguished. There were arguments with regard to the idea that special schools allow the pupils to work at a lower performance level and with less task pressure, and there were arguments with regard to the supposedly better quality and facilities in special schools. Both types of arguments were used (8 and 29 times, respectively). Cross tabulation showed that, in total, six teachers did not use either type of argument.

It seemed reasonable to anticipate that the argument that a special school has more to offer the referred student might be frequently used. However, nine teachers did not use this argument. This was not because the subject was not raised or because the teacher was insufficiently probed. So, this number of 'omissions' has to be taken seriously. In some cases the teachers were quite explicit about their omission of the argument:

> Case no. 39: . . . the school has tried to 'keep' the student in the regular system as long as possible. Looking back at the case it sometimes crosses my mind that it might have been better for the student (now in grade 4) if he were referred longer ago, especially with regard to his socio-emotional functioning. Placement into a special school might have prevented his current failure anxiety and lowered motivation. However, this does not mean that special schools manage to structurally

improve learning abilities and learning performances of the children referred. The school counsellor, who is also present at the interview, states that the special school uses the same methods as in the regular school. Moreover, in the higher grades of the special school, traditional teaching methods (teacher in front of class) are applied in order to prepare the students for secondary education in which similar approaches are standard.

In summary, the majority of the teachers presented arguments which assumed that special schools had greater expertise than regular schools for handling the type of students the teachers had referred. However, details and 'proof' about these assumptions could never be provided.

With regard to the issue of avoidance of negative consequences for teacher and class, 'relief of teacher's task pressure' was mentioned 12 times, 'avoidance of feelings of powerlessness' two times, and improvement of poor class atmosphere six times. Cross tabulation of the data presented in Table 2.5 indicated that a total of 15 teachers used none of these arguments. Besides, 4 out of the 40 teachers could not provide an explanation for referral at all. These cases involved four students with learning or behaviour problems for whom the teachers were unable to describe negative consequences of these problems for the students themselves.

Necessity of Placement

Table 2.6 presents the findings about the variable of necessity of placement. From Table 2.6 it appears that 12 teachers were either in doubt about the referral or placement decisions or even outspokenly negative about these decisions (cases 60 and 98). We consider these 12 cases as particularly relevant in the context of an exploration of the limits of teacher adaptability to student needs. Therefore, brief attention is given to all of these cases.

Table 2.6 *Distribution of majority ratings of 40 interviews for the variable necessity of placement into a special school according to the teacher*

1	Placement was and is not necessary, or is at least considered as doubtful	12
2	Placement was and is necessary	27
	No agreement	1

Case no. 5: The teacher states that despite feelings of doubt about a child's possibilities of being able to learn to read, it would — in general — be better to wait with referral until grade 1 where the child's progress can be carefully monitored. However, this particular child had already repeated a kindergarten grade, and the school guidance service had — at that time — advised to refer the child. Moreover, the fast referral had been reinforced by the parents, because — in their opinion — one of their other children had been referred too late. Nonetheless, the teacher is still in doubt about this fast referral process. On the other hand, the teacher had often experienced feelings of powerlessness because too little time could be spent on the student, although the time that had been spent was not without success.

Special schools can spend more time with students, because their classes are much smaller. According to the teacher, the better facilities of special schools was the most important referral argument.

This particular student was 7 years old when she was admitted to a special school for children with learning disabilities. Before admittance she was in the oldest kindergarten group of the regular school.

Case no. 32: The immediate cause of the referral was the mother's anxiousness about her child being dyslexic. She was worried about the child's progress. According to her, the child could do better, and appropriate steps should be taken. The teacher agreed, because — during the school year 1994–1995 — the child had increasing difficulties with learning, despite having repeated the grade. The hypothesis of dyslexia prompted the mother to ask for thorough assessment by the school guidance institute. At that stage, the teacher was still in doubt about referral to special education. The teacher expected more clarity on these matters from the assessment by the school guidance institute. The teacher regarded their judgement as important, and she had no clear opinions herself.

The assessment session led to the conclusion that the hypothesis of dyslexia was unwarranted, and that the student had a normal intelligence. The admission committee decided negatively about the referral, and in the subsequent school year the student was admitted to grade 2.

Case no. 11: The school guidance institute had suggested referring the student to a special school. The teacher trusted this advice and had no clear preferences himself. Finally, the admission committee came to a different advice, viz., of letting the child repeat the grade, and to seek extra remedial help for the student in the regular school itself. This proposal was executed.

Case no. 28: According to the teacher, it was the student's mother who had speeded up the referral process. The teacher himself had wanted to give it (that is, the situation of keeping the student in the regular school) a further try for some time; although he doubted whether this could have prevented special school placement.

In the meantime, the student had been placed in a special school for children with learning disabilities.

Case no. 86: The student has been admitted to a special school, but for this special school there is a waiting list. According to teacher and parents this postponed placement could result in the placement being cancelled if the current situation of decreased problems remains stable.

Case no. 98: The student was admitted to a special school. Because of a waiting list, this school had advised to temporarily place (for one year) the student in another special school. Because the parents did not want their child having to switch schools twice, the student remained in the regular school. In the new school year, the student got a new teacher who was very much against the idea of referral. This teacher could not detect serious problems. So, the original referral and placement idea will probably be abandoned.

Case no. 95: The school guidance institute's investigations have not finished yet. The teacher has no ideas of his own about the referral and will follow what is recommended by the results of the assessment procedure.

Case no. 48: Referral was initiated in the previous grade. Initially, the current teacher was against continuation of the referral procedure. However, the student's mother insisted on continuation. Moreover, the student's results had deteriorated somewhat, and this had gradually resulted in a change of the teacher's original attitude. The school trusts the opinions and decisions of the school guidance institute. The teacher still thinks that he would not have initiated the referral process. If the mother had not been of a different opinion, the teacher would have had no problems with keeping the student in his class. Meanwhile, the student has been admitted to a special school and will be placed next school year.

Case no. 81: The teacher has been an important factor in the referral process. However, she now doubts the necessity of the referral because the problems seem to have grown less acute. The investigation is not finished yet, and the teacher wants to await its results.

Case no. 60: The student's former teacher considered referral as absolutely necessary. However, the school guidance institute, together with some members of the school team, proposed to keep the student in the regular school for another year, and to help the current teacher with treatment advice. This teacher will also be guided by the special school which the student originally would be referred to.

Case no. 72: The student's former regular school had referred the student to a special school. Due to a waiting list, the student could not immediately be admitted, and the student was temporarily admitted to the present (regular) school. The present teacher would not have referred the student because he does not find evidence for the previously reported problems. If the parents would cancel the original referral decision he would support them. However, the parents are still enthusiastic about the original decision and the teacher trusts the insights of the school guidance institute and the special school's admissions committee. Therefore, the current teacher will keep his opinions to himself. After the summer holidays, the student will be placed in the special school.

Case no. 46: The referred student's mother often takes initiatives about which the teacher is poorly informed. During the interview the teacher finds out that, in the past, the student has already been admitted to a school for children with learning disabilities once! Apparently, this decision has not been executed because the student is still in the regular school. The current referral is for a school for children with mild mental retardation. The teacher's attitude is to wait for decisions by the mother and external experts. The mother has told her that the admission committee's decision is forthcoming, and that the student will be placed in the special school after the summer holidays. The teacher is not against placement; special schools have more facilities that may help to solve learning problems. . . . However, in the course of the interview the teacher becomes not only increasingly unsure about the history of the referrals, but the obviousness of the planned placement is doubted more and more. At this moment (November, last grade level of kindergarten), the teacher thinks that the student is not ready for regular grade 1. However, this might change during the school year. When the question is asked about the possible effects of kindergarten grade repetition compared with the results of placement into the special school, the teacher becomes even more doubtful about the most adequate decision. She had never considered repetition of the first school year. Now that the child is in second K-grade, the teacher does not find it a good idea to place the student back to K-grade 1. However, repetition of K-grade 2 might be an option. . . .

From these case summaries it appears that some teachers are not only unsure about the best decision, but that they are often fairly passive as well. They leave decisions to parents and experts, not so much because of their own uncertainty about the best decision but because they trust the experts and consider their own judgements to be less important and less relevant. In some cases doubtful teachers try to stop an already started referral process before admission and placement. In other cases, however, even when the current teacher would not (yet) have referred, placement can only be cancelled by a negative decision by the admission committee.

Furthermore, from these summaries it appears that waiting lists and other delays of the referral process can positively influence the chance that the student stays in the regular school. It seems that for a number of referrals postponement leads to cancelling the original referral decisions. This situation is understandable if one realizes that the process of referral and admission usually takes longer than one year. The longer the period of referral completion, the greater the chance of regression to the mean. That is, the chance of spontaneous decreases of the problems becomes larger with time, and this also applies to the chance that the student encounters a teacher who considers referral less necessary or even not necessary at all.

Global Referral Categories

The preceding section described in some detail the referral and placement procedures. However, we had also asked the raters to identify a more concise list of eight referral types (see Table 2.7). The (three out of four) majority agreement for this data was .64, which indicates that raters had more difficulty agreeing on this system than on the more extensive categories in Table 2.2. The first category in Table 2.7, preventive referral, seems especially interesting. A disproportionate number of referrals seem to be initiated at moments when problems had no great impact or consequences for the students yet. Referrals of relatively young children are motivated by negative expectations about their future developments and by prevention of referrals that might come 'too late'. Strictly taken, these concern referrals which are not necessary at present. It is possible that for a number of cases the expectations about the students' developments will come true. However, it is also likely that for another number of referred students problems will diminish after the shift to another

Table 2.7   Distribution of majority ratings of 40 interviews according to eight global categories

1 Preventive referral	7
2 Parents want to refer	4
3 Serious academic performance delays and no signs of learning progress	3
4 Serious delays combined with considerable teacher work load	1
5 Delays in learning combined with anxiety failure	4
6 Serious behaviour problems	3
7 Psychiatric problems	3
8 Summation of several minor problems	1
No agreement	14

grade or another teacher, or with a more appropriate treatment in school and perhaps changes in the home situation. In this context the teacher in case no. 98 produced the following statement:

> I do not think positively about my colleagues' statements about *risks* of future stagnations and increasing problems in certain referred students. If all children about whom teachers ever expressed doubts about their future development would have been immediately referred to special schools, then this type of school would already have become larger than regular schools!

Summary and Conclusions

In general, the interviews provided insufficient data of an operational nature, with less detailed descriptions of problems and their consequences than we had wished. Therefore, the theme of 'limits to adaptability' could be treated only superficially. As an additional factor, we should mention the inability of raters to categorize poorly defined information in a highly formalized rating system. Naturally, this is the risk of a set of qualitative data, especially when qualitative analyses are not based on the opinion of a single person or a non-replicable group process in a group of investigators, but, instead, on an analysis of independent judges. In this sense, the present study has added to our knowledge about research methods in a situation where the data are relatively complex and not clearly focused.

As far as the data itself is concerned, an important referral motive seems to involve situations where the regular schools feel that their role in the students' learning progress becomes (too) limited, and that the students' learning performances deviate too much from those of the other students. The five teachers who spontaneously formulated a maximum acceptable degree of learning delays appeared to employ similar criteria. According to these teachers, learning delays of about two years (at the end of grade 6) would be acceptable for regular schools, and learning delays of more than two years would not.

> Case no. 39: A final performance level in grade 6 that is equivalent to normal performance at the end of grade 4, is just acceptable. This is about the norm when poor performances across different learning domains are considered.

Many teachers motivate their referral with the conviction that special schools 'have more to offer' and/or that they can relieve students from the stress of continuous performance pressure in regular schools. According to the teachers the students would benefit more from referral than would the teachers themselves. Special schools have a considerably smaller student–teacher ratio, more specialized treatment can be provided (speech therapist, social worker, and others), and special school teachers have usually followed additional courses of study about the diagnosis and treatment of learning and behaviour problems. Thus, according to many parents and teachers, special education is a superior form of education for children with learning problems. If teachers did not refer students with learning problems, then these students would be denied necessary special treatment, and the regular school would be unnecessarily overtaxed. However, even when extensively questioned, teachers were often unable to indicate *concretely* what the special school would be able to accomplish *more* than the regular school, especially with regard to the particular student they referred.

In the course of the interview, some teachers became more and more *doubtful* about their own reflections.

> Case no. 5: . . . After the interview the teacher indicates that she has appreciated the conversation very much. The discussion about the premises and underlying assumptions of the referral decision has made several ideas more explicit to her. However, the interview also has resulted in increased feelings of doubt about the original referral case.

Additionally, our study indicated that in almost one fourth of the cases, teachers thought that referral was not immediately necessary. However, the finding that the teachers' doubts often did not prevent placement would suggest that admissions in special schools might be too 'easy'. This conclusion is supported by the finding that postponement of placement correlates with its cancellation.

In the interviews, the disadvantage of segregation has seldom been mentioned as a factor that might prevent referral. Furthermore, many teachers appeared to strongly trust the expertise of school guidance institutes, the admission committees and the quality of special schools. A few teachers 'hide' behind the judgements and decisions of experts and parents, and, on this basis, justify their own passiveness. The large majority, however, formulated their own opinions and stated that these opinions generally went well together with those of the experts. Only two teachers distrusted the alleged experts, and preferred their own judgements instead.

The conclusion seems warranted that, for teachers, referral processes can be interpreted as examples of situations where one has to decide in *uncertainty*. In this context, one cannot take seriously enough the statement of one of the teachers that 'it would be wise to let students with problems at least try (regular) grade 1'. This would not only reduce the length of students' stay in special schools, but, in view of the correlation between placement postponement and cancellation of the original referral decisions, letting children complete grade 1 would also lead to a reduction of the number of children entering special schools. The combination of a reduced length of stay in special schools and a smaller number of entries in these schools, can have considerable effects on the size of the special school population on any particular reference date. This is because the number of children attending special education annually is the product of the number of children entering special education and the number of years they stay in special schools.

So, from this study emerges primarily the impression that in a number of cases referral and placement decisions are not always as clear-cut as the involved parties often make it seem after the event. Minor changes in the attitudes of teachers in regular primary schools, possibly resulting in less hasty and more cautious decisions, could make a difference in putting a halt to the growth of the annual turnover of special education in the Netherlands. Voices from inside regular education are of vital importance for change. Teachers in regular schools have the task of not only teaching children with learning or socio-emotional problems but also deciding to label a child as having special needs. Therefore, they are the key persons in the pursuit of integrative goals. Their problems, and their way of analysing and solving these problems, should form the base of any programme to make regular education more adaptive to children with special needs.

Outsiders Listening to Voices from Inside

This research on teachers' motives for referral can be considered as a report based on voices from inside: practitioners working in classrooms give insight into what moves them. It is the researchers' task to invite them to do so, to record their statements and to deduce usable knowledge from the individual statements. In doing so, researchers try to generate knowledge that can be generalized. By presenting this knowledge to students and parents, to practitioners or to policy makers, insight is given into practices which are often taken for granted, and that in itself can serve as a basis for change.

In contrast, we consider the backgrounds, interests and motives of the researchers involved as being irrelevant to the outcomes of the research. And if they were not, we would try to make them as irrelevant as possible. If the characteristics of researchers were relevant, serious doubts about the validity and relevance of research results would be justified. The findings of a good researcher with a particular disability or with other personal motives to perform special needs research should match those of any other good researcher. Any motive will do, even money. Researchers have to listen very carefully to 'voices from inside', but in conducting their research they should operate as independent outsiders.

References

CENTRAL BUREAU FOR STATISTICS, CBS (1996) *Statistiek van het Basisonderwijs, het Speciaal Onderwijs en het Voortgezet Speciaal Onderwijs 1995/1996: Scholen en Leerlingen*, Voorburg: ongepubliceerde tabellen.

MEIJER, C.J.W. (1988) *Verwijzing Gewogen. Dissertatie RU Leiden*, Groningen: RION.

MEIJER, C.J.W. (1994) 'The Netherlands', in MEIJER, C.J.W., PIJL, S.J. and HEGARTY, S. (Eds) *New Perspectives in Special Education*, London: Routledge, pp. 95–113.

MEIJER, C.J.W., MEIJNEN, G.W. and SCHEERENS, J. (1993) *Over Wegen, Schatten en Sturen* (Estimating and Regulating: The Inclusion Policy), De Lier: ABC.

MINISTERIE VAN ONDERWIJS EN WETENSCHAPPEN (1990) *Weer Samen Naar School*, Zoetermeer: Ministerie van Onderwijs en Wetenschappen.

PIJL, S.J. and PIJL, Y.J. (1994) 'Hoe speciaal zijn LOM – en MLK-leerlingen?' *Tijdschrift voor Orthopedagogiek*, **33**, 7/8, pp. 316–25.

PIJL, Y.J. (1989) *Het Toelatingsonderzoek in LOM – en MLK-Onderwijs. Dissertatie RU Groningen*, Groningen: RION.

PIJL, Y.J. (1997) 'Stabiliteit deelname aan LOM en MLK onafhankelijk van WSNS-beleid', *Tijdschrift voor Orthopedagogiek*, **36**, pp. 131–9.

PIJL, Y.J. and PIJL, S.J. (1995) 'Ontwikkelingen in de deelname aan het (voortgezet) speciaal onderwijs', *Pedagogische Studiën*, **72**, 2, pp. 102–13.

POPPING, R. (1983) *Overeenstemmingsmaten voor Nominale Data. Dissertatie RU Groningen*, Groningen: Rijksuniversiteit Groningen.

TOMLINSON, S. (1982) *A Sociology of Special Education*, Henley: Routledge and Kegan Paul.

VAN IJZENDOORN, W.J.E. (1990) *Prognoses voor Probleemleerlingen. Onderzoek naar de Geldigheid van Diagnoses. Dissertatie RU Groningen*, Groningen: RION.

Chapter 3

Parent Voices on Advocacy, Education, Disability and Justice

Colleen Brown

What upsets me is confident articulate parents, well able to work the system, are reduced to quivering wrecks. It riles me that we can do this to people. What about people who cannot speak English and where it is culturally inappropriate to buck [challenge] authority? (Diane, an advocate)

We made front page news when my daughter was five, because the school didn't want her. I home schooled her anyway. I wasn't going to put her into a state system that didn't value her. (Kim)

Being in the education system compromised my soul — it felt like being raped. I have to have eyes in my butt so I can see what they are up to. (Tui, Maori parent of two children with special needs)

I live in a designer community, it is very difficult to bring up a child with a disability in this community. (Kate)

Because we are Catholic we had the naive assumption that our son would be welcome in the schooling system — that had come from the time he was born — when he wasn't welcome our whole belief system crashed — it got right to the core of my soul. (Maria)

I remember being told by a teacher three years ago at our daughter's previous school, 'No one wants your daughter in their classroom next year.' And why does it still hurt so much Colleen? The teacher aide told us that the whole staffroom clapped when they learnt we were leaving the school. (Ann)

I've always been a person who liked justice and that's all I wanted for my child. That's why we have a Human Rights Act so that people get justice, isn't it? (Margaret)

The voices of parents with family members with a disability are rarely heard in the literature on disability issues. This chapter is based on some personal accounts of advocacy in the education system. They are from six New Zealand mothers living with their partners and families in the greater Auckland area, all of whom have a child with an intellectual disability. There is one professional advocate's voice amongst the parent narratives.

As a mother of a son with an intellectual disability I too am a fellow traveller with the parents I interviewed. I live in a quiet Auckland suburb with my husband Barry and our four children, Olivia, Travers, Julia and Jordan. Like many others, I wanted to be an ordinary parent. However, by the time our son Travers was four years old I knew that the distribution of power in our society was unevenly held, and it was certainly not in favour of parents of children with disabilities. I became gradually politicized as I began the struggle to achieve what I believed were my son's rights to the same experiences and opportunities that are available to other New Zealand children. Through contact with other parents, I came to believe that the only way that we would succeed in our goal of inclusion in society for people with disabilities was through supporting one another, accessing and sharing information, and asserting our right to be heard in the development of policy and practice in our society. In these ways I have been involved in disability issues since the birth of our son Travers nearly 17 years ago. For much of that time I have relished the learning curve involved in having to write about special needs and education, dealing with the media, and speaking to parents, professionals, and policy makers in support of our children and their families. I now lecture in communication studies at Manukau Institute of Technology. In this regard there are aspects of my personal and professional life that merge. Nevertheless, even after all of these years involved in the field, undertaking the present study proved to be an emotional, and at times gruelling, experience. Many tears have been shed in the writing of this chapter — tears of sorrow for what might have been; tears for the injustices experienced; tears for the anger; tears for the pain.

In undertaking this work I talked with each of the participants and together we identified the key issues that are presented in this chapter. I focused the study on the issue of advocacy because this is a role that many parents of a child with a disability feel that they must take on. If you have a child who is not labelled by your society, then no one expects you to have to go out into the community and argue for access to the same resources in health, education, and welfare provisions that other children receive as a right of citizenship. Yet for parents of a child with a disability, advocacy becomes necessary because we suddenly confront a society that is so often willing to discriminate on the basis of disability. Many parents and families share similar experiences of advocacy struggles for their children. The parent accounts in the present study contain a number of similarities that will be explored in the paper as key themes about advocacy. At the same time, there are also important differences in experiences and ideas, and these underline the uniqueness of families.

When I was writing this paper I intended finishing with some conclusions from the interviews. However, on reflection I feel strongly that the parent voices must be heard without such an interpretation and that you, the reader, must derive your own conclusions about the state of advocacy as it exists for parents, care-givers and families of people with disabilities both in the community described here and in your own setting. The major feature evident in this exploration is the brutality of the education system towards those labelled as disabled, and their families. Not one of the families interviewed wanted to be identified, and pseudonyms are therefore used in this account.

Disability and Society

English writer and advocate, Len Barton, has stated that people with disabilities have been marginalized by society.

> Oppression is more than a denial of access and opportunity, it is about being power-less and viewed as essentially worthless in an alien society. (Barton, 1992, p. 7)

Such disempowering of people may occur even where legislation is designed to support minority groups. The Education Act 1989 has formed the legislative basis for the New Zealand education system for over six years. This Act gives every child with a disability the same right to education in a state school as any other child. There are provisions for a child to be directed to attend special education, but even these are not often invoked. What seems most commonly the case in New Zealand is that schools simply ignore the Act, have no philosophy or commitment to inclusion, and actively discriminate against disabled children and their families. Hence the need for advocacy.

A common approach to disability in education and community settings has been to segregate and congregate those who are disabled, and to exclude them from mainstream opportunities and experiences. Special schools flourish in certain regions in New Zealand; communities start petitions at the news that people with disabilities will be moving into a residence in their area; some politicians fight to have institutional settings remain open; and families often have to move house into particular school zones where their child with a disability will be welcomed into the school rather than rejected from it. All the parents who have contributed to this paper are survivors in such a society. Their schools and local communities have been unwilling to support the ambitions and endeavours of their least empowered citizens, and are failing to implement legislation and policy on inclusion. Nevertheless, the parents spoken to for this study are considered to be 'successful' by other parents in the disability community. This is because they have managed to overcome many educational barriers and have worked through difficult issues confronting their children, sometimes compromising their ideals in order to access education. Yet these families have inherited and continue to experience the historical stigma of having a person with a disability living with them.

The experiences reported in this paper tell of the struggle parents have endured to access their children's legislated right to an education in the state school system. Because children with disabilities do not have a voice in the system, because they are deemed by the practices of the education sector to have fewer entitlements than regular students, they must have advocates. Usually it falls on the parent to take on that role along with being a teacher, a nurse, their friend, their parent — often forever. Rod Wills has stated:

> It is hard to be the parents of a child that no one else would want to have. It must be even harder for our children, growing up to be the one person that no one wants to be! (Wills, 1994, pp. 252–3)

This view of the parent role would be supported by those parents who understand the challenges of disability in New Zealand society. Parents continue to meet professionals who are not supportive of their children's legislated right to go to a state school and whose views on disability reflect negative attitudes common in our society. As parents, we tell such professionals about the achievements of children with disabilities in inclusive settings. We remind professionals that, not so long ago, children with Down syndrome were institutionalized and had no access to the education system. We point out that now, many children with Down's syndrome are in ordinary mainstream classrooms and are benefiting from involvement in the culturally valued curriculum of their society. These achievements are not because children with Down's syndrome have changed, but because 'our *ideas* about them . . . are different' (Ballard, 1994, p. 15).

The parents interviewed for this study stated that they continually negotiated with their schools about the type of education that the child should receive. It seems that the rights of the child with the disability are 'floating', 'negotiable' items, which is not so for other children in the school. As Ann stated, 'We asked for no more other than what she was entitled to'. They had to keep asking questions:

> Could you find . . . ?
> Could she stay at school . . . ?
> Why can't she go to school on open day like everyone else . . . ?
> Is she welcome back next year or not . . . ?
> For all those things we needed support.

Advocacy was seen by these parents as a necessary and ongoing part of being a parent of a child with a disability. Most parents interviewed were practising self-advocacy and using the support of other parent and professional advocates well before their child entered the compulsory schooling sector. From the interviews, five aspects of advocacy were identified, and the parent experiences are reported under these headings. The key issues discussed by these parents were: what is advocacy?, the need for advocacy, the cost of advocacy to parents and families, the parent/professional relationship and advocacy, and an advocacy wish list for the future.

What is Advocacy?

On the question 'What is advocacy?', Kate stated, 'You are an advocate for your child from day one.' She added:

> I'm the one that loves him. When I am in an IEP [an Individual Education Plan or Programme] meeting there is not one single person in that room who feels like that about my son.

Other parents said that they viewed an advocate as someone who was prepared to work on behalf of the person with a disability, to promote the positive aspects of whatever disability the child might have. All of the parents saw outside advocates as being able to speak for you when you, the parent, become emotionally distressed. As Maria said:

> They are our kids. It's emotional. There are times when I need to say something, but it will upset me. I need to draw strength from someone.

Other parents spoke of the moral support they received from advocates. Kate said that advocates brought with them a wealth of experience and knowledge, allowing them, the parents, to speak with more confidence on behalf of their child.

Tui, who is Maori, felt that any encounter was a weight-of-numbers power game. She saw the problem as being the fact that the principal is under-resourced and the teachers are untrained. For Tui, the advocate helped manage the process of getting everyone through the encounter, with everyone saving face. She stated:

> It is nothing to do with getting resources and problem solving. It is adversarial, with a lot of negotiation happening. I have to feel at the end that I've done my job as a mother. I've dropped [withdrawn from] the system. It doesn't work for me. It's games and subterfuge. It's an IDP [Individual Development Plan] after IDP nightmare. Bureaucracy burns up the resources. I believe it comes back to women and children and family.

All parents stated that an advocate who knew the system and could see both sides was very important. An advocate could be a mediator where required. Many parents said that the physical presence is vital: 'It gives you the strength. The advocate doesn't have to say anything, just be there.' Maria said:

> To me, advocacy doesn't just mean going with someone to a meeting. It means spending time talking about the meeting and what is going to happen, what you are going to say. You spend more time on that than physically at the meeting. Often the parent wants to be in control and be seen by the school to be in control, otherwise they are seen by the school as being weaker. I prefer not to do that. I use the advocate. They speak for me in some situations. Parents can see the advocate in an uncertain light and think that the advocate will take over the meeting.

She added, 'It is hard to advocate for another parent as it brings up issues for yourself.' Diane, who works as an advocate with parents, stated:

> I don't believe parents understand the need for advocates. They don't anticipate the road blocks and barriers. When you have a child who has what the schools see as 'problems', the school professionals look for the worst. The principal only needs to say, 'I don't know whether we can manage' and parents don't hear any more.

Diane had seven years' experience working with families. She said she was there to support parents in whatever way they saw her role as being helpful, whether that be providing information, planning strategies and tactics, or taking people to a range of schooling options, and at the end of a session with school or other professionals, to help the parent debrief. Debriefing can be important in terms of sharing interpretations of what happened; developing strategies for the next meeting; and dealing with emotions that arise from self-exposure of personal issues to others, anger, frustration and relief.

The problem for people in the Auckland region (population 1.2 million) is that there is only one advocate who can assist parents who have a family member with an intellectual disability. This means that the role of advocacy is taken up by other parents. It has been an ongoing observation of parents that, ironically, they are often not listened to concerning their own child, yet as advocates for other people's children they are listened to and can be effective.

Why the Need for Advocacy?

When a child with a disability is born into a family, suddenly life does a U-turn. The existing rules and parameters are changed, without the family's expectation or agreement. The parents who were interviewed for this study may represent a vocal minority. They are people who insist that their voices be heard. Like myself, they would probably be described as 'middle-class' people. I do not think this means that it is only people 'like us' who are advocates or who work for change in our society. Evidence from other New Zealand studies suggests that people from across the range of economic and social circumstances are active in promoting an inclusive society (Ballard, Watson, Bray, Burrows and MacArthur, 1992). In talking with the participants in the present study, what struck us all was the profound shock that we experienced when we found that one of our children was the focus of discrimination. We had not previously seen ourselves as members of a minority group. We had rarely experienced oppression and marginalization. And yet, with the birth of a child with a disability, we found that suddenly we were no longer an accepted part of our community and our local school. Society did not hold great expectations for our child with a disability. Society was not keen to involve this child in the everyday activities of school and sport and other areas of growing up that our other children had automatic access to. We found all of this intolerable. As members of the middle class we had never before had difficulty in negotiating with educational or other professionals. Now we were faced with the need to become politically active in support of our children and our families.

The parents spoken to for this study reported having to combat the beliefs held by many professionals, that it is the professional who knows what is best for the child. The education discourse, like the medical discourse, has promoted the view that the professionals have the best interests of the child at heart and that they can intervene and change the individual who has the problem. In line with the medical discourse, educationalists individualize disability. It is the individual child who is seen as incapable. This professionalizes disability, so that parents confront an array of experts available to offer their opinions and judgements on their, the professionals', terms.

The parents in this study found, as Gillian Fulcher (1989) in Australia also reported, that a language of 'special' needs emphasized professional management and control, diminishing attention to parent wishes, rights and wants. As Tui reported:

> I'm judged as a loser. My [Maori] race is seen as a losing race. We assimilated so quickly into the European way of life. The Treaty [establishing Maori rights under European settlement] states my children will have parallel development. What does that say about my children? See my child, then see the Europeans. I think all Maori children get a bad deal. I got through, I was dyslexic, I was intelligent and able to cover it up. I know people at the local primary school [that my child attended] assumed I was a solo mother. I looked frazzled, I was looking for help, I was a victim. They saw me as creating our own problems. When my white middle-class husband appeared, it made a difference, but it shouldn't.

This parent now teaches her son at home, giving up the struggle to maintain him in the school system. Yet she cannot access the Correspondence School, a national distance-learning agency supporting children in rural areas and children with disabilities. Her child is said not to fit the criteria for enrolment. In order to access this resource a parent has to rely on a professional who will decide whether her son's disability fits the established criteria. Parents see the inequalities of this discourse. The professionals' discourse of criteria is far more powerful than the parent voice asserting needs and rights. The system will not change for one child, therefore the child must change. The views of the parent are given less weight. Some parents see that they cannot change the system, and withdraw their child from school.

The need for advocacy is straightforward for parents. In the education system, schools are still breaking the law.

> We approached the school six weeks before we were due to shift to the area. Our daughter was accepted into the school contingent on two things. First of all, the teacher of her class had to want her. Second, the resources had to be available. Despite the law they were still the criteria. She met the criteria, so our daughter was welcome to stay until the end of the year. Three days before the end of the year we were told she was welcome back the following year. This process happens annually. We couldn't make decisions about intermediate for our oldest child because we didn't know what was going to happen with our daughter with a disability. We felt alienated and discriminated against. Yet [for] my third child I just rang up the pre-school and he is in — simple. (Ann)

The need for advocacy exists because some professionals see parents as threats.

> I was already labelled — I was a stirrer; I knew far too much, more than what they expected a parent to know. They were uncomfortable with that. I was at an IEP meeting eighteen months ago and a professional told me that I was a formidable woman. I replied that I was Y's mother and the reason I'm like this is because I'm his mother and I'll push the barriers. The professional left soon after and never came back. (Maria)

Another parent stated:

> I must at all costs force my child to be normal. I'm seen to be okay if I keep pushing the square peg (my child) into the round hole (the education system). I feel that they (the professionals) are waiting for me to fall over. (Kate)

Parents experience the full brunt of the charity discourse from professionals who appear to adopt the view that because the school has so kindly allowed the student to enrol, then the parents must feel suitably grateful. Parents refer to this as the 'grace and favour' model. Many parents endeavour to repay the school's act of acceptance by joining a Board of Trustees (the parent-elected group that manages each school in New Zealand), being compliant, accepting (illegal) part-time school-ing for their child, anything, just to be included. The fact that their child with a disability is viewed as an object of pity, and that the school appears to be following a moral imperative rather than an educational commitment to provide for those less able, does not escape parents, but they feel powerless to do anything to change the perception. Ann said:

> I've learnt never to go to a meeting without an advocate. The two times I have been to meetings without an advocate have been vicious. I feel vulnerable. If a teacher asks me for a quick word in the playground and if that means going to the office, I will say that I will make an appointment. I was in a meeting where there was the principal and five other people. We were not there to discuss our daughter's IEP as we had been led to believe. We were told that we had to 'express more gratit-ude' to the school. I was darned near destroyed by that experience. . . . Despite the law there are so many barriers.

Margaret said:

> I used someone as an advocate when my son was at kindy — they were having a meeting. There was the itinerant teacher from the Special Education Service, three teachers and two advocates. They asked me if I minded them having their advoc-ates. I said, 'What about little old me!!!' I found out via my neighbour that she had been asked by the kindy staff what my son was like at home. I had a real concern about that. I was told that I shouldn't have taken offence at it. I thought it was an intrusion. They said it wasn't meant offensively. The only person there who agreed with me was my advocate. I expect professionals to behave as professionals.

Diane, the advocate who contributed to this study, said:

> Parents feel grateful for what they are getting, so they don't want to rock the boat. They are scared that if they say 'Hey, my child's the same as everyone else', they will suffer repercussions. There are some degrading and devaluing practices going on out there . . . the child who had to wear a yellow dot on her back in the playground [so teachers could monitor her behaviour] . . . children isolated in the classroom . . . IEPs that go over and over the same thing with no basic teaching principles being aired.

She added:

> A lot of parents have the necessary skills but in this situation those skills go out the window. You put them in that situation and they are disempowered. It is better for me, an outsider, to play the heavy. I can walk away but the parents are there for the next 5–10 years. Parents have to live with the consequences. It is not me living with the consequences, it is that family.

Advocacy is needed because parents want to maintain positive relationships with the schools their children attend. Kate reported:

> We were planning for our son's education from birth. My husband joined the Board of Trustees, because he felt it was the best way to advocate from the inside, to smooth things. When we didn't get the [teacher aide support] hours the school needed for our son to go to school it was a great shock, we brought in some advocates. With my husband being on the Board we didn't want a stand-up row. We wanted to be able to see people on a day-to-day basis.

Advocacy is needed because it appears to many parents that there is a deep-seated fear of disability, which surfaces in the education sector as barriers to inclusion. Many schools speak about the need for 'sluices and ramps', for the rights of the other 28 students in the classroom, over and above the one person with a disability. Fear, ignorance, prejudice and resentment of disabled people are embedded in society's consciousness. Society 'knows' these 'facts' about disability, and rarely examines them unless challenged. Advocacy is needed because teachers are sometimes worried by change, by students who are seen as being different, and the teachers may feel that more is going to be expected of them as professionals. Margaret said:

> The teachers had the attitude that our son would mean extra work and they already had a lot of children's needs to meet. If they had only said they were frightened we could have done something about it.

She added:

> Schools get so tied up with the teacher aide time rather than looking at other options. I know that [some] schools say to parents that their child can come in the morning but there will be no afternoon school unless you come too. Some mums are just so relieved to have their child in the school they will do anything to make it happen. It is just so wrong, it wouldn't happen to anyone else. The teacher just can't visualize having a child there without an aide.

The Cost of Advocacy to Families

Many of the parents interviewed for this study said that having to act as an advocate for their child carried a disturbingly high cost for them as individuals and for their families. When parents challenge deep-seated beliefs about disability in society, often the experience becomes confrontational, and stress is experienced by all participants. Families ask for educational opportunities on the basis of rights, equality and justice. Some educationalists reel back at the unexpectedness of the rights discourse, and sometimes the opportunity for a collaborative partnership between parents and professionals slides out of view. The odds are stacked against parents in terms of power and control, and invariably the legitimated institutions and professionals win.

Many parents can identify with Rod Wills (1994, p. 255) when he speaks of schools and other services as 'The Company', and The Company as being one of 'This is the service. Take it or leave it.' In these settings parents have few rights, few entitlements and few options. They should feel grateful for what is available, and are fearful that it might be withdrawn. Kate said:

> I feel honour-bound to do more as a kind of payback. I feel obliged to these people. This is what society has done to us, when we were young people growing up without people with disabilities in our community. It is all very tiring. I have to smile a lot more for my son, to be on more committees. For a long time I felt I had to be the best mother. I never complain about my son to people. I feel that people think it was our choice because we chose to bring him home.

Kim stated:

> In one interview I taped the entire proceedings. I came home and was an absolute mess. My friends said, 'Can't you put her [our daughter] somewhere?' Overall I'm still angry. We're having counselling. My husband could not understand why I thought the paediatricians were assholes. He could not understand the need to home school, he didn't want to be a part of that. I go through swings saying this is too hard — who wants to get a job, a career, why not jump off the Harbour Bridge? Sometimes I can't be bothered doing this any more.

Ann said that she had been in the system for seven years, both in the pre-school and primary system, advocating for her daughter's needs and rights.

> I have attended at my own cost all the workshops and information groups. I'm tired now, because of the negative experiences. I resent having to constantly fight for her rights when I don't have to do it for my other children. The discriminatory practices are so profound. No one gave me a job description for being an advocate for my child.

Tui talked of how they used her husband to add psychological weight to the advocacy process. She said:

> We call my husband our white soldier. We say, 'Come on, put on your suit', and we trot him out. There are so few men left in our area of disability. Recently we applied for a community grant to provide music workshops for our children. Over

40 per cent of the special needs children are Maori in our community. When we presented our application, a local body councillor said to drop the Maori percentage from the application because there is a lack of sympathy for those kind of statistics. So we did and we got the money.

Maria, who failed in her first attempt to enrol her son at a Catholic primary school, said:

It is about our children. It is emotional, we love them. Schools can turn that around and use it against us. When we first tried to get our son into his local Catholic primary school we had to write a letter to the school board to justify why they should take our son. We were trying to sell him. Looking back it makes me so angry. It disturbs me. We didn't get the support from the priest on the Board we would have expected and it became a personal issue with the Chairman of the Board. It caused a lot of pain in the family and the rift still hasn't healed. I thought my in-laws would understand and support us but they didn't. Even in my own family they asked me why I fought the authorities. They said to me to shift somewhere else, to put him in with other children like himself. My reply to them was to state that they had to understand that we were making choices for our son in the same way that they made decisions for their children. We wanted their support. They found it hard. I didn't ask them to justify their choices. I just wanted our son to get his rights as a kid in the community. It also cost us a lot financially. We live in a part of Auckland I wouldn't normally want to live in, just so we can be in the school zone.

She added:

My husband has had to take a lot of time off work to come with me to the different appointments we've had. It is time away from his business, it is time that he often has to make up by staying at work longer hours, so I have to carry the burden of attending to the children on my own.

Although Maria's son was in a school that welcomed him, she described how:

I'm always checking my role and responsibility at meetings — all the time. I ask myself questions — was I right? I sometimes walk away from meetings and go to my car and burst into tears. It is all new ground. We are always pushing the barriers. My husband always comes to IEPs and he is so positive, he may sit in a meeting and say nothing. I have to make sure that my shoes are always shiny — my husband has to wear a suit. I say to him, 'IEP today, don't forget to wear a suit!' I always wear a jacket.

The Parent/Professional Relationship and Advocacy

For the parents in this study, their relationship with professionals was an unequal one. Many professionals work from a medical model or charity view of disability.

Parents of children with disabilities may also accept such thinking because it is so common in our society. Professionals can then support those parents who agree with their views against other parents over educational issues. When the alternative voices are not heard, the prevailing medical model view remains the common-sense one, with the majority of society buying into the dominant belief that people with disabilities are different and therefore need 'special' provisions. Even those parents who follow a rights discourse on behalf of their child are often manipulated out of the decision-making process by those in power, and persuaded to accept what the system decides to offer. Diane stated:

> Professionals don't realize how much energy and courage parents need. If there is a difference of opinion at the end of the day, parents will back down. Parents are conditioned in the same way as when you see a doctor, a dentist, a principal, that they [the professionals] know the legislation. Parents want to accept things.

Margaret said:

> The relationship with the teacher is critical. We are always the one who works at the relationship. When you are the parent of a child with a disability you are always aware you are not the same as other families. I need a teacher with a sense of humour, to have a chuckle and ignore [the differences between my child and others], not someone who is blown away by the situation. It seems very positive until there is a problem. You hear 'How wonderful for the school to have X at his local school.' Now because there is a problem, it is 'X is a danger to other children.' At the last IEP I asked what was being done about the problem. I was told that the children were telling the teacher when my son did something wrong. I said I would rather the children were taught about assertive behaviour — for them to say 'X, I don't like you doing this.' But I have not been listened to on this one.

Ann, who has had a child in the primary education system for six years, said:

> We depend on the professionals, especially the teacher, the principal and the teacher aide. These people can change from year to year and it becomes very difficult to build up relationships. Last year the principal saw us as adversarial and anything we did was interpreted as aggressive. Not all the information I share with the teacher aide is considered confidential by those professionals — it is shared with a Special Needs Committee. I knew the committee existed and I have to assume that they keep confidences. I merely pointed out to the teacher aide that I'd [now] be selective about what I shared. That gave them food for thought.

Ann added:

> Last year we had a teacher for our daughter who was young, had no children of her own, and didn't want another adult in her classroom. The teacher gave an ultimatum, 'Either she goes [the teacher aide], or I go.' We, the parents, had to ask the teacher aide to leave as the school didn't want an unfair dismissal. This year

we have a different teacher and there are no issues. The whole tone is positive. We have had a change in the teacher aide. The school did not approach us. All the information came via the former teacher aide — the teacher was not informed by the principal. We have no choice but to work with the new teacher aide. We have invited her into our home, we write in the notebook, what choice did we have?

As far as the professionals are concerned, a number of parents saw them as being gatekeepers to whatever part of the system the parents were trying to access for their child. They appear so qualified and they use big words. The system is inflexible and will not change to accommodate the parents' needs. Parents are always trying to get the system to move.

Tui felt that often professionals thought she was 'not a good reflection of their energy'. She felt that often professionals thought she needed rescuing. There appeared to be a cycle of effort being applied to parents like herself, followed by the realization that there were insufficient resources to solve the problem. One professional would disappear from her life, only to be replaced by another who would also see her as a victim and prepare to rescue her all over again.

Diane, the parent advocate, said that teachers and principals have to accept that a child is to be part of the class and is their responsibility, not the responsibility of the Special Education Service (a government agency providing support services for schools), the therapist, or the teacher aide. Diane was aware that teachers were becoming more hard-nosed and cynical about equipment, resources and teacher aide time. Some schools have had one or two bad experiences with help promised and not delivered, and their expectations have become coloured. Parents are then left to cope when a school denies access to mainstream classes or says that a child can attend for only part of a day because support is not available through government services. Diane said that in such circumstances a number of parents will not challenge the system, or they will go to the Ministry of Education, which says 'Go to the Board of Trustees', which may well involve confronting or arguing with neighbours or friends who are in those Board positions. The Ministry of Education has to have teeth to say to schools, 'This practice is illegal. What are you going to do about it?' This rarely happens, so parents struggle on their own. Maria said:

> The school trusts me now. They believe in my son. The principal has transferred his positive attitude to the teachers. There is a confidence in my ability to advocate for my son. It has made it easier for the school. If it is good or bad, I'll take it up. Sometimes I'll put them in the right direction for resources if the school can't find them alone. I know that at the beginning the school thought I was unrealistic in my expectations of my son and therefore of them. I got the feeling that they thought, 'What is she talking about — reading?' They worried that I would blame them if he didn't [achieve] things.

Kim voiced her concern at how professionals treated parents, particularly in the light of her own experience with professionals telling parents what they should do — there was no empathy:

At one Child Development Unit they expected me to leave my daughter there for three weeks with no contact while they carried out an assessment on her. I was so angry. We moved around a lot — Rotorua, Taupo, Whakatane. It was different but the same. In one instance in the medical area, not education, a paediatrician wrote that I was very assertive. If I was a doctor would they write these things about me? If I was anything but a mother would they write these comments?

Changes in the Advocacy System — A Wish List for the Future

As an advocate, Diane summed up her concerns by saying:

> There must be a recognition of family rights and what we are going to do to help them. Parents must be seen as experts and part of the professional team. Parents need to be made welcome by schools. In an ideal world there would not be the need for more advocacy. There are a lot of people out there who neither have the knowledge of nor networks to access advocacy services. Advocacy information needs to be free — the cost of a telephone call can make balancing the family budget very difficult. Often parents of children with special needs are used to assist other parents, but that takes advantage of people who are already vulnerable. It has to be recognized that telling a story yet again to an advocate takes courage. Often people only contact me when they are at the end of their tether — sometimes I've dropped everything and driven to the person, but that is not always possible.

Tui voiced her needs as, 'We need one advocate each and they must be paid an amount of money that gives the job dignity. Parents need to be nurtured and protected.' Maria said:

> Until there is more money in advocacy and more advocates, schools will dominate what happens to parents and children with disabilities. The size of Auckland makes it especially important. Mainstreaming students is becoming a bigger and bigger struggle all the time. No one wants their child in a school where the staff don't want them. Parents live with decisions they don't like. If more advocates were readily available parents could build up a relationship with that advocate and that would provide so much support to parents.

Kate said:

> Ultimately I would like people to assume that my children can go to their local school the same as if he didn't have a disability. I wish that when TVNZ made their community advertisements the faces of people with intellectual disabilities would be shown. We value those who are academically able, we value those who have passed exams — the doctors and lawyers, but people with intellectual disabilities are not valued. There is a place for everyone in society, to be disabled is not such a negative thing — in schools it should be just normal. Society makes you feel as if you have failed as a person. Women in particular have this sense of failure as if we are not 100 per cent.

As Ann explained:

> Advocacy is so many things. It is not just about being there at meetings with parents. It is about talking and writing. And not just in education, but in hospitals, or with landlords, or in prisons. Parents and people with disabilities need to be heard and they need the space to do that in without having their ideas twisted or discounted. It can be so disempowering when an advocate has not really grasped what you've said or not listened to you. I had that happen once and it felt like I was being rescued. The impact on me was profound. I would like to see parents learn the skills so they can do it themselves.

References

BALLARD, K. (1994) 'Disability: An introduction', in BALLARD, K. (Ed.) *Disability, Family, Whanau and Society*, Palmerston North, New Zealand: Dunmore Press, pp. 1–27.

BALLARD, K., WATSON, M., BRAY, A., BURROWS, L. and MACARTHUR, J. (1992) *The Otago Family Network: A Report on the Research Contract to the Research and Statistics Division, Ministry of Education*, Dunedin, New Zealand: Donald Beasley Institute and University of Otago.

BARTON, L. (1992) 'Disability and the necessity for a socio-political perspective', in WOODS, D. (Ed.) *Disability and the Need for a Socio-political Perspective*, Monograph No. 51 of International Exchange of Experts and Information in Rehabilitation, Durham, NH: University of New Hampshire, pp. 1–14.

FULCHER, G. (1989) *Disabling Policies? A Comparative Approach to Education Policy and Disability*, London: The Falmer Press.

OLIVER, M. (1990) *The Politics of Disablement*, London: Macmillan.

WILLS, R. (1994) 'It is time to stop', in BALLARD, K. (Ed.) *Disability, Family, Whanau and Society*, Palmerston North, New Zealand: Dunmore Press, pp. 247–64.

Chapter 4

My Kid, and Kids Kinda Like Him

Linda Ware

The aim of this research was to enlarge the framework for the study of inclusion by inviting eight parents to participate in a series of four critical dialogues on progress towards inclusion in the urban school district in which their children were enrolled in both general and special education.

Tapping into the parents' subjective experiences as the unit of analysis to inform inclusion proved to be a challenge for several reasons. First, the parents varied by age, gender, socio-economic status, education, and by their own parenting and advocacy experiences. Naturally they reported a range of perspectives. Although many advocates are quick to dispel the notion of the 'parent perspective' as a unifying standpoint, the notion persists, especially among special educators. From the outset, my goal was to avoid essentializing the input of the participants, and to minimize all attempts to fix them into boxes. Further, as a feminist researcher who strongly endorses the belief that the inquirer be located on the same critical plane as the participants, I felt uniquely situated for understanding given my own experience as a parent in active pursuit of inclusion for my son. It was ironic, then, to discover that this very resonance silenced my voice in the early stages of data collection — as though the Goddess Hera had been summoned to condemn once more, as she had to Echo, 'You will always have the last word, but no power to speak first.' Over time, I realized that the tensions I struggled with originated from multiple sources discussed in the chapter, chief among them that which Heshusius (1994) describes as abandoning 'the possibility of objectivity as a life option' (p. 15).

Critical Dialogues

Critical dialogues are an approach to evaluation that seeks to engage research participants and researchers in open-ended discussion specific to an identified research problem. The assumption is that, through dialogue and the articulation of positions, participants will, with greater confidence, attempt to fill in the gaps between understanding and action (Ware, 1994b, 1998, in press). Critical dialogues are structured as small group interactions, with five to ten individuals who collectively consider change, or the components of change, such that interpretation, reflection and evaluation emerge in a natural progression. Initially, the group meets to share their own awareness or understanding of a given problem and, in this way, they begin to develop group identity. Over time, rapport is forged through focused meaningful exchange.

The role of the researcher is critical as a creative mediator, but not necessarily the *leader* of the dialogue. Carefully posed questions by the researcher prompt the participants to reflect on their own perspectives and practices, their students, peers or clients, and their beliefs and motivations, in an effort to more comprehensively contend with reform or change. During this discourse with self and 'other', rapport increases among the group members, and the participants probe one another with the same degree of interest and insight as the researcher. A central feature of the critical dialogue approach is the recognition that individuals as persons possess a point of view and the power of self-evaluation, such that self-interpretation becomes central to understanding and thus to change (Ware, 1994b).

In this research, the four critical dialogues occurred over 10 weeks during the summer of 1996. Each dialogue lasted approximately 90 minutes and was tape recorded and transcribed. After each meeting the entire transcript was mailed to the participants along with brief memos and one-page summary reports of the dialogues. Participants were free to challenge or amend the contents of each, and the memos and transcripts were then used to inform subsequent analysis by the participants and the researcher.

Research Setting

The study was undertaken in a university community with a population of 70,000. The participants had resided from one to 21 years in the community, and most viewed themselves as life-long residents. They attended typical school functions, including school orientations, grade-level recognition events, band concerts, plays, holiday programmes, school picnics, carnivals and parent/teacher conferences. Although these parents 'rarely' attended school board meetings, many cited frequent communication with the newly appointed special education administrator. They reported daily or weekly contact with their child's teachers, support staff and/or administration, either in person, on the phone, or in written daily notebook correspondence. These interactions were generally friendly, a descriptor which stood in marked contrast to their interactions with the previous director, whom many described as 'highly unavailable and generally unresponsive'. Some of the parents also reported community involvement with advocacy organizations such as the ARC (formerly known as the Association for Retarded Citizens), and various district committees such as the Parent Advisory Council, the Special Education Advisory Council and the Transition Council. Also, because these dialogues occurred during the summer, parents reported 'exhaustive' participation with their children in city-wide league sports (for example soccer, T-ball, softball) and community recreation which included programmes for special populations.

The Inclusion Context

The recent appointments of an enthusiastic pro-inclusion district Director of Special Education and an equally enthusiastic State Board of Education Director of Special Education, heightened awareness of inclusion at the local and state level. During the previous school year numerous articles appeared in the local newspaper which spurred further interest about inclusion. Community presentations on inclusion sponsored by the district Special Education Advisory Council coincided with the publication of the district's inclusion policy outlined in an informational brochure titled *Inclusive Schooling Means Belonging* (District Public Relations Document, 1995). Similar to the national and international controversy generated by inclusion, local concerns focused on resources, personnel preparation, staffing, policy, curriculum and the need for a clear definition of inclusion and its goals (Brandt, 1994; Lipsky and Gartner, 1997).

The Participants

Twenty parents were nominated as likely participants by teachers and principals throughout the district, and of this group, five mothers and three fathers agreed to participate in a series of four critical dialogues. The parents were between the ages of 30 and 49, and their children ranged in ages from newborn to adolescence. Alane gave birth to her second child during this research, while Emma and Sandy had children in high school. Emma's three children spanned high school through elementary school, which created the chaos of shuffling between school schedules, enrichment lessons, sports activities, leisure activities and doctor's appointments, and all the while she worked at a 'snail's pace' to complete a masters degree in social work. Sandy had two sons in special education, one in the high school resource programme, and one in the middle school gifted education programme. 'Mama Mona' (as she was known in her neighbourhood) had four children — one adopted child with significant disabilities, two foster children with significant disabilities, and her biological daughter who was identified as learning disability/gifted. Paula, a general education teacher, had two children without disabilities, both of whom were enrolled in inclusion classrooms in the district.

Among the fathers who participated, Ben had two young children, a daughter who was home-schooled by his wife, and a younger son with Down syndrome, who was enrolled in a Montessori kindergarten affiliated with the university. Jack had two daughters in general education, and one son with Down syndrome who attended his neighbourhood school. And finally, Gray, like Emma, had three children in three different schools. His oldest son was in high school, the second eldest had Down syndrome and was enrolled in a pull-out programme at the district's 'cluster site', and the youngest, a daughter, was in second grade in their neighbourhood school. Among these participants, I had prior interactions with Ben and Jack through research for the ARC. Because I worked as a consultant in support of inclusion in all of the schools represented — at the request of either the school district, or the State Board of Education — I was acquainted with several participants and/or their children.

Multiple Perspectives and Parent Sensibilities

One of the important features of the critical dialogues reported in this research was the diversity of the group, and the various assumptions they held about schooling, the needs of their children, and of all children. Some parents reported that their children began public schooling in special education at a time quite unlike the present. Today, according to current district policy, the right of every child assumed 'going to your home school with brothers, sisters and other kids from the neighbourhood' (District Public Relations Document, 1995). Services previously provided in cluster sites staffed by specially trained personnel using special techniques and individualized curriculum were inspired by the previously unquestioned assumption that individualized education equalled separate education. In contrast, parents moving from a pre-school service delivery model with an Individual Family Service Plan (IFSP), were more apt to assume that their children would 'receive special education services through collaborative teaming by special and general educators, related service personnel, paraprofessionals, parents and administrators' (District Public Relations Document, 1995).

In the space between the history these parents did not share and the present in which they came together in dialogue on inclusion, a variety of lived experiences and richly diverse perspectives were threaded together in a process that clearly exposed the myth of an essentialized parent perspective. Although there were strands of a common language between the parents, there was a noticeable absence of authority in what they told the group, a phenomenon similar to that described in the construction of women's agency by Hartman (1991). That is, 'when women move to *subjective knowledge* [emphasis in the original], they know themselves as knowers but experience their knowledge as warranted only to themselves by themselves' (p. 20). The particular, local and regional quality of this knowledge is further described by Foucault (1980) as 'subjugated knowledges', which, in fact, depict two separate knowledges. The first refers to the 'historical contents that have been buried and disguised in a functionalist coherence or formal system' (p. 81). The second refers to a 'whole set of knowledges that have been disqualified as inadequate to their task or insufficiently elaborated: naive knowledge, located low down on the hierarchy, beneath the required level of cognition or scientificity' (p. 82). The critical dialogues reported in this research enabled parents to excavate new meaning in this 'disqualified knowledge' not only to themselves but to one another. Through this genealogy, they recovered knowledge that 'owes its force only to the harshness with which it is opposed by everything surrounding it . . . [and] it is through the reappearance of this knowledge . . . [that] criticism performs its work' (p. 82).

This chapter will serve as an instrument of criticism that borrows from the voices of the parents. I will foreground the material context derived from their harsh accounts of struggle, resistance and conflict in a system itself in struggle to make sense of inclusion. Informed by the parents, my primary task is to underscore the value of parent sensibilities in our efforts to inform the progress of inclusion; and to this end, to legitimize their historical knowledge borne from struggle and survival. From this subjectivist viewpoint, infused by a postmodern consciousness, I aim to inform and broaden the discourse on inclusion.

In addition, the data presentation departs from the more traditional 'first-then-after' linear narrative, to one in which I intertwine exchanges in a [re]structured textual representation (Ellis and Flaherty, 1992; Ellis, 1997; Richardson, 1994, 1997).

Ellis describes a process of condensing several scenes into 'evocative composites' which result in a story greater than the conventional 'mirror representation of chrono- logically ordered events' (1997, p. 128). In support, Richardson urges that such narrative play is essential to the construction of the experimental representations needed to interrupt traditionally staged research. In this research, the narrative was reordered to the extent that exchanges from the fourth dialogue may be reported as part of the second or of the third dialogue, and the reverse. Blending these exchanges, I altered time, but not the content or the exact wording exchanged in our dialogues. For example, throughout the critical dialogues, the parents described their children in various contexts, which became the lines in verse I crafted to introduce their chil- dren. [Re]structured in this way, the verse renders succinct details which invoke the reader's sensibilities with greater immediacy. And as one parent commented during our final member check, the poems 'tell the readers upfront — here's my child, this is who we're talking about, this is how I know her'.

The Subject as the Object of our Affection

I have a son, Ian. He'll be thirteen this month.
He has Down syndrome.
In the early years
we had all the medical complications
stunted growth, diminished overall ability
healthwise we're rolling now.
He's moving into seventh grade in the fall.   *(Gray)*

I have a six year old. Second grade.
Amy's hearing impaired. Profoundly,
deaf from birth.
My husband is also deaf.
Amy went to Willowtree
on campus.
Then in Utah, Bright Beginnings
on campus.
Last fall when we moved back
our options were the school
for the hearing impaired,
or our neighbourhood school.
We didn't want Amy in either one.
Guess we have a real unique situation
with Amy's school
our neighbour works there.
She signs.
The chances of ever finding
a regular ed teacher who signs,
it's a gift from God.
So Amy's in.
Fully included.   *(Alane)*

Jon is eleven.
Has Down's.
He'll be in third grade.
Real handsome.
Girls love to be around him.   *(Jack)*

I have two sons. They aren't disabled.
One is Amy's classmate.
We're lucky to have so many worlds of difference
to understand now.
That's why I'm here.
I used to teach when we called it mainstreaming.
Now I've seen it from both sides.   *(Paula)*

Zach is five, his last year at Willowtree.
A pretty happy kid overall.
Sometimes I get the feeling that he knows
more than what he lets on.
Maybe we're fooling ourselves
but we expect first grade
should be as good or better.
He has Down syndrome,
did I say that?   *(Ben)*

Among the three parents with more history in special education, Mona opened with an apology for her inability to be 'brief'.

We have four children,
three are severely, multiply, handicapped.
Debra, the youngest, is six.
They say she has Ingerman's syndrome.
We don't necessarily agree with that.
Christopher is eleven, going into Jr High.
He has spastic CP, severely microcephalic.
Della is twelve, at the Jr High too.
She has spastic CP.

They say our children are severely retarded.
We don't necessarily agree with that.
Our thirteen year old, is LD/Gifted.
She just opted out of the program this year.
Teenagers have their own ideas about school.

Since second grade, Chris and Della
were always included.
We were really happy with that,
back then the staff was very accepting.
Now it's issues like the lack of para training,

substitute paras, equipment breakdowns,
it all falls on one teacher to fix.
Mr Swan tries. We all know that.
But there's not much team work at the Jr High.

Debra has some behavioural issues,
we're working on them.
We've done a lot of consulting with people.
It'll probably be a while
before we get inclusion for her.   *(Mona)*

Nate is sixteen, a freshman in high school.
For years we searched for a label
now we have one,
'pervasive developmental disorder'.
A whole galaxy of differences,
academic and social emotional problems,
so many things could be impacted.
I don't want to know
any more.
He's aware he's different.
Jr High drives your differences home.
All at once everyone isn't so nice any more.
Nate wants to go to college,
then to graduate school.
That's what he talks about,
but, I don't think it can happen.
School work has been real hard,
always has.
This summer he's working.
His job coach comes out,
checks in, says,
'everything is working well'.   *(Sandy)*

Kara's a freshman. Eighteen.
From early on I would go in
'larger than life' to make sure
her needs were known and met.
I didn't want to work for systems change.
I didn't have time for that.
I couldn't wait for inclusion
to trickle down and be accepted.
I won't let Kara's life dwindle away.
I mean, her school life.
We didn't call it inclusion back then,
but that's what it was.
Social skills are her strength.
She's a self-advocate.
Powerful.   *(Emma)*

49

'Is any of this going to make any difference down the road?'

Although the parents were willing participants in this research, and each voiced a unique stake in the future of inclusion, their initial comfort level sharing with one another was uneven. Some disclosed only immediate details about their lives and their children, others traced back through history to paint a backdrop to situate their perspectives. However, as the dialogues progressed, shared understanding and common beliefs about their children's needs emerged, although constant negotiation and tinkering with the boundaries for each participant's zone of comfort continued.

Alane, the youngest parent, was quick to acknowledge the value of sharing experiences. With great enthusiasm, she volleyed a round of critical questions immediately following our introductions.

> ALANE: I want to ask you guys about your IEP [Individual Education Plan] teams ... I mean, about the dynamics of the team. As I listen to you all describing your kids I'm thinking, 'wow, I'd love to sit in on your IEPs and find out how all this really works for you. Like for instance, have administration techniques changed over the time? Have any of you ever felt that there were people on your IEP teams or IFSP [Individual Family Service Plan] teams that you didn't necessarily want on the team? Persons that maybe weren't really contributing? Because the idea of having a dream for your child, it's got to be essential that it's unanimous among the team. But that isn't always the case, and while everyone can have a different dream, having someone on the team that is in extreme opposition — not even in the same boat with you — makes all your work that much harder over time. Doesn't it? How has this worked for you all?

In the unbearable silence that followed Alane's explosion of questions, I grew anxious wondering who would hazard a response. Finally Mona offered, 'You know, it's rare for me to lose my temper, but I have.' She described an incident with a speech therapist whom she insisted be removed from Debra's support team based on prior experiences with her son, Chris. The therapist disputed a previous assessment of Chris, and urged that her recent evaluation (which detected significantly lower ability) take precedence. Mona described her discomfort at the confrontation, but since then, her approach has been to persist with her demands, and to follow up with a support call to the district administration. Mona was known throughout the district and the community as a parent who made 'reasonable' demands and visibly supported teachers. 'Mona is definitely a team player, I have a lot of respect for her', recalled Mr Swan, who taught both Chris and Della. The new district director agreed with this assessment and was equally supportive and responsive to Mona's calls for help.

Emma insisted that she learned early in her daughter's schooling, to 'make a big entrance at the beginning'. As she explained it, 'I fade back real quick, but I want them to know who I am, that Kara's got a lot of concern focused on her, in that we're a very caring family.' She described a recent episode with a 'teacher who did not want Kara in his classroom'. Emma explained that the teacher had prior experience with the family, and was once again 'targeting our family — his grudge began before Kara, and would likely continue after her'. For that reason, Emma and her husband urged Kara to handle the situation 'as best she could', in the same way they had urged her siblings before her to negotiate with this teacher.

> EMMA: We knew nothing bad was going to happen to Kara, and we wanted to see how she handled things that were not fair or just, things that were unpleasant. It wasn't a perfect situation, I don't think all of hers get to be perfect. We knew she wasn't going to be learning much history, but we figured she would be learning how to deal with someone who didn't want to include her, in much the same way an employer might reject her in the future, or any number of different people in her life — we looked at it that way.

Emma spoke with a clarity informed by 18 years of parenting, which captivated Alane. Although Alane would later apologize for monopolizing the first dialogue, she was convinced there was little time to waste getting to the 'real issues'.

> ALANE: That brings me to my next question as far as inclusion is concerned — there's this whole other side of the coin that we deal with as parents — socialization. It's such a sensitive issue for us as parents because it's a double edged sword. Are we robbing Peter to pay Paul just to get our kids included? In some ways inclusion is great, but we all know that in some ways, it's not so great. My big heart pain as a mom is, 'how important is inclusion right now, or is it something that is going to bene-fit Amy down the road?' Like you said, Emma, you let Kara learn from discrimination in hopes that she'll have thicker skin later in life. But, it seems like every year once school ends, I think, 'great, I'll never have to face these problems again.' Right? But then, when the same thing happens the next year, I catch myself knowing this is going to keep happening forever — with future job opportunities, or in college, or whatever, down the road. Won't we always be fighting to get our kids included? Always fighting to have our kids considered as full human beings? Is any of this going to make a difference down the road?

As Emma prepared to respond, Gray interjected a lengthy monologue about the administrative process of the IEP and its connection to the success or failure of inclusion. He made no effort to respond to Alane's concerns. As a leader in opposi-tion to inclusion in the community, Gray proposed another form of theft — that inclusion robbed parents of choice — because their children were forced to attend their neighbourhood schools that were unprepared to deal with diversity. As an example, Gray held that despite his son's IEP which specified support services, Ian lost needed services as therapists travelled between schools. Gray's concerns then prompted a lengthy exchange about the inherent value of the IEP, which con-tinued in our second meeting in something of an 'IEP show-and-tell'. The parents were anxious to exchange IEPs, given that most reported familiarity only with their own IEP, something that stood in marked contrast to the fact that teachers, school psychologists, and school administrators get to see numerous IEPs. That the parents desired to exchange IEPs for analysis was apropos of everything this research sought to accomplish: the open-ended design of the critical dialogues invites consideration of numerous forms of data, as it emerges from the context of the dialogue, initiated by the participants rather than the researcher.

Silencing the Parent/Researcher

At the conclusion of the first critical dialogue, I reflected on my less than active participation in dialogue. This was curious. Given that I felt comfortable with the parents and versed on the topic as both parent and researcher, my lack of engagement was perplexing. I shared my politics on inclusion as 'core values' that informed both my parenting and my research, and I described my son, Justin, who resides in another state:

> 22, cerebral palsy-like symptoms / high verbal, high wit / when attempts to force him into a group home, Justin mocked: 'You guys are acting like Nazis and you're expecting me to be a Jew and accept your concentration camp', drafting an auto- biography of his life marked by the impact of music / Paul Simon, Crosby Stills and Nash, Eric Clapton, Garth Brooks.

Also, in my reflexive journal entries, empathy, affiliation and signs of blurring the lines between the role of parent and researcher were evident:

> These stories are rich, rich, rich, these moms, these dads, they're treasures. Do they know that? Does the system? Do they know what lies ahead? Will they hear? Be heard? They want for answers, they want for guarantees, they want for comfort, they want for hope eternal.

In response to selected phrases made by the parents, I elaborated at length, in very personal and confessional writing informed by personal parent knowledge. Like Heshusius (1994) who discovered the need for 'merging' with research particip- ants in order to be 'fully attentive' (p. 19), I too was wholly aware of the merger, and yet silenced by it in the early stages of this research. Somehow, it seemed inappropriate to access my parent voice until I could unpack its seeming threat to my research. Although there is a long history of interpretivist researchers merging events from their personal lives, not so much for confessional purposes, but in contribution to sociological understanding, the response to this work has tended to be a critique of its methodological soundness (Ellis and Flaherty, 1992; Heshusius, 1994; Richardson, 1992; Smith, 1997).

Later, when I reviewed the transcript, I noted another difference between this dialogue and my previous research using critical dialogues. Typically, in earlier studies the participants were less forthcoming in the initial meeting than Alane, as group dynamics necessitate that sufficient time be provided for participants to ease into one another's zone of comfort and safety. Often, differences across age, across status, those of gendered communication patterns, and those related to political ideology impact the rate of interaction in critical dialogues. It was also Alane with whom I initially engaged in my reflexive journal entries, captivated by her straightforward communication style and her desire to 'seize the moment' and move the discussion forward (something which ultimately became the standard for the group!).

Also, as I reviewed the transcript I was reminded of a recent conversation with my son, Justin, who struggled to understand why his co-workers in the music store appeared put off by his attempts to socialize. 'I invite them to my apartment, or to meet at a movie, but they always say they're too busy with school.' In resignation, he added, 'I'm kinda thinking that's not it.' Justin's voice was lodged in my memory where the '*heart-pain*' accumulates. Despite our many successes at inclusion and Justin's personal independence in particular, I still wonder, as Alane asked, 'is any of this going to make a difference down the road?' Prior to this research project — the first to recover my own struggles as a parent — I believed that I stridently talked back to this 'great heart pain'. Now, I wanted to relate that *the 'heart-pain' never stops*. After 22 years, that much I could claim with authority. Perhaps that is why I fell silent.

Unfortunately, as a result of complications that arose from her pregnancy, Alane was confined to bed rest, and unable to attend our remaining dialogues. In an attempt to keep Alane's presence viable in the group, I posed questions as she might, piecing together her concerns as she related them to me in phone conversations. Over time, our voices seemed to merge, which allowed me greater participation in this research, and less pressure to speak from the authority of my own parenting experience.

'I've never taken the thing seriously'

When the second dialogue convened, Emma returned empty handed, without an IEP, and Sandy having lost hers, with a new copy from the school. Between Emma and Sandy the laughter was heartfelt, but among the other parents I sensed discomfort as they proudly returned with their IEPs. In a more solemn tone, Emma and Sandy attested to their dedicated attendance and participation in the IEP meetings. Nonetheless, they concurred that the document itself was all but meaningless.

> SANDY: I feel really awful saying this, but I've never taken the thing seriously, not at all. I suppose that's a terrible thing to say, but it always seemed to be something that didn't really relate to anything Nate did.

With her 12-year history of special education to draw on, Sandy amended her comment and reflected back to a time when she felt the IEP was relevant. 'When the IEP was written out in long hand . . . I really had more of a feeling that the teacher was in touch with Nate.' Flipping through the 12 pages of Nate's current IEP, she criticized his current computer-generated IEPs as 'just a bunch of gobbeldegook. I don't even know if they [school personnel] take it seriously.' She read a few goals as examples and this fuelled an exchange.

> Given 10 word problems involving money using amounts equal to or less than a dollar, Nate will write number sentences to solve the problem with 100% accuracy.
>
> Given 30 clocks set at minute intervals of time before the hour, Nate will state the time with 100% accuracy.

'With so many of these tasks I can't imagine how they even get Nate to attempt them', Sandy mocked. Jack was quick to agree, 'It's all too mechanistic. My kid rebels against this sometimes. He gets into this feisty mode, or maybe it's just boredom, and says, "I'm not going to do this any more!"'

'Exactly! For Nate, this is not the stuff he does well. None of it. Performing is his weakest point. A lot of his abilities don't surface when he's asked to perform on command', Sandy snapped. The exchange shifted to wonderment as to how such myopia could have prevailed across the state and the nation in support of computerized IEPs. Mona recalled the claims made at the time the district adopted this computerized approach:

> They insisted it would save money and free teachers to spend more time with our kids, I remember that clear as a bell. And, what a joke. You know why? Because I've seen how much time Mr Swan has to put in to make his IEPs meaningful. He has to search forever to find goals that make sense, or he just makes up new ones. I bet he'd agree the whole process takes up more time, not less.

On this, Jack explained that he and his wife raised concerns similar to those of the district administration, and the offer was made to create an alternative IEP for Jon. Together, with district personnel, and the state director of special education, they wrote an *integrative* IEP for Jon in which goals and objectives were cross-referenced to daily activities aligned to ongoing classroom instruction. In Jack's estimation, the process of writing the IEP was the most crucial component because it enabled the school staff to assume greater investment in Jon's education and more meaningful ownership.

> It was the most incredible IEP meeting we ever had. We discussed Jon's most successful classroom activities, his favourite ones, and the ones for his home activities too. We also talked about the frustrating ones, and what is reasonable to expect from him in school — based on how we deal with the same matters at home. We came out of the meeting feeling really very good about what's going to happen next year for Jon.

Mona was quick to retort, 'So what kinda strings did you have to pull?' Her scepticism was understandable. It was unusual to have the participation of the state director in planning an IEP. He was, however, also a parent of a child with disabilities, and both he and his wife were leaders in the local and regional ARC. His vision for reform in special education across the state included the [re]vision of IEPs to underscore the belief that special education was a service, not a place.

This exchange served to inform the critique of the IEPs, as well as to demonstrate their status as artefacts that marked changes in the material context of the

10-to-15-year histories with special education and public schooling that separated Sandy, Emma, and Mona from the others. These moms shared a history shaped by compliance rather than cooperation, and by the 'parody of collaboration' which all but ensured standardized, routine parent interactions in place of meaningful engagement (Ware, 1994a). At the time, I identified with the cynicism that edged their perspective. It called to mind the claim by another mother with whom I conducted research with families. In a confident voice, without any suggestion of apology, this mother said, 'I hope you won't think I'm always this aggressive — it's just that I've had to learn to keep my balance, by staying "on guard"' (Ware and Howarth, 1998). These parent struggles across generations, across communities, across states, were as predictable as the IEP protocol regulated by policy. In contrast, Ben, Jack, Gray and Alane were the benefactors of the conflicts and struggles that preceded them, and they could cite instances of meaningful collaboration and alliances with school personnel and administration. In dialogue the parents unpacked the complexity of moving from an era of meaninglessness, to one in which meaningful inclusion need not place them '*on guard*'. In the section that follows, a narrative block is provided for readers to draw their own conclusions from our exchange.

My Kid, and Kids Kinda Like Him

As Jack described it, he was hopeful that his son's IEP would shape inclusion in both the classroom and the school, to be utilized as a tool of both practice and policy — a goal consistent with the original purpose of the IEP (Smith, 1990). In contrast, Sandy's 12-page IEP was all but meaningless in the context of her son Nate's science inclusion class. Her hopes diminished as larger concerns surfaced about Nate's needs being met prior to graduation from high school.

SANDY: What I worry about is that Nate's going to be included in a bunch of classes, and that the material will be way over his head — which has happened a lot already. And every time, I feel like I should rewrite the curriculum he needs, or rewrite the class, or even these materials to better suit Nate. I feel that if I could spend a year to write this course very differently, I could come up with content that he would understand. But I don't have a year to do it — he's only there a year, and then the next class comes along and we start all over. Now that he's in high school, the semester is less than a year. So why is he taking classes that he can't understand? That's not inclusion to me.

JACK: That's what we wanted to avoid with Jon, guess it's probably easier to do in third grade than in high school. But when we started the IEP we knew there were going to be some things he's just not ready for, but then there are some things that he can be learning along with his class. So when they're doing things that he can't understand just yet, he's doing things that are similar, but not *exactly* the same. That way he's included in an instructional task, learning the same thing, but maybe not at the same level.

SANDY: But, I'm not sure that I even believe that my son should be going to those classes. Just going to those classes and trying to sit still for 45 minutes and listening to the teacher talk about science, chemistry, physics — that just seems too incredible. And it was really hard for him at first, he would come home with homework that I didn't even understand. I felt like it was like a test, not to see how much Nate knew, but how much I knew.

LINDA: Did things change over the course of the semester?

SANDY: I suppose. We did the homework! I'm one of those driven, responsible people, and if the teacher sends home this homework, well, by golly, we're going to do it. So what I tried to do was break the material down for Nate. These were very interesting concepts, so I worked to present them in ways that I knew made sense to Nate.

LINDA: That sounds great, but it's real unfortunate that the opportunity was missed to share those modifications for other kids.

SANDY: What do you mean? He was the only one from special education in that class.

LINDA: I mean, earlier you said you could have written a better course, and you probably did. I know regular education teachers that would love to have someone make those adaptations — whether it's the special education teacher, a paraprofessional, or the parent — just seems that the opportunity was missed to use what you created with other kids.

SANDY: Oh, I don't know about that, they'd probably just say, 'Nate's level isn't the next kid's level.' Nate has a certain, definite level that isn't the level of the student sitting next to him. It's like the goal becomes how do we write a curriculum to suit everyone? There ought to be some middle ground for my kid, and kids kinda like him.

LINDA: You're exactly right — I'm convinced most teachers know the need exists for your kid and kids kinda like him, so why is this point missed? We could also utilize the curriculum that's already there too. I'm working with some other teachers in the district with a hands-on science curriculum — very high interest content with lots of physical exploration that would likely be very well suited to Nate. It's an elementary curriculum, but that isn't to say it couldn't be the springboard for hooking students into more challenging content that is *like — but not at — the exact same grade level.* Jack's right, for inclusion to work at the curriculum level, the goal has to be parallel instruction which is 'like' but not necessarily the same. We spend so much time and money on 'adaptations' that are commercially produced, but they're edged in neon, signalling different, different, different.

SANDY: That sounds good, Linda, but you know what? I never know how much to push for, how much I should insist on. I always hang back and think, 'How can they do this much for my child, when resources are so scarce?'

BEN: I'm sitting here wondering the same thing. How the heck is the school district going to be able to afford all this?

SANDY: That's why I didn't scream real loud. I don't think that the district can do it all.

JACK: But don't you think it can be done one piece at a time? I mean, they're not going to just come up with three million dollars and just like that modify or adapt the whole curriculum. But inclusive neighbourhood schools has to mean changing the IEPs and modifying the curriculum.

BEN: I guess maybe, if you gave teachers the latitude, because they know the child and the child's capabilities — giving them the latitude to come up with the curriculum — they could do it. But I expect it'll scare the heck out of some of them even if it's like you said, Linda, with the science curriculum that is already there.

SANDY: Yeah, I think there are good people out there. They just don't know what's expected either, or how to accomplish so much in a short amount of time.

LINDA: Guess that's where I lose patience because I know teachers are already making an effort in curriculum reform and inclusion. Most started out to do one or the other, but they soon realized the goals overlapped. I think Ben is right, given the latitude to figure this out, teachers could be very successful, and with help from parents, even more could happen.

GRAY: Everyone here seems to be forgetting an important piece. I didn't bring a copy, but I can, my petition to stop inclusion in this district has over 150 signatures. Teachers don't feel they've been trained for it. A two-hour in-service is not going to prepare teachers for inclusion. So let's say you have 20 teachers, Linda, I have 150 who don't want to touch it!

LINDA: But think about everything we've talked about here, what's to train for?

EMMA: Exactly! The first thing we always hear about is, 'Oh, no, not with me, I don't have any special training.' My response to that is, hey, neither do I! Nobody gave me any special training, I'm still making it up 18 years later. I think if you just get in there and do it, you'll see that all you really need is a little confidence and a lot of compassion.

LINDA: Great point, Emma! So much of this turns on letting go how we've done things in the past, assuming that we *want* to see all kids in their neighbourhood schools.

GRAY: But not if they can't be provided for. We moved Ian from our neighbourhood school after second grade to the cluster site, and they're doing a great job by him. The other school couldn't meet his needs.

BEN: What about the socialization issue, is that something that comes up for Ian?

GRAY: I think the socialization issue can be argued both ways. Having a child with special needs, there are adults in this community I work with from ARC, or with Families Together — but I don't invite them to my house for dinner, we don't go to Chiefs football games. Does that mean I'm a bigot or that I discriminate? No, it's just that we tend to move to the people that we feel comfortable with. And no matter how hard they try to get the kids to affiliate with Jeff, he can 'high-five' them, but he can't dribble a basketball like a regular sixth grade kid. By the end of recess the groups have migrated to where they're most comfortable. Not just the regular ed kids, but the special ed kids too — I see that as just pretty natural. The kids are showing their preferences the same way we adults do. I'm not convinced that forcing everyone together will accomplish better socialization.

PAULA: I'd say it does! My older son has been in classes with kids with varying kinds of disability, from behaviour problems to autism. Now my younger son is with Amy, Alane's daughter. Sometimes, he'll sign to us at home because it's something he does at school with Amy. This experience, I think, is opening up his world to see how many different ways there

are to include others. Amy's more like him than she is different. She gets
in trouble, just like my son, she runs out on the playground, just like my
son, they play together, and write notes to one another. We're lucky to
have so many worlds of difference to understand now.

GRAY: So the greater benefit to your child has to come at the expense of receiving better services for my child? Shouldn't I, as a parent, have some say
in that?

PAULA: I don't know that that's what I was saying.

BEN: I think Paula has a good point. The benefits can be for all kids but it's
going to mean that we start doing things differently so we can make inclusion work for *all* kids. I think we'll need to get newer and hopefully,
better ideas about educational practices that work for *all* kids, and not just
kids with disabilities. Inclusion is forcing us to rethink how education for
all kids should be done and how it should have been done all along.

Among these parents, inclusion was fraught with as much complexity as when
it is discussed among educators. Curriculum considerations were central to the debate,
the preservation of services as hard-won entitlement, and the unyielding issue of interrupting authority in a functionalist organization. Ben's appeal for larger goals that
might impact the system as a whole were all but dismissed at the moment, but served
well when the dialogue moved on and Emma argued for inclusion as an issue of
social justice.

'Civil rights, affirmative action, social justice, isn't that the core of it?'

'You know what?', Emma opened the exchange in our third dialogue. 'I kind of
look at this as an affirmative action kind of thing. It's about basic human rights.'
She raised this issue specific to athletics prompted by a human interest story on the
evening news.

EMMA: Did any of you catch that news report where a child with Down syndrome
played on a high school football team in California? He wasn't the manager.
He wasn't the water boy. He played football. For just a moment, I thought,
'Maybe Kara can actually play volleyball, and not just be the manager', you
know? I know she would like to be on the volleyball team, but I can't see
the coach ever, ever, ever letting *anybody* that's less than a perfect athlete
grace her gym, or her locker room. It's more than annoying. But I could
also see Jon playing football, couldn't you, Jack?

Jack and Mona agreed without the slightest hesitation, laughing that Jon would
agree as well.

EMMA: Let's say, for the sake of argument, that I concede that your child's
better than mine, but why isn't mine on the team? Well, because kids like
mine have never been allowed to be on the team. That's it. It's no more

complicated than that, except that also means that we've never had teams experience the less-than-perfect fellow athletes. Civil rights, affirmative action, social justice — isn't that part of the whole inclusion thing? Can we have somebody with less than normal IQ in a regular classroom? Can a teacher teach to diversity? Can a classroom function with less-than-normal IQ kids? Of course they can! And teams can — maybe not win the state championship, but they can go on and play the game. You know the Forrest Gump thing! Everyone raved about that movie — so why can't life be more like the movies? Kara tried out for volleyball this year and during the try-out process (which she didn't make), somehow or other, she generated this will inside of her — you know, '*I just might make the team!*' I was so proud of her. In the process, she really put some of the teachers on the spot. She'd ask her teachers, 'Do you think I'll make the team?' One teacher was really positive and said, 'You know, Kara, you've got really strong legs.' You can't hit that ball, but you've got really strong legs. Kara would come home and say, 'I'm going to try-outs tomorrow, Mom, because Ms Leonard says I have really strong legs.' And I'd say, 'Well, you do, Kara.' I knew that she wasn't going to make the team, but I thought, you know, there's a million other kids trying out that aren't going to make that team either. Sure she came home and cried because she got cut. And I said, 'Well, you know, you still get to be part of the team, because they asked you to be manager. You'll still get to go to the parties, you'll still get to leave school early when they do. It's good to do all those things.' But in all honesty, I'm thinking, wouldn't it have been nice if she could have been on the team, not on a Special Olympics team, but on Carter's ninth grade varsity basketball, volleyball, whatever — real team. Wouldn't that have been OK?

Lodged within Emma's argument was the need to move the conversation beyond framing disabilities as functional impairment — as something that was wrong with Kara. From a sociopolitical perspective, Emma suggested that the boundaries of Kara's present interactions and her environment would have to be stretched beyond the current context of schooling. Inclusion necessitated conversation to address bias, prejudice, segregation and discrimination — themes that Emma raised throughout the dialogues. For the most part, the parents were quick to chime in agreement, and reason through similar points, but it was Sandy who voiced doubt.

SANDY: I have to tell you, I don't know how to handle this conversation. Last summer Nate was on a basketball team and I still remember the great anxiety I felt watching him play because he really didn't know how to play and these kids were cut-throat. They were good to him, and the coach was good to him. Nobody was mean or anything, but he'd get the ball and he'd run the wrong way, or he'd get the ball and completely mess it up, which I guess you'd expect. But my anxiety was so intense, I could hardly stand it. I kept thinking, 'Who is going to get mad first?' You know, somebody's finally going to have enough. Then what?

EMMA: Well, I don't know that I would have picked sports for Kara if that wasn't her niche. In our family, we're all a bunch of dumb jocks, so it's our family cultural thing, and she's always been a part of it. But if music was what my family was all about, and we were all taking music lessons, and enjoying that piece of the arts, I would've been going after orchestra for her — someway, somehow. Or if it had been in art — same thing — but in our family, it's sports. Kara has been exposed so much to athletics in every way, professional on down, you know? I sometimes wonder what this does to her identity within our family.

LINDA: This reminds me of what Jack said when they were planning Jon's IEP, considering what Jon does well at home in order to contextualize the IEP, remember?

JACK: Sure, that's a good point — but are you saying Kara's identity could be threatened because she doesn't get to be a real athlete?

EMMA: Exactly.

BEN: I might agree with that — funny that's not something I would have come up with. But I can buy it with Jon in the classroom more easily than with Kara in sports, but it is the exact same issue.

LINDA: You know, the first time we met, Alane asked the question, about whether moving mountains now would make much of a difference in the future. I'm wondering, how possible would it be to urge policy change for 'no-cut sports' all the way through high school. This is new practice at the Junior High anyway, isn't it? Wasn't the argument to encourage everybody to join a team because team experience is valuable? Would our input help shape the district to move on a similar issue?

MONA: That might be a stretch . . . a good idea, but a stretch.

JACK: I don't know, sports — especially winning — is a big deal in this state. And everywhere.

EMMA: Like I said earlier, I can't wait for a systems change. Kara's in school right now. I don't have time to convince people to see what I see.

LINDA: So how's it happening in California? And in Vermont, they make similar considerations, according to Rich Villa [former special education administrator, Winooski Public Schools, prolific writer/advocate for inclusion].

JACK: I'd have to agree, sports likely won't change to include our kids — unless you want to count special olympics. But is your other question — the one from Alane — whether we think we're doing what we're doing largely for other people — for someone else's children?

LINDA: Does it feel that way? Do your efforts pay off right now? I think her point was, you move mountains because today that's the scale of change needed — but when does the scale change for you and your kids?

JACK: I guess I never thought that way. I'm sure there's an element of truth to that. I'm sure it's going to be easier for kids in three or four or five years because of what we're doing now for Jon, but in honesty, I can't say that's my motivation.

MONA: But you know, Willowtree is a perfect example. Della was the first special needs child to be included there over 10 years ago, before Zach was even born! When you were describing his success stories, I kept thinking about how much was partly a consequence of Della!

BEN: In the long run, isn't that what education is about? I think the system is learning. I want to count on the system to help my child to learn to be an independent citizen that hopefully can have a job, be productive, and be happy. States are in the process of shutting down institutions, and putting everybody back into the community, and isn't this also what inclusion is supposed to be about? This is a starting point for all of us, because the kids who are, I guess you'd call them the normal kids — if they have kids with disabilities in their class — the experience will become more of a common experience. When they grow up, they'll be more accustomed to differences so it's going to be a lot easier, in the long run, for our community to be inclusive. They'll be the ones who will hire Zach because they'll already know him from school. Isn't that how a lot of kids get jobs?

JACK: Right, it's easier to change the attitude of kids than adults — we all know that.

BEN: You know, I'm on the Board at the group home where the long-range goal has shifted to supported employment, meaning we'll eliminate the sheltered workshops. That's a change from institutionalization under way right now.

LINDA: Exactly. I guess that's why Emma's expectation for sports to be another vehicle for inclusion doesn't seem too far fetched to me. Inclusion has to be about more than the classroom. Life is about more than work, so why should that be the only goal for inclusion?

MONA: I'd be willing to bet that teachers like Mr Swan and Ms Lawrence would support this idea.

EMMA: Have you met them? Mr Swan is pure gold, and not just as a teacher. Ms Lawrence too, she can handle somebody like Dana, and a gang-banger in the same classroom, and still be a very effective teacher.

MONA: She's pretty amazing, they both are. And there's lots more at Carter.

LINDA: For sure! There are a lot of stellar teachers across the district; if we'd just focus on the teachers who are doing a good job with inclusion, they could become the *advocate leaders* for co-training and cross-training of other teachers. Let's seek out their support because they've figured it out and they're doing it! Rather than arguing about differing ability and awareness levels, or the unwillingness of some to make the change, we can look at where it's happening.

EMMA: Well, that's the strengths perspective from the School of Social Welfare speaking there. They're really into that, you know. Not 'what's going wrong', but what we're doing right, and move those practices forward, move that information forward, rather than focusing on all the negative stuff. There really *are* some tremendous teachers at Carter. Although Mr Swan hates it that so many kids are all transferring to his class, but as a parent, I don't blame these parents for seeking him out. I have to think about Kara's needs, not the system. I'd recommend that school to any parent who wanted the best for their child's personal growth, even if it meant leaving their neighbourhood school.

SANDY: Here I go again, speaking against the party line here, it's not like me to challenge this way, but I guess I'd like to hear what you all think about this. I'm one of those parents who made a decision to keep Nate in Mr Swan's class even though Fillmore is our neighbourhood school. I agree with everyone here, Rick's an outstanding and caring teacher, but as far as friendships go, Nate is really losing out because he's not in our neighbourhood school. When I heard Fillmore was real into inclusion, I got this brilliant idea and went to see the counsellors there. I was hoping they could suggest a friend for Nate — maybe a few kids that might be willing to hang out with him — or whatever. But they can't give out names. They promised to talk with other parents, so I left my name and number, but no one ever called. Nate is in desperate need of friends. He's sociable, but he's different. It's really hard for him to find a friend.

Throughout the research, Sandy pulled at my heart, as her efforts paralleled my own struggles with my son. I wondered if it would be useful to mention that limited friendships was the current norm? And if I looped this back to Emma's points, it might be easier to consider the subculture of disability and disability rights issues — and strive for hopefulness. And then there was the Fillmore story — this school was a stunning structure, built to accommodate the tremendous growth and development on the city's west side. My first-hand experience was that administration and staff advocated full inclusion and worked in cooperation with the District Special Education Advisory Council to sponsor public meetings in support of inclusion. No doubt Sandy had been enticed by all that she heard about the school's progressive inclusion practices, and yet when she ventured an effort to relieve the 'heart pain' about her son not having friends, her hopes were extinguished once more. Surely the principal could not have known about her call for help, right? As Echo, I did not engage these issues but continued to wonder: *Would it serve to probe Sandy's still raw feelings in response to this event? Would it serve to explore how she recovered from this event? Was it relevant to this research?*

Interrupting my reverie, Jack launched into an excited description of Jon's experience with Circle of Friends, a classroom-based programme that focuses on the development of friendships in inclusion classrooms (Forest, Pearpoint and O'Brien, 1996). Jack's enthusiasm was contagious as he explained, 'this programme fosters exactly what you're wanting, Sandy. A class begins by discussing why we have friends and who are our friends.' Jack drew the visual map of friendships (concentric circles) used when presenting Circle of Friends in classrooms. Again Jack credited the newly hired district special education director who conducted Jon's Circle of Friends. With little hesitation, Sandy jabbed with sarcasm, 'Do you know this guy personally, or something?'

Amid the teasing that followed, Jack registered no offence, but was quick to praise, 'I've gotten to know him pretty well. He's real interested in making inclusion work. Since Jon was one of the first students to be included in our school, I think we're getting extra support from him.' Somewhat withdrawn, Sandy offered in a more quiet voice, 'When Nate was younger, socializing wasn't as big a deal, I guess it's really an issue for every adolescent.'

It was not difficult to read Sandy's resignation as she attempted to diminish her initial appeal for help, and her efforts to gloss over the issue of difference between Nate and other adolescents. It often seemed that hope, for Sandy, was all but extinguished in the face of a formidable history she continued to survive with decreasing optimism. Unlike the other parents who experienced support from the district, and who could count on administrators as allies in a larger reform effort,

Sandy and Emma worked without advocates in a system that had long pitted parents on one side and administrators on the other. The bulk of their experiences had been with the previous special education director who was far less visible in the schools. As Jack characterized it, 'I think parents and teachers have seen more of the new director in one year than we saw of the previous director in over 10 years!' Although an exaggeration, the cultural story Sandy, Emma and Mona survived during the previous decade was one in which 'pulling strings' to get special attention for their children was far from an exaggeration. It was evident that there existed a need for a new collective story that not only addressed parents, but one that brought into its audience those seeking a greater understanding of the mechanisms of power masked by functionalist or systematizing thought (Foucault, 1980).

Knowing the Knowers, Hearing the Knowledge

At the conclusion of each dialogue, the parents would linger afterwards, continuing in dialogue. Despite differences of opinions and contrasting life experiences, they had engaged one another in affirming knowing and their knowledges. However, a goal for this research was to enlarge the framework for the study of inclusion, and thus moving beyond local understanding and the wisdom gained/confirmed by this research, it was important to ask '*so what?*'

Borrowing from feminist theory suggested that analysis of these parent dialogues could be informed by a poststructuralist deconstruction of the unified subject, and by drawing on Foucault's (1980) genealogical approach, in which 'the union of erudite knowledge and local memories . . . allows us a historical knowledge of struggles to make use of this knowledge tactically today' (1980, p. 83). Genealogies, according to Best and Kellner (1991) are attempts to 'foreground the material context of subject construction, to draw out the political consequences of "subjectification", and to help form resistances to subjectifying practices' (p. 47). This research portrayed parents as active agents intervening in and transforming their social environment. However, the parents were, for the most part, unaware of their impact on the larger project of inclusion. Recall Emma who insisted, 'I can't wait for systems change.' And Jack, who in response to Alane and Emma realized the possibility of simultaneous transformation of the social context of schooling and the community for all children. Similarly, Mona claimed some credit as Ben described Zach's success in school building on the risks she took with Della's inclusion a decade earlier. Their accounts were central to understanding inclusion in all of its complexity.

Although this research exposed the harsh accounts of struggle, resistance and conflict of those who live the experience, it was clear that the parents' agency remained untapped by the larger system of schooling. Simultaneous tinkering with multiple solutions, attempted in the absence of broad understanding of the outcome, assumed a constant invention of solutions — a course of action central to parenting. It is, as well, a process central to the success of inclusion (Ware, 1995). Parents know their child in the everyday context of life, and not simply against a standardized test score or rate of performance on an isolated skills inventory. Their particular knowledge affords a unique understanding of inclusion in a humanizing context essential to the success of inclusion both inside and outside schools. Although large systems do not rely on such inventive and intuitive approaches to change, it would seem evident that in the example of inclusion, schools will have to reconsider this reluctance.

Building on this research, I modified my pre-service teacher preparation courses to include shadowing experiences which placed pre-service teachers 'in community' with students with disabilities, their families, friends and support networks, prior to classroom instruction experiences (Ware and Howarth, 1998). The goal for this experience was to provide pre-service teachers with early experiences coming to know students with disabilities and their families in more humanizing contexts than schools often afford. In a related outcome, the success of this experience led to my own efforts to encourage the university to enlarge the influence and presence of parents and their children in our curriculum, as my colleague on this project was a parent and community activist. Prior to this assignment my efforts to offer a new course, *The Construction of Disability: Piss on Pity* was dismissed by special education colleagues who held that an existing course titled *Techniques of Parent–Teacher Counselling* served the same ends. Armed with the testimonies of pre-service teachers and community members, I reasoned that working *with* parents was qualitatively, ideologically and radically different from working *on* parents in the functionalist tradition that has grounded special education knowledge for the past two decades (Ware and Howarth, 1998).

Conclusion

When considering the value of this research, I return to the question, 'where do our interests lie?' What is the value of 'knowing the knowers and hearing the knowledge?' Parent stories differ across class, racial and cultural lines as well as across disabilities. Parent stories are many, not one. They represent some, but not all that education reform must attend to, and yet, the system all but silences parents. I would argue that more stories of parents are needed because parents *live the experience* of their child's disability in ways that many professionals cannot know despite all good intentions otherwise. That is what parents can teach. As a researcher, my responsibility to parents is to chronicle their knowing and their knowledges so that as their children move into adulthood, alliances across age groups, disabilities and experiences can be more easily made. Parent advocacy will likely continue throughout their lifetime, and thus their voices from within remind us that the goals for their children, like those of inclusion, cannot be measured in conventional outcome terminology. The complex outcomes for inclusion must instead be considered on a human scale, with an ever-shifting gaze towards the realities of life after school. As Ben related this:

> It was good for me to hear the perspectives of other parents that have older kids, even though it kinda shook me up a little bit because it made me realize that there are a lot of things changing, but lots of changes still need to be made.

And several weeks after our final critical dialogue, Mona shared that she continued to reflect on the wisdom she came to know:

> It was as if I was still inside that bubble of conversation, all the dialogues seemed to have merged in my mind like a guide book, a reference of some sort that makes me feel stronger, more confident about being a parent.

References

BEST, S. and KELLNER, D. (1991) *Postmodern Theory: Critical Interrogations*, New York: Guilford Press.

BRANDT, R. (1994) (Ed.) 'The inclusive school' (Special Issue), *Educational Leadership*, **52**, 4, pp. 1–95.

DISTRICT PUBLIC RELATIONS DOCUMENT (1995) *Inclusive Schooling Means Belonging*, Lawrence, Kansas: Lawrence Public Schools.

ELLIS, C. (1997) 'Evocative autoethnography: Writing emotionally about our lives', in TIERNEY, W. and LINCOLN, Y. (Eds) *Representation and the Text: Reframing the Narrative Voice*, New York: State University Press, pp. 115–39.

ELLIS, C. and FLAHERTY, M.G. (1992) (Eds) *Investigating Subjectivity: Research on Lived Experience*, Newbury Park, CA: Sage.

FOREST, M., PEARPOINT, J. and O'BRIEN, J. (1996) 'MAPS, Circle of Friends and PATH: Powerful tools to help build communities', in STAINBACK, S. and STAINBACK, W. (Eds) *Inclusion: A Guide for Educators*, Baltimore, MD: Brookes Publishing, pp. 67–86.

FOUCAULT, M. (1980) 'Two lectures', in FOUCAULT, M., *Power/Knowledge: Selected Interviews and Other Writings, 1972–1977* (Ed. C. Gordon and trans. C. Gordon, L. Marshall, J. Mepham and K. Soper), New York: Pantheon Books, pp. 78–108.

HARTMAN, J.E. (1991) 'Telling stories: The construction of woman's agency', in HARTMAN, J.E. and MESSER-DAVIDOW, E. (Eds) *(En)Gendering Knowledge*, Knoxville, TN: University of Tennessee Press, pp. 11–34.

HESHUSIUS, L. (1994) 'Freeing ourselves from objectivity: Managing subjectivity or turning toward a participatory mode of consciousness?', *Educational Researcher*, **23**, 3, pp. 15–22.

LIPSKY, D.K. and GARTNER, A. (1997) *Inclusion and School Reform: Transforming America's Classrooms*, Baltimore, MD: Brookes Publishing.

RICHARDSON, L. (1992) 'The consequences of poetic representation: Writing the other, rewriting the self', in ELLIS, C. and FLAHERTY, M.G. (Eds) *Investigating Subjectivity: Research on Lived Experience*, Newbury Park, CA: Sage, pp. 125–37.

RICHARDSON, L. (1994) 'Writing: A method of inquiry', in DENZIN, N.K. and LINCOLN, Y.S. (Eds) *Handbook of Qualitative Research*, Thousand Oaks: Sage, pp. 516–29.

RICHARDSON, L. (1997) *Fields of Play: Constructing an Academic Life*, New Jersey: Rutgers University Press.

SMITH, J.K. (1997) 'The stories educational researchers tell about themselves', *Educational Researcher*, **26**, 5, pp. 4–11.

SMITH, S. (1990) 'Individualized education programs (IEPs) in special education — from intent to acquiescence', *Exceptional Children*, **57**, 1, pp. 6–14.

WARE, L. (1994a) 'Contextual barriers to collaboration', *Journal of Educational and Psychological Consultation*, **5**, 4, pp. 339–57.

WARE, L. (1994b) *Innovative Instructional Practices: A Naturalistic Study of the Structural and Cultural Conditions of Change* (unpublished doctoral dissertation), Lawrence, Kansas: University of Kansas.

WARE, L. (1995) 'The aftermath of the articulate debate: The invention of inclusive education', in CLARK, C., DYSON, A. and MILLWARD, A. (Eds) *Towards Inclusive Schools?*, New York: Teachers College Press, pp. 127–46.

WARE, L. (1998) 'Sometimes I wonder if we're fooling ourselves', in BOOTH, T. and AINSCOW, M. (Eds) *From Us to Them: An International Study of Inclusion in Education*, London: Falmer Press, pp. 21–42.

WARE, L. (in press) 'What we have done to ourselves by doing these things to them', in GABBARD, D.A. (Ed.) *Education in the Global Economy: Politics and the Rhetoric of School Reforms*, New York: Lawrence Erlbaum.

WARE, L. and HOWARTH, S. (1998) *Tapping the Source: Preservice Teachers Learning from Parents*, paper presented at the Annual Arc NM/SUN TASH, Albuquerque, New Mexico, 23 April.

Chapter 5

I Don't Need This: Acts of Transgression by Students with Special Educational Needs

Julie Allan

The main voices in this chapter are those of four Scottish students with special educational needs (SEN). Seventeen-year-old Raschida and 15-year-old Laura, both of whom were visually impaired, attended a secondary mainstream school. Specialist teachers of the visually impaired accompanied them to lessons and gave them individual tuition (for example, in Braille) within the school's special unit. Special units are a common feature of SEN provision in Scotland, offering both intensive specialist support and participation in mainstream classes. Susan, an 11-year-old wheelchair user with spina bifida, spent part of her school day in the special unit of her mainstream primary school and the remainder with her mainstream peers. Eleven-year-old Peter, who had been identified as having social, emotional or behavioural difficulties and who attended the same school as Susan, experienced a similar pattern of special unit and mainstream provision.

The students' accounts reveal their attempts to challenge the kinds of identities and experiences that are constructed for them within formal school regimes and the informal discourses of teachers and students. These efforts are described by Foucault as 'technologies of the self' (1988, p. 18), which are transgressive, and involve not direct confrontation but a kind of playful struggle against those who attempt to label them as either disabled or normal or restrict their participation within mainstream classrooms. Foucault (*ibid.*) wrote that these practices

> permit individuals to effect by their own means or with the help of others a certain number of operations on their own bodies and souls, thoughts, conduct, and a way of being, so as to transform themselves in order to attain a certain state of happiness, purity, wisdom, perfection or immortality.

The practices of the teachers who supported the students in the present study were based on a discourse of need. This often acted against the students' attempts to transgress fixed identities and to practise alternative forms of conduct. Furthermore, the legal framework of the Record of Needs allowed teachers to negate officially the students' transgressive practices. The Record of Needs is the Scottish equivalent of a Statement, in operation in England and Wales. It sets out the special educational needs of an individual and the measures proposed by the education authority to meet them. Each of the four students in this study had a Record of Needs. Their official designation as 'special needs' undermined some of their efforts to transgress their assigned identity, but certainly did not usurp their efforts, as their accounts reveal.

This chapter begins by addressing the question of what counts as transgression, then reports the four students' accounts of this process. Their voices, and those of their teachers, are presented as overlapping and competing discourses of the students' desires and the professionals' perceptions of their needs. The voices of mainstream students who feature in the four students' accounts are generally supportive of them. In so far as they do not appear to challenge or undermine the students' transgressive practices, they are not explored in detail here. It is important to recognize, however, that they are instrumental in shaping the identities and experiences of students with SEN, within their mini-regime of governmentality (Foucault, 1982; Allan, 1997). There are considerable challenges for schools and teachers in helping students with SEN to express their desires and find ways of resolving conflict between these and their own considerations of the students' 'best interests'. These are explored towards the end of the chapter.

A project of this kind, which privileges normally subjugated voices, carries two major risks. First of all, my own reading of the accounts reflects personal values and theoretical perspectives, which reconfigure the voices within particular onto-logical and epistemological frameworks. A second danger relates to the impact of foregrounding the voices of pupils and others on those doing the speaking. In the final part of this chapter I shall make my own voice explicit and explore the price of speaking out.

What is Transgression?

As Foucault (1977a) reminds us, the individual is a disciplined object formed by 'a policy of coercions that act upon the body' (p. 138). This means that 'we are objects of social institutions and processes while we intentionally engage in behavi-our' (Cherryholmes, 1988, p. 35). At the same time, however, Foucault urges us to break out of the individualizing and totalizing power structures and to 'promote new forms of subjectivity through the refusal of this kind of individuality which has been imposed on us for several centuries' (1982, p. 216). One way of doing this is to transgress.

Foucault (1977c) looked forward to the day when transgression 'will seem as decisive for our culture, as much part of its soil, as the experience of contradiction was at an earlier time for dialectical thought' (p. 33). One of the difficulties in trying to examine the nature of transgression concerns the absence of a language in which to describe it. It is possible, however, to say what transgression does. Most importantly, transgression, says Foucault (1977c, p. 37), involves the challenging or crossing of limits or boundaries, imposed by others:

Transgression opens onto a scintillating and constantly affirmed world, a world without shadow or twilight, without that serpentine 'no' that bites into fruits and lodges their contradictions at their core. It is the solar inversion of satanic denial.

Foucault suggests that transgression has its entire space in the line it crosses and recrosses. It is a continuing and playful act, of agonism rather than antagonism, a kind of taunting, which Simons (1995) likens to a wrestling match. It seeks to laugh in the face of those who have tried to impose limits:

There, at the transgressed limit, the 'yes' of contestation reverberates, leaving without echo the hee-haw of Nietzsche's braying ass. (Foucault, 1977c, p. 36)

Transgression is an ambivalent act of non-positive affirmation which 'neither repudiates the place from whence it came nor welcomes the place to which it is bound' (Boyne, 1990, p. 82). Foucault likens transgression to Blanchot's notion of 'contestation', which 'does not imply a generalized negation, but an affirmation that affirms nothing' (1977c, p. 36). Transgression, according to Foucault, does not transcend limits, since that would be to end being, nor transform individuals; rather, it provides an unstable space where limits are forced. Simons (1995), however, argues that the effort of going beyond limits can paradoxically reinforce them.

For those who transgress, 'otherness lies ahead' (Boyne, 1990, p. 82) in new forms of subjectivity. It allows individuals to shape their own identities, by subverting the norms that compel them to repeatedly perform, for example, as gendered or disabled subjects (Butler, 1990). The important task, then, is not whether to repeat these performances, but how to vary these repetitions, producing an identity that is 'always in *process*, producing itself in response to and being produced by the contingent antagonisms and alliances that constitute the social' (Schrift, 1995, p. 39; original emphasis). Lloyd and Thacker (1997) warn against reifying transgression such that every transgressive act or practice is praised for its own sake, and Foucault (1984b) emphasizes the need to maintain the option to transgress. He urges caution in the pursuit of transgression, as it may not be possible or desirable for all. Indeed, acts of transgression by individuals may conflict with the interests of others, as was the case with the four students in this chapter. These costs need to be evaluated against the freedom acquired through new forms of subjectivity.

Raschida, Laura, Susan and Peter: Transgressing into and out of Disability

Raschida and Laura made considerable efforts to transgress out of the disabled identities they felt they had been assigned. Susan and Peter, in contrast, seemed to try to transgress *into* disabled identities. The precarious nature of this process, however, required the students to engage in a kind of policing of boundaries around their own selves. They also needed to work on their mainstream peers to encourage them to 'catch' the ordinariness of their transgressive actions.

Both Raschida and Laura spurned the long white cane given to them to assist their mobility. Raschida giggled as she told how she managed to lose hers in a lake, by testing the depth of the water. She had subsequently been given a smaller one which could be folded up when not in use. The students refused to undergo mobility training with a rehabilitation officer anywhere at home or at school where they might be seen by friends. Controlling their peers' awareness of their impairment, for instance by appearing to be coping with everyday tasks, was important to the girls and this would be spoiled if they were 'seen with a white stick or a dog — I'd die on the spot', said Laura.

Both had become so accomplished at making their way around the school that, as Raschida claimed, 'nobody really can tell, hardly'. Outside school, Raschida still tried to control the information others had about her by not letting on that she was visually impaired until she knew someone well. This included a boyfriend, who 'never realized that I couldn't see for ages'. She was only able to do this in an environment which, like school, she knew well, but even then her cover-up was elaborate:

> I usually met him at nights and that and he was pissed [drunk] and, like, I used to always pretend that I was drunk as well. I wasnae really, but I was just saying that so that he'd think, if I couldn't see anything, he'd realize [laughs] . . . I decided to tell him. Because we used to meet up at my friend's house and I knew her house quite well as well, so I never used to bang into things or anything, I'd just act normal, casual.

She eventually told him when she realized she could not keep up the deception. Her anxiety was not just about how he would react to being told that he had been lied to, but how he would feel about her being unable to see, and so she worried about 'spoiling things'.

> He couldn't take it, he couldn't believe it . . . It changed things for a while, then we got closer I think in a way, I don't know. It was just better in a way, but I was really worried then.

Raschida and Laura indicated that pupils in their mainstream classes found their 'difference' difficult to deal with. One effect of this was that issues about seeing and not seeing became taboo in their presence and the girls were aware of the difficulty and embarrassment caused by trying to deny the existence of their impairment:

> They're frightened to mention about my eyes and that . . . like in first year they used to be dead wary in case they said anything. (Laura)

As a result of this, Raschida and Laura had developed pedagogic strategies, aimed at educating their mainstream peers out of any discomfort over their impairment. This mainly involved self-deprecating humour:

> Sometimes people are uptight . . . in the beginning everyone was uptight about
> your eyes, but you just make jokes about it all the time and just forget about it.
> Especially Raschida and me, we always seem to make a fool out of each other.
> (Laura)

They said this had worked well, as 'everybody's so used to laughing now, like, they
treat it as a joke'. Raschida also said that a 'slagging off' she had received from
mainstream students for ignoring them in the street, even though they knew she
could not see them, signalled a breakthrough in her relations with them. Laura cited
an example of how her best friend had not only responded to her jokes, but had also
begun to make some of her own.

> In first year, they used to be dead wary in case they said anything, but I remember
> a couple of weeks ago, Linsey was going on about OIS [Office and Information
> Skills]: she's always looking at the keys and she's always getting into trouble. I
> says to her, 'I never look at the keys, I just look at the screen' and she says, 'I
> know, you'd get caught.' She never used to be like that, she used to be dead wary,
> but she's used to me now, because I'm always saying something like that.

Things were much easier for them, they said, if people were not constantly 'up-
tight' or 'falling over themselves to help or say the right thing'.

The students' transgressive actions were not singular accomplishments that
guaranteed them a particular identity or experience; rather, they had to be constantly
monitored and repeated. This required a high level of vigilance, patrolling what
Goffman (1971) calls the Umwelt, 'the region around which the signs for alarm
can come' (p. 297). They had to be ready to repair their own mistakes (or failed
transgressions), such as the one Laura describes here:

> There was one time when I went out for a meal with my mum and dad and my
> sister and instead of pouring vinegar on my chips I actually poured the water from
> the flower vase on my chips. I could hear everyone stop eating and they were all
> looking at me, thinking 'what a shame', I could tell. I just wanted to disappear.
> The only thing I could do was burst out laughing, then everyone else did as well.

The looks, she said, were coming not from her family but from other people in the
restaurant, but her family did nothing until she rescued them by laughing. This erased
the immediate pity which she sensed they felt for her, yet left them with a feeling
of admiration for the way her humour 'saw her through' difficult moments.

Susan's efforts, in contrast, appeared to be directed towards transgressing into
a disabled identity. 'One good thing about being in a wheelchair is that you get to
meet lots of people', said Susan, listing the 'important people' who had been to see
her. She said she had been in the newspapers, as part of publicity to raise money
for a trip to the Peto Institute in Hungary. She had also been the focus of a visit
from the Scottish Home and Health Department, initiated by her mother in a bid
to secure physiotherapy provision for her. According to the head teacher, she had
'wrapped them around her little finger' and they had been 'absolutely captivated by

her'. A physiotherapist had been provided a few days after the visit. 'People will always do things for me because they know I can't walk', said Susan. As a kind of celebrity figure, she was made welcome and fussed over whenever she came into the mainstream classroom.

Susan seemed comfortable with an identification as a kind of 'star', although, as Shapiro (1993) notes, this is an oppressive view that is located within charity discourses. She created an obligation among her mainstream peers to help her, and they responded positively to her dependence on them. One student said of Susan that, 'She asks if she wants something. She'll just come out with it . . . She's not scared to say anything. It just comes out.' They seemed to appreciate her ability to rely on them, which they compared with a more passive person who would 'just sit there'. Susan spoke of how she felt her status within the school and her self-image had suddenly been threatened when another member of the unit was given an electric wheelchair. Until then she had been the only one with a wheelchair of this kind, and she said 'it makes me a bit special — [mainstream students] make jokes about it, asking me how fast I can go in it'.

Teachers described how 'furious' she had been when the other pupil received his wheelchair. As one said, 'It took a lot for her to admit it but she finally said to me "I'm actually jealous of Alan."' Susan seemed to view the second wheelchair as a threat to those transgressive actions that enabled her to stand out from the other disabled pupils.

Peter, like Susan, also seemed to try to transgress into, rather than out of, a disabled identity. 'I sometimes say things to shock people', he said. 'Like I tell them I'm going to kill myself but I don't mean it.' In the past, he had opted out of activities at school and home, claiming that he couldn't do them because he was a 'spastic'. According to his mother, this seemed to occur when he sensed a lack of sympathy for his behavioural problems from his mainstream peers:

> There was a while when he had this thing about being a spastic, you know. 'I can't do that, pick my cup up, because I'm a spastic.' You know you ask someone to pass over something — 'I can't do that, I'm a spastic.' 'I can't feed the rabbit, I'm spastic' — I think because he was being teased at school.

Peter may have picked up the notion that children were more favourably regarded if they had a discernible impairment, and so tried to acquire one. Peter's fellow students seemed disposed towards excusing his behaviour or giving him the benefit of the doubt. For example, when he failed to contribute to a practical activity, a member of his group said 'he's not lazy, but when it's, like, using your hands or making stuff, he doesn't like doing it. I expect that's his worst subject, making things.'

In Need of Support? Transgression and the Teacher

Teachers seemed to present the greatest challenge to the students' transgressive practices, by subjugating the students' desires within their professionally expressed 'needs'. The teachers who worked with Raschida, Laura, Susan and Peter seemed either unaware of the significance of their strategies or saw them as counter-productive to the support they were offering. Raschida's practices were read not as transgressions (successful or otherwise), but as evidence of her failure to accept her impairment and the support they could offer. Laura seemed to receive less criticism because she was more 'cooperative'; her teachers also acknowledged her efforts to transgress her disabled identity. Susan's efforts at cultivating a kind of obligation among her peers was simply indefensible in the eyes of staff, who were seeking to encourage her to be independent. Peter's claim that he was a 'spastic' and his other 'bizarre' behaviour was pathologized as arising from low self-esteem and other failings, including those of his parents. The teachers' readings of the students' trans-gressive practices appeared to contradict and threatened to undo some of them. The teachers, however, were responding within a professional discourse that privileged special educational needs over the desires of individual students, and these need to be understood as part of the multi-layered discourse operating within the classroom.

Raschida and Laura said that their teachers were more uncomfortable than their mainstream peers were with their visual impairment. Raschida, for example, mentioned a student teacher's attempt to avoid the taboo associated with seeing and not seeing:

> She's really nice, but she never says 'see' to me — she says 'I'll give you this and you can listen to it' and it's a sheet of paper and she never likes to use the word see, or anything to do with the eyes, and you can tell when people are trying to avoid that. It puts you off.

Raschida thought this was amusing and indicative of the embarrassment her impair-ment had caused. She drew parallels with a famous television sketch from *Fawlty Towers*, in which Basil Fawlty is told that a party of Germans are visiting his hotel and he is warned not to mention the war, but he ends up goose stepping before them. Both girls found that most teachers drew attention to their impairment, for example by checking that they were able to see something properly, but said that this was often unnecessary:

> They always move you to the front of the class when you don't want to and you don't even need to be at the front sometimes. (Laura)

The effect of this was that some teachers went 'over the top' in their efforts to be as helpful as possible:

> They always ask you to come down to the front, in front of the whole class and things like that, and I don't really need to be at the front because I can't see the board in the first place anyway and if it's television, I prefer sitting at the back, because I've got tunnel vision and I can see it better. (Raschida)

Raschida's comment illustrates the paradox of inclusion for her: the teachers, by trying to help her, were disabling her by making it more difficult to see and by drawing attention to her impairment. Her teachers, however, were critical of her for failing to 'accept' her impairment, and in a report for the review of her Record of Needs they had stated that:

> Raschida is being extremely difficult about accepting that she requires help and is trying to pretend to be able to read print which we are aware is too small or too obscure. However, she does not like to fail and we are hoping that she will come to appreciate . . . that she must accept support in order to succeed.

Her teachers also repeated with grim bemusement the tale told by Raschida of how she dropped her long cane in the lake to illustrate the 'difficulty she had in accepting her disability'. Laura's teachers, on the other hand, were more positive about her attitude to her impairment and wrote:

> In all respects, Laura is a normal girl. Her parents and teachers will continue to ensure she maintains her relaxed and balanced attitude towards her visual impairment . . . She is independent, but able to accept help which she needs.

They seemed to recognize, however, the significance of her transgressive practices:

> Her mobility is good in that she sensibly stays with the limitations imposed by the severity of her VI. However, she does this so skilfully that there are few apparent differences between Laura and her peers.

One of the specialist teachers, referring to Laura's reluctance to use a long cane, said she understood 'the vanity thing . . . and the whole teenage reaction'. This could be interpreted as a positive act of self-formation, yet the teachers regarded it as vanity, on a par with concern over spots or wearing a brace. The students' refusal to undergo mobility training where they might be seen by their friends posed problems for their teachers, since 'the point of the training' was to teach them 'independence in their home environment'.

Susan's mainstream peers had praised her dependence on them. Her class teacher, however, took a rather different view:

> When she first comes in, they make a big fuss and ask 'can she sit at our table?' and I have to say 'look, Susan is part of the class, she's not here to be made a fuss of, she's here to come in and be treated as . . .' [pauses] you know . . . There's a few of them there that like to mother her and Susan likes that you know. Susan sits back and lets them mother her and you've got to try and get away from that and onto the idea that she's got to do things independently.

The specialist teacher agreed with this:

> Her own personality can be a barrier — it's a double-edged sword, because she won't sit back and not get. She'll ask and she'll make friends and enemies that way.

Criticism of her tendency to 'sit back' was recorded officially, and in her Record of Needs it was stated that:

> Participation in the wider activities of the school is important and a reasonable degree of firmness will be required to discourage Susan from being too dependent on others.

Susan's teachers saw her transgressive actions as posing a direct threat to her achievement of independence. They gave no indication of seeking to understand the possible motives behind her practices, for example as a means of cultivating affection among her peers or as a response to the inability of others to deal with her disability (Sinason, 1992). Instead, staff had dismissed them as countermanding their own incontrovertible goal of independence. Susan's jealous reaction to the 'competition' from another electric wheelchair user was seen as illustrating a conceit which they sought to discourage.

Peter's teachers read his adoption of a disabled label not as an act of transgression but as something he had picked up from his parents.

> I feel that at home that is being said to him because a child doesn't pick that up about themselves, that they are handicapped, you know, using those kinds of words, so whether that's how they've punished him or taken out their own frustration on him, I don't know.

They also attributed his 'bizarre' behaviour to his lack of self-esteem and a failure to be accepted by his peers:

> Peter is very anxious to be accepted and his own lack of self-respect and self-esteem hold him back; he is desperate to be liked and appear grown-up but he is unsure as to how to go about this — he is immature in this respect. He finds it difficult to conform to others' behaviour, therefore he tries to get others to be like him.

The teachers' responses are understandable, particularly where their efforts have focused on the students' impairments and ways of circumventing them in order to maximize learning opportunities. The negative response to Susan's practices is also easily recognized within special education discourses in which 'independence' is the stated goal for all pupils to aspire to, even though the validity of this heuristic has been questioned (Corbett, 1989; French, 1993b). Attributing the source of an individual's difficulties to their parents, as in Peter's case, is not unusual either: as Galloway et al. (1994) have noted, the culture of assessment allows professionals to 'explore the deficits in the parenting role' (p. 77). The teachers' practices, framed within SEN discourses, construct individuals as passive objects of their professional knowledge, with impairments and needs that require 'fixing' (Ballard, 1996, p. 38). This is reinforced with the Record of Needs, in which teachers can report the responsiveness (or submissiveness) of students to the support offered. The four students' practices, on the other hand, defined them as active subjects, with desires rather than needs. Perhaps it is not surprising, then, that the practices of the teachers and students conflicted. Schools face the challenge of trying to resolve this conflict in ways that recognize both needs and desires.

Challenges for Schools

Many of the practices described by the students would be unnecessary if schools were less oppressive spaces. A major task, therefore, has to be to effect 'deep changes in the way schools work' (Pignatelli, 1993, p. 411). Teachers must also

> avoid discourse-practices that essentialise categories of deviance in the minds of students and themselves; discourse-practices that cause students to internalize and monitor their deviant status — in effect blaming themselves for their own marginality. (Pignatelli, 1993, p. 420)

Raschida and Laura's accounts illustrated how teachers, by trying to avoid the taboo of seeing/not seeing, often made things worse. If teachers avoid such practices, there may be less need for the students to react with the kind of defensive strategies reported here, where 'the constant fear of discovery makes *normative* social interaction difficult and adds to the barriers faced by disabled people' (Barnes, 1996, p. 43; original emphasis). As French (1993a) points out, however, social remedies can never 'truly eliminate disability' (p. 19), and others (Finkelstein, 1990; Oliver, 1987) have commented on the unsuccessful efforts to remove barriers created by public attitudes. That is not to say that these should not continue to be tackled; it is clear, however, that students need to be helped to cope with the real situations in which they find themselves, and to find ways of overcoming the barriers that remain. In short, they need to be taught how to transgress.

The challenge for teachers is to listen to students and to ensure that the student voice is not then silenced by the teachers' professional discourse of needs. Teachers should be able to express what they understand to be the needs of individuals, based on their experience and professional judgements. Rather than see these as contradictory demands of student desires and teacher-assessed needs, it is perhaps more constructive to acknowledge these as separate layers, from which solutions can be found. But this can only happen if there is dialogue between teachers and students.

Teachers might help students to explore their sense of self — with this expressed as desires rather than needs — and to analyse constraining and enabling factors. This could then lead to the removal of some constraints or the enunciation of strategies to circumvent others. Teachers could also specify the kind of support they perceive to be necessary, with both parties exploring the consequences of receiving this kind of support. It may be possible to evolve strategies that recognize both needs and desires, for example by providing support within classrooms, which does not disturb peer interaction. Dialogue of this kind may encourage students to try to evade the process of categorization and to practise alternative forms of conduct. At the same time, however, they can be helped to understand the tariff that comes with certain actions, such as doing without specialist help or becoming dependent on one's peers.

Listened to But Not Heard?

The 'voices project', as we initially envisaged it, set out to privilege those accounts normally silenced within the professional discourses of special education. Our aim was to listen to students, parents, teachers and others who, in our view, had a great deal to say. We were not wrong: the stories they told us stretched our emotions as well as our intellects. Speaking personally, the accounts of the oppression experienced by parents in Colleen Brown's Chapter 3 and by Marilyn, whose story is retold by Keith Ballard and Trevor McDonald in Chapter 7, moved me much further towards an emotional and political engagement with disability. It made me ask why these voices have been silenced so completely and how they can be not only listened to but acted upon. But what is the price that comes with speaking out? It depends on who is doing the listening. In undertaking this research project, each of us interacted with our participants and retold their stories in good faith. But we came to these interactions with our own particular values, beliefs and theoretical perspectives which, inevitably, coloured the retelling of the story. Many of us have long ago stopped worrying about the neutrality of research, but it seems essential, in a project such as this, that we should articulate our own value positions. So here is mine.

Including Ourselves

Just in case it has not been obvious, I have an interest in Foucault. I have only recently stopped apologizing for this and started to enjoy, and even invite, the gentle teasing that comes the way of anyone with an obsessive interest. This particular 'obsession' is one which I've pursued in moderation, unlike other things (but it's not appropriate to go into those here). Indeed, far from being a slave to Foucault, I think I have used his theoretical perspective as a 'box of tools' (Foucault, 1977b; Allan, 1996) to help understand the voices of students and explore new productive possibilities. I was anxious that the students' voices should not be heard as essentialist accounts of what it is *really* like to be disabled or to experience inclusion. Instead, I felt that they should be taken as partial stories within a complex power/ knowledge knot (Simons, 1995). The voices seemed to reveal a great deal of that wider context through their discourses and it was important, I thought, to try to unpick some of the power relations within it.

One of the major criticisms of Foucault's work has been his pessimistic analysis of the way in which individuals are constrained. The problem with this is that it offers no recipes for change, and undermines the possibilities of resistance. Listening to the accounts of Raschida, Laura and others, however, has made me realize that they were more than capable of challenging their oppressors, through their transgressive practices. That has made me much more confident about the possibility of helping students to find new ways of being a subject that both recognize limits and test them. So power continues to interest me, not in terms of its constraining effects, but in its playful possibilities (Simons, 1995) and opportunities for challenging limits (Hutchings, 1997).

And it is with this optimism that I have faced my new responsibilities for special education within the teacher education programme in our university. The student teachers are given a fairly bleak picture of the pressures on mainstream schools imposed by financial cutbacks and policy reforms, which is echoed by the professionals they encounter during their school experience. My main message to student teachers, however, is that there is a great deal that they can do to help students with special educational needs overcome the many barriers they face. Fundamentally, they need to examine their own practices and ensure that they do not contribute to these barriers. They also need to be prepared to listen to their students.

Shaken and Stirred: Helping Students towards Practices of the Self

Although I am convinced that studies of this kind are of fundamental importance, I still have some concerns about the impact upon those who speak out. As Ligget (1988) points out, disabled people who speak out are placed in a double bind of participating in the normalizing society that creates the labels they also seek to resist. In other words, in order to have a voice, they have to speak as disabled people. This concern has been countered, however, by organizations of disabled people and individuals who have expressed pride in their disability and demanded greater respect (Corbett, 1996; Oliver, 1992). We need to give them that respect and take our responsibilities, which come from the privileged positions we occupy (Barton, 1995), much more seriously, by listening to and acting upon what students, parents and others have to tell us.

A second concern I have is that encouraging individuals to articulate the ways in which they are constrained could raise false hopes about breaking free or might further entrench the 'object of the research' (Fulcher, 1995, p. 9). It would be wrong of us to promise to find solutions to problems identified by students and others, since these are unlikely to be within our grasp. Yet the students' accounts illustrate that it is possible to resist certain constraints while accepting the limitations of others. We have an important role in assisting them to explore these possibilities, through what Foucault (1984a) calls an ethic of permanent resistance:

> My point is not that everything is bad, but that everything is dangerous ... If everything is dangerous, then we always have something to do. So my position leads not to apathy but to a hyper- and pessimistic activism. I think the ethico-political choice we have to make every day is to determine which is the main danger. (p. 343)

The major task for all of us is to help students, parents and others to acquire new forms of subjectivity in which they are no longer 'docile bodies . . . used, transformed and improved' (Foucault, 1977a, pp. 135–6), but active agents in their own transformation.

If we are to help in this process, perhaps we too need to transgress in our daily lives. This need not involve radical changes in ways of working, but it does require us to begin 'surveying the closure and repetitiveness in our own thinking' (Roth, 1992, p. 695). An example of 'useful' transgression was described by Colleen Brown at our research group meeting in Auckland. Hearing of obstacles placed in front of a parent by officials, she simply 'made a phone call' which removed them. She was using her own privileged position to subvert power relations, something which many of us are capable of doing. We might also celebrate publicly individuals' acts of transgression, by writing and speaking about them. These actions challenge limits and extend notions of what is possible, producing a kind of freedom in which individuals are both constrained and enabled:

> Freedom, therefore, becomes the practice of inventive, resourceful, strategical moves along an axis of power, moves that possibly anticipate but cannot terminate the play of power. (Pignatelli, 1993, p. 427)

References

ALLAN, J. (1996) 'Foucault and special educational needs: A "box of tools" for analysing children's experiences of mainstreaming', *Disability and Society*, **11**, 2, pp. 219–33.

ALLAN, J. (1997) 'With a little help from my friends? Integration and the role of mainstream pupils', *Children and Society*, **1**, 3, pp. 183–93.

BALLARD, K. (1996) 'Inclusive education in New Zealand: Culture, context and ideology', *Cambridge Journal of Education*, **26**, 1, pp. 33–45.

BARNES, C. (1996) 'Visual impairment and disability', in HALES, G. (Ed.) *Beyond Disability: Towards an Enabling Society*, London: Sage, pp. 36–44.

BARTON, L. (1995) 'Conclusion: Many urgent voices', in CLOUGH, P. and BARTON, L. (Eds) *Making Difficulties: Constructions of SEN*, London: Paul Chapman, pp. 143–7.

BOYNE, R. (1990) *Foucault and Derrida: The Other Side of Reason*, London: Routledge.

BUTLER, J. (1990) *Gender Trouble*, London: Routledge.

CHERRYHOLMES, C. (1988) *Power and Criticism: Poststructural Investigations in Education*, New York: Teachers College Press.

CORBETT, J. (1989) 'The quality of life in the "independence" curriculum', *Disability, Handicap and Society*, **4**, 2, pp. 145–63.

CORBETT, J. (1996) *Bad Mouthing: The Language of Special Needs*, London: Falmer Press.

FINKELSTEIN, V. (1990) ' "We" are not disabled, "you" are', in GREGORY, S. and HARTLEY, S. (Eds) *Constructing Deafness*, London: Pinter/Open University, pp. 265–71.

FOUCAULT, M. (1977a) *Discipline and Punish*, London: Penguin.

FOUCAULT, M. (1977b) 'Intellectuals and power: A conversation between Michel Foucault and Giles Deleuze', in BOUCHARD, D. (Ed.) *Language, Counter-Memory, Practice: Selected Essays and Interviews by Michel Foucault*, Oxford: Basil Blackwell, pp. 205–17.

FOUCAULT, M. (1977c) 'A preface to transgression', in BOUCHARD, D. (Ed.) *Language, Counter-Memory, Practice: Selected Essays and Interviews by Michel Foucault*, Oxford: Basil Blackwell, pp. 29–52.

FOUCAULT, M. (1982) 'The subject and power', in DREYFUS, H. and RABINOW, P. (Eds) *Beyond Structuralism and Hermeneutics*, Chicago: University of Chicago Press, pp. 208–26.

FOUCAULT, M. (1984a) 'On the genealogy of ethics: An overview of work in progress', in RABINOW, P. (Ed.) *The Foucault Reader*, Harmondsworth: Peregrine, pp. 340–72.

FOUCAULT, M. (1984b) 'What is enlightenment?', in RABINOW, P. (Ed.) *The Foucault Reader*, Harmondsworth: Peregrine, pp. 32–50.

FOUCAULT, M. (1988) 'Technologies of the self', in MARTIN, L., GUTMAN, H. and HUTTON, P. (Eds) *Technologies of the Self: A Seminar with Michel Foucault*, London: Tavistock, pp. 16–49.

FRENCH, S. (1993a) 'Disability, impairment or something in between?', in SWAIN, J., FINKELSTEIN, V., FRENCH, S. and OLIVER, M. (Eds) *Disabling Barriers — Enabling Environments*, London: Sage/Open University, pp. 17–25.

FRENCH, S. (1993b) 'What's so great about independence?', in SWAIN, J., FINKELSTEIN, V., FRENCH, S. and OLIVER, M. (Eds) *Disabling Barriers — Enabling Environments*, London: Sage/Open University, pp. 44–8.

FULCHER, G. (1995) 'Excommunicating the severely disabled: Struggles, policy and researching', in CLOUGH, P. and BARTON, L. (Eds) *Making Difficulties: Constructions of SEN*, London: Paul Chapman, pp. 6–24.

GALLOWAY, D., ARMSTRONG, D. and TOMLINSON, S. (1994) *The Assessment of Special Educational Needs: Whose Problem?*, London: Longman.

GOFFMAN, E. (1971) *Relations in Public*, Harmondsworth: Penguin.

HUTCHINGS, K. (1997) 'Foucault and international relations theory', in LLOYD, M. and THACKER, A. (Eds) *The Impact of Michel Foucault on the Social Sciences and Humanities*, Basingstoke: Macmillan Press, pp. 102–27.

LIGGET, H. (1988) 'Stars are not born: An interpretive approach to the politics of disability', *Disability, Handicap and Society*, **3**, 3, pp. 263–75.

LLOYD, M. and THACKER, A. (1997) *The Impact of Michel Foucault on the Social Sciences and Humanities*, Basingstoke: Macmillan Press.

OLIVER, M. (1987) 'Re-defining disability: A challenge to research', *Research, Policy and Planning*, **5**, 1, pp. 9–13.

OLIVER, M. (1992) 'Intellectual masturbation: A rejoinder to Soder and Booth', *European Journal of Special Needs Education*, **7**, pp. 20–28.

PIGNATELLI, F. (1993) 'What can I do? Foucault on freedom and the question of teacher agency', *Educational Theory*, **43**, 4, pp. 411–32.

ROTH, J. (1992) 'Of what help is he? A review of Foucault and education', *American Educational Research Journal*, **29**, pp. 104–19.

SCHRIFT, A. (1995) 'Reconfiguring the subject as a process of self: Following Foucault's Nietzschean trajectory to Butler, Laclau/Mouffe, and beyond', *J'Accuse*, **25**, pp. 28–39.

SHAPIRO, J. (1993) *No Pity: People with Disabilities Forging a New Civil Rights Movement*, New York: Times Books.

SIMONS, J. (1995) *Foucault and the Political*, London: Routledge.

SINASON, V. (1992) *Mental Handicap and the Human Condition: New Approaches from the Tavistock*, London: Free Association Books.

Chapter 6

The Impact of Hospitalization on School Inclusion: The Experiences of Two Students with Chronic Illness

Jeff Bailey and Belinda Barton

This chapter identifies potential issues and problems confronting children and adolescents who have a chronic illness. The two students we interviewed have cystic fibrosis. Their perceptions and feelings about having the illness, taking frequent absences from school for hospitalization and returning to school after these, were examined in terms of the impact of the illness on their inclusion in school. Children with chronic illness confront problems of being included in schools that may be similar to those experienced by children with disabilities, but often with less support and with little recognition of their integration and reintegration needs.

A largely unrecognized group, children with chronic illnesses include those with cancer, haematology problems, haemophilia, cystic fibrosis, congenital cardiac conditions, chronic renal disease, spina bifida, muscular dystrophy, sickle cell anaemia and juvenile diabetes. Some of these illnesses are more typical of the 'disability' groups we usually think of in the provision of special education support and programmes, for example spina bifida. Others, however, with low incidence rates and often with invisible impairments, may languish largely unnoticed in the education system. Their needs for support and inclusion, though, may be as great as or exceed those with more obvious conditions.

It is acknowledged in using the terms chronic illness and cystic fibrosis that we are labelling the students, worse, we are medicalizing their condition and creating 'difference'. We recognize this problem and believe that the labelling is justified in this study because of the need for inclusion researchers to cast their net widely to assess the impact of intra-individual characteristics which might be responded to in ways that create exclusive conditions.

So, in this chapter, we explore the views of a male and a female adolescent who have to live with a potentially disabling, terminal condition. We examine the impact of the illness on them, with particular reference to feelings of alienation and isolation resulting from the illness and from absences from school as a result of repeated, significant periods of hospitalization. Our task in this chapter is to allow the students' voices to tell of their concern about having a specific chronic illness in terms of their growth, development, interaction with peers, and progress and life at school.

A Personal Profile

Part of our justification for selecting and categorizing our participants on the basis of a medical condition can best be seen in the work the authors do. We both work for the largest and most respected paediatric hospital in Australia.

Jeff Bailey: I am a Professor of Special Education and currently hold a joint appointment with the University of Western Sydney, Nepean and the Royal Alexandra Hospital for Children. At the Hospital, I am the Inaugural Director of a new research centre established in 1996 — the Children's Hospital Education Research Institute (CHERI). I have an extensive background in education and particularly in working with children and adolescents with disabilities and learning difficulties. An educator and psychologist by training, I have been a teacher, school principal, special education consultant and academic. My doctoral training was in a university affiliated research centre, the Cincinnati Center for Developmental Disorders. Attached to the Children's Hospital and the University of Cincinnati, this experience gave me insight into the importance of taking a comprehensive, transdisciplinary view of children's problems and developments. Recognizing the need to treat children as children, I realize, nevertheless, that to provide the most effective services to children with disabling conditions, it is essential to embrace a wide range of perspectives and disciplines.

Belinda Barton: As Coordinator and Research Associate I was the second appointment to CHERI. I am a psychologist in training, with an honours degree in psychology. My previous research undertaken at other hospitals has been in the areas of depression and anorexic individuals. I have also spent some time working in a refuge, counselling female adolescents who, as a result of past unfortunate experiences, have a number of emotional and behavioural difficulties.

CHERI: The mission of our research institute is to conduct studies into medical, psychological and developmental problems associated with children's health, especially in relation to the interface between health and education. For this reason, and as CHERI has a particular advocacy role for children with disabling conditions not typically dealt with in 'special education', the selection of cystic fibrosis as a representative illness for consideration as an inclusion challenge, is logical and important.

Understanding the Extent of Chronic Illness in Children

Before we listen to the students' voices, it is important to reflect on the extent of chronic and severe illness in Australia. We should consider how many children and adolescents have chronic illness and also understand the typical problems that might impact on their full acceptance in school.

While there is some debate about what characterizes a chronic illness, it is generally defined as a condition which:

lasts for a considerable period of time;
or has sequelae which persist for a substantial period;

Table 6.1   *Changing prevalence — survival rates*

Disease/Condition	Changed from	To
Cystic fibrosis	2.5 increase from 11 years in 1966	30.1 years in 1996
Acute lymphoblastic leukaemia	In 1960 only 1% survived to 5 years after diagnosis	70% disease-free for 5 years
Sickle cell disease	14 years in 1960	In 1994, 42 for men and 48 for women
Very low birth weight infants	<1500g — 1960 few survived	Increase in survival from 27% to 72% by 1989

Source: Thompson and Gustafson, 1996

> may be progressive;
>
> is sometimes fatal;
>
> might have a normal life span, although there could be impaired functioning (physical or mental); or
>
> persists for more than three months; and
>
> requires continuous hospitalization of a month or more (see Thompson and Gustafson, 1996).

The occurrence of chronic illness can be identified by looking at the current population of Australia, estimated to be 17.9 million (Australian Bureau of Statistics, 1997). Of that number, 22 per cent are in the 0–14 year group. Incidence rates per 1,000 live births for chronic childhood illnesses (Gortmaker, 1985) suggest that about 2,000 Australian children will have cystic fibrosis (the incidence is 0.50 per 1,000 live births); 39,380 children will have asthma (10 per 1,000); 31,504 congenital heart disease (8.0); 7,876 chronic kidney disease (2.00); 3,938 spina bifida (1.00); 1,575 juvenile diabetes (0.40); and 1,418 children will have sickle cell anaemia (0.36 per 1,000 incidence). In Australia, the estimated frequency of children with a chronic illness is approximately 90,000. Further calculations reveal that nearly 20,000 of these children are in the city of Sydney, where the authors live and work. While the specific medical details of the illnesses are well-known and documented, there is almost no literature on the impact of these illnesses on the children's academic, physical or social inclusion at school.

These figures were chosen to demonstrate the extent of the problem in just one city of Australia — Sydney. Before proceeding to sketch an argument for examining the inclusion support needs for these students, other important background information from an epidemiological and historical point of view will be outlined. While estimated frequencies have been used to suggest the scope of health problems in the Australian population, it is important to add that the prevalence of children with chronic illnesses has doubled in the 20-year period from the early 1960s (Thompson and Gustafson, 1996).

It can be seen from Table 6.1 that over recent years there has been a significant increase in the life expectancy of children with chronic illnesses. As a result, these children now have the opportunity to attend and complete schooling, which demonstrates further to us why we need to examine inclusion issues in the school environment. For many children with chronic illnesses, the school environment provides a setting where they may be viewed as children and adolescents rather than as patients (Sexson and Madan-Swain, 1993).

Medical Perspectives and Models — Anathema to Educators?

One of the problems recognized by the authors of this paper is that the medical labels used tend to be aetiological, pathological and exclusive. The situation is complicated with chronic illness because the main paradigm for classification and intervention is medical, a perspective that many educators find limiting and even demeaning for children for whom they are advocates. It is not the place to explore this theme fully in this chapter, but it is important to recognize some of the traditional problems with what is called the medical model because the paradigm affects the well-being and perspectives of the children whose voices are revealed later in this chapter. For children with a chronic illness, the way their condition is medicalized may limit their full functioning on their return to school. One of the major limitations of the use of medical labels for these students is that teachers may presume that the medical condition is unrelated to education, is being handled by other professionals, and because of this does not require any specific intervention by educators. While such a world view does not of itself mean that students are excluded, it is possible that steps to effectively include them are not taken by the students' teachers.

The medical model can be narrow and reductionist. Patients are viewed in terms of a 'pathology'. Diagnosis and treatment can be fragmentary, and more holistic community-oriented approaches may be bypassed (Reed and Watson, 1994). There are criticisms that the medical model overlooks the rights of the client, and that parents and patients assume passive, recipient roles instead of being able to take charge of their own lives and therapies (Chewning and Sleath, 1996). The dominant paradigm of scientific medicine with its emphasis on technologies to repair damaged bodies has been said to violate patients' rights and to promote helplessness (Stambolovic, 1996), while nursing and medical routines may further disempower patients (Schroeder, 1994).

These criticisms should guide us in our consideration of children with chronic illness so that we might ensure that our approach is client-centred, holistic, healthy, empowering and enabling. While the use of 'illness' terms may involve a social construction that suggests fragility, helplessness and pathology, the use of diagnostic terms is of less importance than the development of an argument to consider the inclusion needs of these children as a special group. To some extent, educators need to build bridges with health and medical professionals to ensure the best provisions and outcomes for the child with a chronic illness. Educators must also be aware that the symptoms and complications that are part of having an illness may require the educators to take the initiative in thinking about, and actively including, these students in the daily life of the classroom and school.

What is Cystic Fibrosis?

Cystic fibrosis is a chronic life-threatening illness and one of the most common genetic diseases affecting Australian children. Cystic fibrosis affects about 1 in every 2500 children in Australia (New Born Screening Clinic, 1996; Harbord, Cross, Botica and Martin, 1987). There are approximately 800 children and adolescents in New South Wales with this disease, and 2500 nationwide (New Born Screening Clinic, 1996). Improvements in health care have dramatically increased the median survival age from 11 years in 1966 to 30.1 years in 1996 (Cystic Fibrosis Foundation, USA, 1996).

Cystic fibrosis affects the exocrine glands of the body, resulting in the production of thick, sticky mucus secretions (except for the sweat glands) that can block passageways. The two major areas of the body affected by the disease are the lungs and the pancreas. Patients with cystic fibrosis experience significant respiratory problems and virtually every one of these patients develops lung disease. Problems with digestion result in malabsorption, and poor growth and nutrition. The reproductive system is also affected in both males and females, with the majority of males being sterile.

The Voices

For the purposes of this paper, we shall refer to our two participants as Peta and James. We interviewed Peta and James while they were in hospital. Peta is a 15-year-old female of Anglo-Saxon descent. She attends a neighbourhood high school in the south-west of Sydney, New South Wales. Enrolled in Year 10, she has two more years of high school to complete. Peta is from a family of four, with one older brother. At the time of the interviews, Peta was in hospital for three weeks. She is hospitalized about four times each year for a period of three to four weeks each time.

James is 12 years of age. He attends a specialized performing arts high school in which he is enrolled in Year 7. This is his first year of high school so he has had to cope with the transition from primary (or elementary) school to secondary school. James's parents are divorced and his mother has remarried. James sees his biological father from time to time. James has a total of four stepbrothers and stepsisters, and his mother is expecting another baby shortly. He also has a great deal of contact with his grandfather. At the time of interview, James was in hospital for two weeks. He attends hospital between five and seven times each year, generally for a period of two weeks each time.

When interviewing Peta and James we wanted to understand their life and experiences, particularly with regard to their feelings of being isolated and excluded as a result of their illness and/or hospital experiences. We wanted to know what happens to them when they are hospitalized. For example, does the teacher provide them with school work, how do they feel, and do their friends come and visit them? More importantly, we wanted to understand what happens when they return to school, the classes they have missed, the reaction of their teachers and peers, and their apprehension about returning to school. By listening to the voices of these students we hoped to find some answers to these questions.

Our Assumptions about Having Cystic Fibrosis

Prior to the interviews, we reviewed the information on cystic fibrosis and developed a list of issues and questions that we believed might characterize the participants' views about their illness. The following list provided a frame of reference for our interviews. In terms of their personal development:

> Did they feel different because of their illness?
> Did they feel disadvantaged in any way?
> Were they unhappy because of their illness?
> Did they feel excluded in any way at school?
> Did they have difficulties with their peers and teachers?
> Were they worried about the future and the terminal nature of the illness?
> When they had to go to hospital, did they feel anxious or worried?
> Were there any school-specific problems created by either leaving school to go to hospital or returning to school after the hospitalization?

We were also interested in their accounts regarding the amount and type of support provided by teachers. Specifically, we wanted to know:

> How much teacher support did they receive based on their illness?
> Did the teacher(s) know about the chronic illness?
> Did the teachers foster positive attitudes about the children with chronic illness in their class?
> Were compensatory arrangements made for their illness, for example, being able to go to the toilet when feeling ill, having special consideration in physical education?
> With regard to the hospital absences, did the teachers provide extra homework and study materials, did they check on the work upon the student's return to school?

Some of these issues are addressed in the transcripts which follow.
When James was asked about his condition he replied:

> Well, I have cystic fibrosis, um . . . my brothers and sisters don't have the cystic fibrosis because my mother is with another man now and cystic fibrosis can only be formed when two people must have the same gene and my mother and my father were married and they had me, and that's how I have cystic fibrosis.

James indicated that he was diagnosed with cystic fibrosis at about eight weeks of age but he didn't know about it until he was five years of age. When asked whether he understood what it meant then, he replied that he didn't. We were interested to know what cystic fibrosis meant to James now. He told us that cystic fibrosis was:

> a form of asthma and bowel problems together . . . [which] . . . interferes a fair bit actually, because you can sit down and about to have lunch and you see the other kids when they can just start eating and you have to stop and take some medication then you can eat and it's very hard.

James indicated that he meets many other children with cystic fibrosis in the hospital. When asked whether these people talked about having cystic fibrosis he responded:

> No. They're too busy. They talk about other things — they don't really worry about it.

This lack of concern could be how children with this terminal illness approach their condition. Alternatively, the children may suppress their real feelings to ignore the inevitability of the disease. The following account gives another insight into James's approach to his illness. He was talking about coming into the hospital.

JEFF: If you had to pick out the best thing that you're really pleased about, what would it be?

JAMES: Probably the Starlight Foundation . . . you know, the Wish Foundation. They're going to grant me a wish.

JEFF: How does that work?

JAMES: Terminally ill kids, like, you can't get it if you have asthma or a cold because you have to have an illness that will be with you until you die.

JEFF: Right.

JAMES: That they can't cure yet.

The Clinical Team working with young people with cystic fibrosis speak of their resilience and bravery. It is difficult to know from the foregoing transcripts just how worried James is about his condition. He seems to adopt a matter-of-fact approach to the problem but, obviously, he is aware that he has a terminal condition. He does end with a note of optimism, though, when he adds that cystic fibrosis is a disease that 'they can't cure *yet*' (our emphasis).

We asked both participants what it was like to be in hospital. When we first asked Peta how she felt about coming into hospital, she told us:

> I don't mind, I still get stuff, it's sort of . . . it's not that much different from home, except I can't play sport.

However, when later we asked her to give us some reasons why she liked coming to hospital, she stated:

JEFF: Do you have any contact with your school teachers while you're away?
JAMES: Umm . . . no.
JEFF: Not at all?
JAMES: No.

What about Family and Friends?

Peta had regular visits from her family and friends while she was in hospital. At least one of her parents, or both, visited Peta in hospital daily, and her brother visited occasionally. Peta generally went home for one day on the weekend while in hospital if she was well enough. Peta's school friends visited her sometimes after school or on the weekend:

> they [friends] come at least once or the whole group comes at least once and but then like . . . umm . . . people from my primary school come more because I'm better friends and then a few of my better friends from high school come more as well, a few times, while I'm in every weekend and then sometimes after school.

One of Peta's friends telephoned her daily, and other friends sometimes made telephone contact with her two or three times a week. When we asked her about how she felt when her friends told her what had happened at school that day, she stated that she didn't mind not being there, and that 'school gossip' was interesting.

James did not appear to have as much contact with his family and peers as Peta. His mother rang him daily and visited occasionally, although she lives 15 kilometres away. James stated that it was difficult for his mother to come and visit him because of the other children in the family. James has a close relationship with his grandfather who visits him every two or three days and telephones daily.

When we asked James about how much contact he had from his friends, he replied that he could not call them as they did not have telephone numbers. He did not mention that any of his friends came to visit him. James said that he had only one good friend, Steve, who also went to his school, that he had known for two or three years. His best friend knew that James had a chronic terminal illness. James felt that his friend understood him.

> We can talk to each other, we know what we're going through.

Steve also suffers from a condition, epilepsy, which perhaps accounts for some of the understanding between the two of them.

Life at School

Some of the major difficulties experienced by both participants were feelings of tiredness, a lack of energy to get through the day, and weariness walking to classes and around the school. Peta stated that one reason she didn't like school was 'walking around', as she expressed with humour:

BELINDA: What don't you like about school?

PETA: Walking around. They should have all walkways, automatic walkways, like escalators, and press a button, and hop on and travel around.

Peta stated that she felt tired and out of breath from walking up and down stairs, even just one flight of stairs, particularly when she was sick. James also experienced tiredness from the demands of walking around the school, and felt weary at the end of the day.

JAMES: I'm like on energy tablets, salt tablets, give me more energy because I can hardly walk to school now.

JEFF: You just feel really tired all the time?

JAMES: And all worn out.

Management of this chronic illness is an everyday part of life for children and adolescents affected, involving various treatments and therapies. As mentioned by James, he needs to take salt tablets for energy and cannot sometimes participate in sports as do his peers:

I have options because of cystic fibrosis, because of the sun like, because like when I sweat I'm losing a lot of energy, like salt out of body, that's what the salt tablets are for, to pour energy back into me . . . and umm . . . if it's too hot, I have the option, that I can either play or sit it out and just watch or something like that.

James stated that he likes to participate as much as he can, but it doesn't worry him if he sits down and watches the others play. James told us that his peers do not say anything to him if he decides not to participate.

James told us that he also coughs frequently in the classroom and may need to expel a build up of mucus and sputum from his lungs. He goes to the toilets sometimes to expel the sputum, but sometimes the toilets are locked in between classes, so he uses a bin. In a role-play situation, we asked James to pretend that we were a student asking him why he was coughing, what would he say to us.

It's a bit worse than asthma but with this, it's called cystic fibrosis, you may not have heard of it but . . . umm yeah it's got a lot to do with asthma but I don't have to carry inhalers and stuff around.

This form of disclosure or telling strategy is common among adolescents and young adults with cystic fibrosis. After disclosing, individuals generally provide an explanation and descriptive details of the illness, sometimes followed by a comparison to a less stigmatized condition. Potential complications and the terminal nature of the disorder are rarely mentioned (Admi, 1995).

James believed that adolescents were more accepting of him having a chronic illness than the teachers. He based this decision on the fact that the teachers showed more concern for his health than his peers. He found it annoying that teachers asked frequently whether he 'was all right', while kids forget about it.

> When the kids just say 'Oh yeah, you OK?' and you just say 'Yeah, yeah, sure' and they just don't worry about it really.

Perhaps this indicates that James feels more comfortable with his peers than his teachers. It is possible that children and adolescents normalize an experience much better than adults. Children and adolescents often show interest by asking an initial question, but don't persist with the questioning when the peer responds. James's response may have also discouraged further conversation from his peers, thereby avoiding further explanation about his illness. Responses regarding an illness may be determined by the social situation and the audience (Admi, 1995). In addition, teachers' expressed concern may also attract attention towards James and identify him as being different from his peers.

Taking tablets and medications is a part of life at school for students with cystic fibrosis. Enzymes and vitamins are necessary to assist in digestion and a special dietary intake may be required. As James stated, it is difficult when you have to take medication before you start eating, while others have already started. Although James gave the impression that all was going well at school, he said he felt lonely there. His true feelings about school can perhaps be gleaned from the answer he gave when asked why he was happy to be missing out on school.

> Well, because sometimes you get a bit bored sitting there listening to the teachers talk and then there's nothing to do in the playground when you get out there, your friends are always busy, so better off being in hospital, have something else to do.

Returning to School after Hospitalization

After a significant period of time in hospital, both Peta's and James's thoughts of returning to school and home were dominated by concern about school work and the need to 'catch up'. As they said, what worried them was:

PETA: I've got so much work to catch up on.
JAMES: All the work I'm going to get to do when I get back, all the work I'm going to have.

James told us that he was at the top of his class, but because of his absence he would now probably be middle of the class.

> Well I'm not really worried about being at the top of the class, just how much work I've got to do when I get back, like a whole lot when everyone else is like 20 times ahead of you, they've done all that work when you're there trying to cope with it.

Trying to make up for missed school work and falling behind can result in anxiety for the young adolescent. Subsequently this may interfere with the child's cognitive and concentration skills (Weitzman, 1984), making 'catching up' and learning even more difficult. James's attitude was that it was *his* responsibility to try to 'catch up'.

> Oh they [teachers] don't help you out with school work — you've got to get back into the thing and learn how to do it, you know, you've got to expect that. You've got to expect, like the stuff that they've already teached you they expect you still to remember that, they're not going to run it over again like 20 times, they might run over some new things they have done but I think that would be about it. They won't do anything old again that you've already done.

James's worries were also heightened by the fact that this was the first time he had been in hospital since starting high school. He did not know what it would be like returning to high school. He thought it would probably be confusing, finding out where to go to for classes and having a lot of school work to do. When James was asked what it was like for him when he returned to primary school after hospitalization, he responded that it wasn't that hard, but his friends had 'made new friends and other things and they're a lot more busy than usual'.

Peta was looking forward to seeing her family and friends, the family dog, sleeping in her own bed and just doing her 'normal routine'. Peta felt that going back to school felt like beginning a new term.

> It feels like, you know, like you're starting a new term . . . because you haven't been there for a while.

Peta told us she felt happy the first day at school to be seeing her school friends.

> Well you feel glad that you can see them again and, well, you feel happy because you're seeing them . . . but then . . . you kind of just feel normal because it's just back to the way it was . . . so mainly feel happy and kinda of relieved that I can go back and do the stuff again . . . school and see everyone.

Most of Peta's friends that she had spoken to on the telephone while in hospital were aware beforehand that she was expected back at school. On her first day back, Peta identified a different reaction from the friends that she had contact with compared with others who had not kept in touch.

> 'cause I talk to them [friends] on the phone, so you know, how are you, and it's not like 'oh, you're back', it's not really exciting and the people I usually haven't talked to them, and just talking to them go 'you're back' [high inflected expression] so just sometimes you just see people and they realize you haven't been there for a while but then most people just say 'oh you're back, how are you' and stuff [normal tone].

Peta's teachers generally enquired about how she was and where she was up to in her school work. Peta did not feel anxious or 'left out' when she returned to school. If the class was working on a project in small groups when Peta returned, her friends did not mind if Peta joined their group. Depending upon the size of the project, sometimes Peta did not participate, but would just sit and watch her friends.

Discussion

The voices of Peta and James have provided us with some insight into their life at school and at the hospital. From their comments it seemed that they did not feel significantly excluded in any psychological or educational way at school. It is probably realistic to add, though, that there appeared to be no special efforts made by the teachers to positively include Peta and James. The failure to be proactive in considering the needs of students whose 'condition', regardless of whether it is a physical or psychological illness, or a disability, or another form of disablement or difference, could be construed as a passive form of exclusion. It is important that those studying inclusion consider this possibility.

To create an inclusive curriculum and an inclusive classroom we need to take into account the differences and needs of all the students, including those who are regularly absent and/or who have a chronic illness. Educators need to be aware that regular absences from school can contribute to the student's feeling of disenfranchisement and alienation. Unless special assistance is available from teachers, the absences have the potential to make the students feel neglected. Within the school setting, the particular problems that attend the illness (problems with energy, diet and eliminative processes) can mark the chronically ill student as different, thus contributing to their feelings of being excluded. Perhaps leaving students to fend for themselves can promote resilience and self-reliance, but experiences surrounding chronic illness also have the potential to leave these students alienated and isolated. Potential exclusion may also vary with the age of the individual. Some of the literature reports that students with cystic fibrosis have been teased at school, experienced difficulties in forming friendships, expressed concern about coughing in the classroom and were worried about their physical appearance (Boyle, di sant'Agnese, Sack, Millican and Kulczycki, 1976; Christian and D'Auria, 1997).

Another problem that can create feelings of exclusion and alienation is failure to thrive academically. Students with a chronic illness, particularly one like cystic fibrosis which sometimes requires frequent hospitalization, often have high levels of absenteeism from school. This then leads to the possibility of them falling behind in their school work and becoming under-achievers. Again, teachers need to be sensitive to the potential problems that can occur from frequent absences.

Because of the contagious infection Peta was carrying, she lived in an atmosphere of exclusion at the hospital and was unable to talk and meet with other people as she did at school. This exclusiveness was broken down to some extent through regular telephone contact and visits from her school friends.

As for James, he had no contact with his friends while in hospital, and to some degree appeared socially isolated at school. He had only one good friend at school, who also had a medical condition. James expressed his feelings of loneliness both at school and at the hospital, although it is unclear whether this was associated with having an illness and with frequent absences from school.

Nevertheless, it seemed likely that Peta and James have a relatively normal school experience, and perhaps this is how they normalize their condition and life. For Peta, returning to school was returning back to her 'normal routine'. However, both admitted to some difficulties caused by their illness, which differentiated them from their peers. They felt very tired at school and lacked energy; they had specific dietary and eliminative needs; and they could not participate fully in physical activities.

Both Peta and James were very concerned about missing out on school work while they were in hospital. In terms of the teachers' recognition of their illness and needs, few concessions were made. There appeared to be no specific arrangements for either student regarding their school work while in hospital and Peta relied on her friends and parents to provide her with school work each week. James had no contact with his school peers or teachers. In addition, neither student reported any additional academic support when they returned to school.

The picture that emerges is that the students themselves accepted responsibility for coping with their absence from school, collecting work and catching up on their work after hospitalization. This picture of the 'solitary coper' leads us to conclude that subtle forms of exclusiveness may characterize their school life. Even if this is the case, the two students in this study seemed to adapt and accommodate both to their illness and to school demands.

While Peta and James have given us a glimpse of their life experiences at school and at the hospital, we have heard only what they decided to share with us, and this may not be the complete picture. Many adolescents and young people with cystic fibrosis seldom express their fears or concerns when interviewed (Admi, 1995). There may lie more deeply seated problems which have not been addressed in this study. For example, the students seem to 'normalize' their illness and related problems in a way that could be seen to be too clinical and matter-of-fact. It is possible that they are not coping as well as their responses would suggest. Alternatively, they may cope by maintaining a positive outlook and by denying the existence of their illness and associated problems.

The voices of two adolescents with a chronic illness in this study suggest that these students are self-managing to some degree, and appear to be coping well. Although different in some aspects from their peers, there did not appear to be any obvious 'exclusion' at school, although when they were not attending few efforts seem to be made by teachers to include them in school work. The insights we have gained form this study may lead to a more comprehensive study and we believe that it is important that we continue to listen to the voices of children and young people with a chronic illness. We also believe that it is essential to ascertain whether the absence of proactive inclusive measures does not lead, involuntarily, to a form of exclusion by neglect.

References

ADMI, H. (1995) 'Nothing to hide and nothing to advertise: Managing disease-related information', *Western Journal of Nursing Research*, **17**, 5, pp. 484–501.

AUSTRALIAN BUREAU OF STATISTICS (1997) *1996 Census of Population and Housing* (No. 3101.0), Canberra: Australian Demographic Statistics.

BOYLE, I.R., DI SANT'AGNESE, P.A., SACK, S., MILLICAN, F. and KULCZYCKI, L.L. (1976) 'Emotional adjustment of adolescents and young adults with cystic fibrosis', *The Journal of Pediatrics*, **88**, 2, pp. 318–26.

CHEWNING, B. and SLEATH, B. (1996) 'Medication decision-making and management: A client-centered model', *Social Science and Medicine*, **42**, 3, pp. 389–98.

CHRISTIAN, B.J. and D'AURIA, J.P. (1997) 'The child's eye: Memories of growing up with cystic fibrosis', *Journal of Pediatric Nursing*, **12**, 1, pp. 3–12.

CYSTIC FIBROSIS FOUNDATION (USA) (1996) 'Facts about cystic fibrosis', http://www.cff.org/factsabo.htm.

FOWLER, M.G., JOHNSON, M.P. and ATKINSON, S.S. (1985) 'School achievement and absence in children with chronic health conditions', *The Journal of Pediatrics*, **106**, 4, pp. 683–7.

GORTMAKER, S.L. (1985) 'Demography of chronic childhood diseases', in HOBBS, N. and PERRIN, J.M. (Eds) *Issues in the Care of Children with Chronic Illnesses*, San Francisco, Calif: Jossey Bass, pp. 135–54.

HARBORD, M.G., CROSS, D.G., BOTICA, F. and MARTIN, A.J. (1987) 'Children's understanding of cystic fibrosis', *Australian Paediatric Journal*, **23**, 4, pp. 241–4.

LARCOMBE, I. (1995) *Reintegration to School After Hospital Treatment*, Aldershot, UK: Avebury.

NEW BORN SCREENING CLINIC (1996) 'Fact sheet for cystic fibrosis patients', The Royal Alexandra Hospital for Children.

REED, J. and WATSON, D. (1994) 'The impact of the medical model on nursing practice and assessment', *International Journal of Nursing Studies*, **31**, 1, pp. 57–66.

SCHROEDER, C. (1994) 'Community partnerships and medical models of health? I don't think so . . .' (Editorial), *Public Health Nursing*, **11**, 5, pp. 283–4.

SEXSON, S.B. and MADAN-SWAIN, A. (1993) 'School reentry for the child with chronic illness', *Journal of Learning Disabilities*, **26**, 2, pp. 115–25.

STAMBOLOVIC, V. (1996) 'Human rights and health within the dominant paradigm', *Social Science and Medicine*, **42**, 3, pp. 301–3.

THOMPSON, R.J. and GUSTAFSON, K.E. (1996) *Adaptation to Chronic Childhood Illness*, Washington DC: American Psychological Association.

WEITZMAN, M. (1984) 'School and peer relations', *Pediatric Clinics of North America*, **31**, 1, pp. 59–69.

Chapter 7

Disability, Inclusion and Exclusion: Some Insider Accounts and Interpretations

Keith Ballard and Trevor McDonald

For this study, three people worked with us to write about their experiences of inclusion and exclusion in the New Zealand education system. Our goal was to present some insider accounts and interpretations of disability in the school years and beyond, listening to the voice of those who had direct involvement with enabling and disabling people and settings, and reflecting on some of the longer-term implications of these.

For our part, we did not see ourselves as recording devices gathering information around predetermined questions to be treated as text data for analysis (Tripp, 1983). Our interviews were extended conversations with people who undertook to work with us in creating a shared understanding of aspects of their lives for this project (Limerick, Burgess-Limerick and Grace, 1996). Nevertheless, as part of the ethical procedures of informed consent, we provided a list of possible questions that participants might respond to when we first met. These asked where they went to school; whether they had experience of special education; friendships at school; how they thought that disability affected their schooling; and their involvement in education beyond the school system. Divergence from this outline was encouraged, and, as we talked, both the researcher and participant would seek clarification and explanation for accounts and interpretations of events and issues.

The participants knew us from our work in the area of disability and education, and through our involvement in community-based groups concerned with support and advocacy. We think that this made it possible for us to achieve the level of trust that is required for collaborative work of this kind, which involves self-exposure, for the participants especially, and the critical scrutiny of motives and findings that is central to research thought and practice. We agree with Clandinin and Connelly (1988, p. 281) that such studies require a relationship 'akin to friendship'. Time is needed to establish understanding and a shared purpose. We acknowledge the power relationships involved here (Scheurich, 1995) but we attempted to give the participants a voice in the research in ways that were not exploitative and that met with their wishes (Lincoln and Denzin, 1994). This was how we included ourselves in this work, aware of the need to examine how our experiences — as former school teachers, psychologist (Keith), and assistant principal in a special school (Trevor) — and preferences — in support of inclusion, for example — might shape the project. We tried to be sensitive to our 'passions and limitations' (Lather, 1986, p. 272) and to test interpretations against alternative plausible ideas and explanations (Schön, 1991).

After two or three interviews the participants each indicated that we had achieved an initial coverage of the experiences and issues they wanted to present. We then transcribed this material from the audiotape recordings and gave this to them to read, although Paul and Karen chose to listen to the audio recordings. Moving from oral speech to the written word is a significant transformation of the data, in which it is decontextualized, and information and meanings available in the nuances and complexities of personal interactions may be lost (Scheurich, 1995). We talked with the participants to further clarify their accounts and develop them in written form, deciding on verbatim material that would be used, and the organization of material in a way that would make sense to the reader. Once we had written each person's narrative up into a form that could be presented in the chapter, we gave this back to them in written and audio format for their further comment.

In this way, through several drafts of the chapter, we wrote the accounts and interpretation of experiences presented here. In Wolcott's (1990) terms, we have not set out to 'discover a ready made world' but 'to understand a social world we are continuously in the process of constructing' (p. 147).

Care was taken in the use of personal information. What is revealed in situations where people work closely together and believe in the importance of a project can lead to comment about relationships, for example, that might not warrant inclusion in the public record. Only a few instances in this study proved of that kind, and they have been left out of this chapter. The 'gift' (Limerick et al., 1996) of self-disclosure should not carry the cost of later regret by the participant, unless they decide that the cause may justify this. The choice of anonymity by the participants is also part of that protective approach in the study. Apart from our own, all the names in this chapter are pseudonyms.

Marilyn

Marilyn is a woman in her thirties who is married, has a university degree, and is employed full-time in a professional position. She describes herself as 'not as disabled as a lot of other people'. Nevertheless, her mobility is by motorized chair, and, as she says,

> I can't completely dress myself. I need assistance basically for everything. . . . I am reliant on everyone about what time I go to the loo [toilet], if I want to get a drink. If somebody puts something out of my reach I can't get it.

As Marilyn explained, there are people in residential settings for the physically disabled who are more independent physically than she is. What she has is a background that includes a good education and, related to this, the opportunity to have control over her own life. Nevertheless, as she said, 'take away the support systems that I have got, the people . . . [and] it would be very scary [for me]'.

Marilyn described her childhood as being that of a very active, able-bodied child until age 11 when 'I got really sick really fast.' For three years she was hospitalized, for much of that time in wards with aged and sometimes terminally ill patients. Hospital rules were that children under the age of 12 were not allowed to visit, and she subsequently learnt that her former school friends thought that she had died. The interaction of severe pain and medications meant that she did not continue with school work during her hospitalization. Nevertheless, when she was ready for discharge, her medical specialist worked with her parents to ensure that she went 'to the best school academically' in her community and that she was enrolled with her age group. Participation with her age peers involved Marilyn starting school in the last three to four weeks of the year and still being expected to sit examinations that usually determined progression into the next form level. On failing these, Marilyn recalled that she cried because she would be separated from people that she had got to know in the preceding weeks. Yet this did not happen. She was moved on with her peer group and, as she said, 'I don't know what happened [but] from that day I never looked back.' In reflecting on this, Marilyn indicated that a key element seemed to be that she was not seen as someone 'with a disability'. Marilyn remembered that 'the teachers kept pushing me. I was in the top stream except for the languages. . . . I don't ever remember having trouble adapting. Because I was just in with all my friends and allowed to [just keep] going.'

Marilyn said that until she was 18, she, along with others, believed that she would 'grow out' of her impairments. She thought that for this reason her teachers did not treat her as a disabled child. Instead,

> I was a child with an adult's disease. My wheelchair was bought for me so that I could grow into it. I never fitted it. My school uniform was bought so I could grow into it. I looked hilarious. My wheelchair was too big for me, my uniform was too big, and . . . I never grew because of the drugs that I was on.

Although this state high school had a segregated class for disabled students, Marilyn was never located there. She said that had she been labelled with a disability then this, and the fact that she had missed three years of schooling, could have seen her assigned to the special class. Instead, her medical practitioner ensured that she 'had the same expectancies to be the same as everybody else. . . . He was my best advocate as a child.'

At the end of high school, Marilyn saw her friends going off to get jobs or going on to university. There were a number of uncertainties for her at this time. She became more withdrawn and quiet because of anxiety about social relationships now that a secure peer group was no longer available to her. Her guidance counsellor recommended botany and biology for study at university because those were her highest grades at school. The irony of this, said Marilyn, was that she had received virtually no assistance that allowed her to actively participate in sciences at school. The chemistry tables were 'up above my ears', and in this and other science classes she was expected to 'just watch and learn'. The expectation, said Marilyn, was that people with physical disabilities would not be competent in science areas, which is 'really sad because especially when you have an alternative way of looking at things you would make a great scientist'. Nevertheless, Marilyn did not think that she had the physical ability to work in these areas. She described her decision at that time as

> looking at striking out [to be] independent. So when everyone else was looking at settling down, I decided that my options were into varsity to get a career to finance myself and then get into a house so that if anything happened to my parents, God forbid, I was self-sufficient. But that was a really unsettling time. I can't remember a lot about it. But I knew that I was really scared. 'Cause everyone else was [taking a] great jump off into a new career, but to me, I was thinking of the realities for the rest of my life. Because school was very much a protected area and those things [planning for the future] aren't addressed.

Marilyn described going to university from high school as a difficult time. In this period in the late 1970s, she met only one other person with a disability on campus. Because of problems in getting around in her wheelchair, she described sitting outside lecture rooms for three or four hours waiting for a lecture to start. This was easier than moving to another part of the campus and coming back. In any case, she was unable to get into the cafeteria and other areas because of steps and stairs. After three unhappy years, Marilyn described meeting two (non-disabled) people with whom she became friends and 'started to enjoy a social circle again'. As Marilyn said,

> which is interesting because they were both people that couldn't see the disability, they just liked me for who I was, and they kept pulling me in. It was them contact[ing] me, saying 'come on, let's do something. . . .' It just happened at the right time.

Of her time at university, Marilyn reported only failing one paper, and that in a year 'when I broke my neck'. She remembers the indignities of a system that would not adapt to people with disabilities. This included, 'I had my Dad carrying me upstairs to get to examination rooms' because the person responsible for the location of exams would not make arrangements that met the needs of people in wheelchairs. Years later this administrator praised Marilyn for not being one of those disabled people who 'demanded change'. In lectures, her feeling of isolation was exacerbated by always being at the front of the room with no facilities for her to be included in the seating arrangements. Marilyn said that by this stage in her life, everyone else had continued to grow physically but that she now 'was really tiny'. As she said, at university, 'people didn't know how to react to me. Or any person with a disability.' While lecturers might ask if they could help, both they and students had little idea of how to meet the needs of someone in a wheelchair. She remembered students who failed to think of her physical safety while helping her, people who did not realize that she 'was sore, and I knew if I fell I would break something'. She also recalled a related difficulty at school. This involved a teacher who assigned children to a roster for helping Marilyn get around. As she said, this forced her to be with students that she did not want to be with, people who 'didn't like me or I didn't like them, or who were unsure of me and I was unsure of them'. Such experiences indicate that the provision of support systems is more than simply an arrangement that ensures physical movement or the availability of equipment. The social implications of a helping relationship clearly need attention.

What is also evident in Marilyn's account is the significant impact that an individual teacher can have on a student's life. The teacher who had created the roster for helpers also presented Marilyn with some other challenges, and resulted in what Marilyn described as 'the most miserable year I ever had at school because of this woman'. In contrast, another teacher had told students about a person in a wheel-chair who was coming to their class, and that people should be friendly and make her feel welcome. As Marilyn said,

> This 'worked', and I made some of my best friends and I have still got them. In that class I was included, I was allowed to sit at a desk, and everybody treated me really well. And I made friends there, and also my friends brought other friends around. That is how I met my first ever boys, who when I was hospitalized after that became regular visitors every day. I learnt a lot about motorbikes. They had bikes, and so they would come up to [the hospital] and visit me every day. Spent four or five hours a day. . . . Because I had that good doctor by that stage, I was allowed, people were allowed access to me all the time.

Marilyn was 'just friends with anybody who would want to be friends with me. And luckily I picked the middle-to-in crowd.' The importance of these social relationships was that Marilyn saw them as 'a really good peer group, which sustained me right through . . . until I was about 18 or 19 [years of age]'. Nevertheless, as she got older, she felt more uncomfortable at parties and other social gatherings, and gradually withdrew into her studies. She described this as a 'typical defence mechanism' used by disabled people. While talking about friendships in the teenage and early adulthood years, Marilyn commented that no one had ever discussed close and intimate relationships with her until she was in her late twenties. In her view, she had been lucky even then in meeting good people who, as professionals, were able to give her confidence and understanding about interpersonal issues. Other people with disabilities that she has met have had very little help and support on issues of sexuality and related matters.

For Marilyn, the social contexts that she experienced emerged as being critical for her well-being in several ways. In her first few years at university she said that she became 'very quiet and very very insecure', but that it was 'people that pulled me out of it', and with friendship came involvement with a range of activities and social groups. These friendships were initially with non-disabled people. As Marilyn said, she thought of herself as 'an able-bodied person in a disabled body'. When she first met some people who were blind, she responded 'hell, what do we do here? But that was the beauty of it, I just stopped and I said OK, what do we need to do. I was an open book in some ways, no preconceived ideas.' These people became friends and worked together on disability issues on campus and in the community.

As she did this, Marilyn then found that, because she was in a wheelchair, she was expected to know about disability and its social and political implications. In fact, she said, she had to learn about such things for herself in what became a consciousness-raising experience. Contact with other physically disabled people introduced her to issues that she had not previously confronted. As she said,

> [Until recently] I hadn't really had any contact with people with disabilities. I didn't consider myself as having a disability. I just happen to be in a wheelchair, and I lived in an able-bodied world, and I had an able-bodied job, able-bodied friends. So it is only in the last six or so years, that I actually met a lot of these people. And it scares me when I see where they are. Some of them, a large majority of them, can read and write, but they have never had any career expectations. Now people are starting to think, hey, these people can do things. In the case of some that are in their forties it's too late, ones in their thirties no one will ever expect them to get jobs or employment. It's more how can we keep them occupied? Which is really sad.

Increasingly Marilyn has come to see education as the key to inclusion in mainstream society. She described emerging technology that would, for example, allow the blind 'to hear' chemical reactions, opening up science and other areas in ways not previously envisaged. She saw value in non-disabled students providing support for disabled peers, noting that their initial caution, even fear, 'dissipates quickly on direct' contact with disability. Those without disability, said Marilyn,

> have got a really big role to play. The key, I think, to inclusion is making people without disability comfortable with disability, [but also to] accept that they have got a responsibility to help remove the barriers and the fact that when they do that it is the same thing that they do for their own children, for their own relations. If they see an animal in distress or whatever. Not that I am equating animals with people with disabilities. But [it's] what you do if you see something wrong, you don't walk away from it.

Also, Marilyn emphasized the need for those training in professional areas to confront disablism in their lives and work places. She described some of her experiences as a teenager in hospital being 'stripped down to the waist in front of [a lecture hall of] doctors' along with other indignities. While the move to emphasize patient rights may reduce such incidents, ignorance and prejudice remain. In this regard Marilyn said that 'the key to everything now is education'. Today's students are tomorrow's professionals and parents, 'so if we can just get them thinking at whatever level or mixing with people with disabilities on campus in their classes or as part of the curriculum . . . the ice is broken, the questions are being asked'. These people are also citizens who may influence policy and action at national level. They may, through the democratic process, support or profoundly harm disabled New Zealanders. As Marilyn said,

There's barriers for me if my support system falls down. Which I don't want to think about. The biggest concern is which way the social system and the government is going to go. How much it is going to retrench things like attendant care and home help and those things. Which for me could make or break my lifestyle very quickly.

Paul

When Paul contributed to this study he was 18 years old. Since finishing full-time school he had attended a sheltered workshop for four days of the week. On the fifth day he joins a group of senior students from a special school for children and young people with intellectual disabilities. This group spends part of its time engaged in community-based activities, and on other days works on community, leisure and recreation skills with tertiary students who are completing a full-time professional course on supporting people with disabilities.

Paul described people who have a disability as those who 'have problems . . . like they can't walk properly . . . hands are always bent . . . and they have problems talking'. He identifies as having a disability himself. He says that he has had some learning problems and was not allowed to do the same work as other students at school.

TREVOR: So, at intermediate [school] other kids did things like social studies and science . . . but you didn't?

PAUL: No. I used to do painting and that . . . I used to draw pictures when I felt like doing it.

TREVOR: Do you think it would have helped [to study the same things as other students]?

PAUL: Yeah.

TREVOR: Why do you think that they wouldn't let you do the same stuff?

PAUL: Because they wouldn't let me control myself, they wouldn't let me do other things . . . they won't let me try what I wanted to do and that . . . I didn't like that much . . .

Paul has attended a number of schools and has experience of both segregated and mainstream education. At 5 years of age he was enrolled at his local school by his foster parents. At approximately 7 years he was transferred to another school and enrolled in a special class for children with intellectual disabilities. He continued in that class until he was 13 years old. At that point he was enrolled in a mainstream class at an intermediate school (for children aged 11 to 13 years). This was in his home community, but through all of his primary and intermediate years Paul was taken to school in a taxi. After less than one year at intermediate, he was moved to a residential special school for boys with learning difficulties some 400 kilometres away from his foster parents. For the three years he attended this school he saw his foster family only during school holidays.

Paul has few memories of his first primary school except that he was in a regular class and that he used to walk there from his foster parents' home. He also has no recollection as to why he was moved from this first school to the special class . . . 'I just ended up there.' He did, however, report vivid memories of his teachers in the special class.

> Like Mrs Brown doesn't do anything, she just sits and does her work [but] Mrs Green, she used to hit me all the time, so if I didn't do anything right she used to push me.

Paul said that he experienced similar treatment from some teaching staff at the residential school.

> Mr Pink, me and him, oh I got angry one day and he pushed me down on the ground, because I think I lost my temper . . . and he grab me down on the arm down on the ground and put my hand behind my back and that.

The regime of the school made it clear what was acceptable and what was not

> If you don't do your job, you do your job, if you hit someone immediately you are on the hot seat . . . and into bed . . . into your pyjamas in the corner, no normal tea, Marmite sandwiches and you had to do heaps of jobs. You are not allowed to talk to other people. Twenty-four hours, that is how long it goes for. If [you] mucks up [and] you talking . . . the isolation goes up further, like they extend it . . . you weren't allowed to go anywhere . . . we sat there in a wee corridor till our staff member comes and picks us up . . . not even funny, so I got really pissed off about it.

Some of the incidents that Paul described suggested that emotional, physical and sexual abuse occurred at his residential school, although he said that he was usually protected from this by his friendship with a member of staff for the villa in which he lived. Aggressive interactions between students seemed common. He talked about an incident where he was punished.

> John came up behind me and jumped on my back, and I said, ah you little prick and he and I was flat down like a pancake . . . and he, he, I got up and turned around and smacked him in the face, because he hit my back real badly, I think he put my back out of place out of shape . . . I got sent away to hotseat again, like um . . . we weren't allowed to hit anyone.

People who have been isolated into environments away from the usual scrutiny of parents and the community report similar experiences of abuse (Sobsey, 1994), although for Paul unpleasant experiences were not restricted to segregated settings. Of his time at intermediate school he talked about how miserable he felt, about how isolated he was from his peers, and about how they and some of his teachers upset him.

because the kids were making fun of me, calling me names. I turned my chair around to my teacher, um Mrs Blue, and she would say 'come here' and [I] would just storm out of the room because she and them were making fun of me.

He maintained that because he was separated from other students in class work and received some of his instruction away from the rest of the class, he was seen as different, unacceptable, an interpretation supported by research on discrimination in mainstream settings (Llewellyn, 1995). From Paul's account it would also seem that the physical and emotional insults he received were condoned by at least some of the teaching staff, reflecting the kind of sociocultural prejudices reported in other studies of students with learning difficulties (Goodley, 1996). As at the residential school, Paul said that even where there had been provocation he was often the one who received the punishment.

And . . . they say to me, all you are Paul is just a fat, but a pig. That is what they used to call me . . . because I was real fat . . . and that and they used to make fun of me and that, so I get real angry and went up and hit one of the kids. They were getting me real angry . . . so I walked out of the . . . so my teacher grab me by the arm and took me outside to the headmaster's office and that.

Much of Paul's time at school he remembered as protecting himself from harm from others.

They used to give me hidings, used to beat me up all the time and I didn't like it . . . I used to run away, I used to run away. I used to go over to the river, go down the river and crawl in [to a hiding place] and that, they used to call me really nasty names.

In spite of these difficulties Paul is adamant that there were some people at his schools who were there to support him. He noted that he had not wanted to go to the residential school.

PAUL: Because I didn't want to go to [boarding school] really . . . I wanted to stay here because of my school. I had to leave this school, I had to leave my next door neighbour . . . leave all my friends.
TREVOR: Even though there was a lot about the school you didn't like?
PAUL: Yeah . . . because it was closer to home and everything.

He talked about recently meeting up with a friend from his time at intermediate who is now a supervisor in the sheltered workshop Paul attends. Meeting this friend again has been important to Paul, and has had a significant bearing on his desire to remain in the workshop. He also talked of one teacher, Mr Grey, whom he remembers:

Yeah, there was a guy called Mr Grey . . . he was one of Glenn's old teachers . . . he used to go to intermediate as well. And he used to give me a wee real trick, because I was so friend to him, nice to him. He used to be one of my best friends.

Paul also spoke with affection about a number of his social workers in the residential school and has maintained telephone contact with some of those people. Although his experiences of friendship and affection seemed limited at that time mostly to those whose paid work it was to care for him, he recalled his time at the institution as being a relatively settled period of his life, 'because I had more friends, heaps of friends'.

A recurring theme in talking with Paul has been the importance of friendships and friendly relationships with people. It is these links that make him happy.

> Um, when someone laughs, when they say 'Gidday mate, how are ya?' If I see a friend of mine, like Mike, I saw him not so long ago, I said 'Gidday Mike, how are ya mate?' and he says, 'Oh good'. He is a father and he has got a wee baby. He didn't tell me what his name was. He said, 'I'm a Dad. Didn't you know I'm a Dad?' I said, 'No, oh congratulations.' He told me he had a wee kid.

Of the educational opportunities that came Paul's way he is certain that he has missed out by comparison with his typical peers. At primary and intermediate school he talked about access to a physical education programme, which included swimming and games, to whole-school activities such as assemblies, and to vocationally oriented activities such as woodwork and metalwork. A high point from his time at intermediate was involvement in sports. On the sports field Paul felt more like a typical student than he did in the classroom. He also felt accepted by his peers:

> PAUL: . . . I didn't have a . . . disability, like to play games and that.
> TREVOR: It was OK playing games?
> PAUL: Yeah . . . I did games and they reckon I had a disability in the classroom.

Aside from some reading, which at intermediate took place away from the rest of the class, Paul has little recollection of access to the regular curriculum. He talked about spending a great deal of time on painting and drawing, on reading to himself in the classroom, and on being alone a lot of the time. Paul said that he asked to be involved in social studies, science and maths activities at intermediate but was told 'to get stuff[ed]' or 'get lost' by fellow students and staff. For some time while at the intermediate school he did not attend school for the full day.

> They just decided they didn't want me around, the teachers [didn't] wanted me around . . . I had to go home for lunch all the time . . . and I had to go home and that mucked up my day . . . and couldn't go back to school until tomorrow.

At the residential school Paul recalls 'actually quite a lot' of work experience in the gardens and in the laundry, and various recreational and community-based activities. Classroom-based activities seemed to revolve around maths, which Paul really enjoyed. When asked about other curricular areas like science or social studies, Paul recollected only 'heaps of reading' that he did by himself.

Paul was not sure about the merits of one form of schooling over another. On the one hand he saw it as important that people who have a disability should have the opportunity to get their particular needs met. His experience tells him that the place for this to happen is perhaps a special school or special class. However, if support was available in regular schools, Paul thought that this was a good option:

> PAUL: They should go to special schools, like they could get some help . . . like special help . . . when they got disabilities when they can't talk properly . . . they should go to prop[er] different schools.
>
> TREVOR: What if the help was in ordinary schools?
>
> PAUL: Probably go to a normal school or something . . . like that.

When Paul talked about going to a 'normal' rather than a special school, he spoke mostly about people going to schools 'closer to home and everything' so that they would be with their family and friends. Now that he is back in his home town, he clearly values the opportunity to see and interact with people he has known over long periods of time.

Paul felt strongly that schools have a responsibility to value all of those attending. In talking about his experience at intermediate, he explained what schools needed to do to ensure that they are welcoming environments. He said that students should be able to

> PAUL: . . . sit down and talk about it, how they feel and not how the, like, how they are feeling and how they don't feel.
>
> TREVOR: So, who should do that?
>
> PAUL: The school, talk [to] the kids, should talk to the kids, teachers should talk to the kids and say, What is wrong with you? . . . [The student might say] I don't like you treating me like I'm a bit of shit or something, like I'm a bit of dust . . . and that. And that is what they should do . . . talk to the kids . . . and sort it out.

With respect to his future, Paul knows that he is going to live in an IHC house (an organization providing residential and vocational services for people with intellectual disabilities in New Zealand) but did not know when or who with. He has recently found out where the house is located:

> PAUL: The house, I know where it is now . . . it is in David Street . . . that is what I got told.
>
> TREVOR: Do you think that people give you enough information?
>
> PAUL: Yeah, they better, because I asked them if I could have a look, and they say, 'I don't know where about it is.' I haven't seen the stuff . . . all I have heard is this street, David Street. Where the hell is David Street? I keep on thinking, I better have a look at a map, they never show me the map.
>
> TREVOR: Is it OK by you not to have that information, or do you think you should have it?
>
> PAUL: I think I should have that information . . . because I want to leave. I was meant to leave this year, last year. [I think] . . . they made this house up!

One of the recurring themes in talking with Paul was the lack of information that he had been given about the changes that had occurred to him during his life. He did not know why he was moved from school to school and, although he sees himself as a person with a disability, he did not know why his educational programme should have been different from that of other students. Nevertheless, Paul is an optimistic person who seeks out and values friendships. Had he remained at school in his local community it seems possible that his friendship networks might be less fragmented, more sustaining, and might have helped him with gaining an understanding of options available to him and decisions he could make.

Karen

Karen is in her twenties, has recently finished a tertiary qualification at her local university, and is now engaged in job hunting. Karen is 'totally blind'. She describes this as a disability in that

> if society was set up so that I could contribute as much as anyone else then it would not be as much of a disability as it is, but as things stand, it is a disability because of things such as accessing information, I cannot drive so am not as capable of getting around, street signs in general are not available to me . . . and also people's attitudes are still negative in general to blindness, and people think that blind people are not able to contribute as much as able-bodied people, that is how I see my disability . . . it is a social and environmental thing.

Karen said that people in general lack information about adaptive equipment that people who are blind can use around the community and in employment settings, and therefore thought of her and others like her as less capable than sighted people. Karen's experience was that employers especially were often 'not prepared to go the extra mile to see if things will work out'. The result of these attitudes was that Karen, like others in her situation, has to be 'very self-confident' and 'able to sell yourself even more than other people'.

Karen said that in New Zealand there was something of an acceptance among the blind that the availability of resources and equipment to support people in the community was, and would probably remain, problematic. 'There are just not enough of us to make it viable. It should not be an issue but it usually is.' Karen's education reflected the difficulty of maintaining relatively small numbers of blind students in their local school. After attending a regular pre-school in her local area, she went to a special residential school for blind children when she was 5, the age when children in New Zealand begin school. As this was over 1,000 kilometres from her home, Karen had to board during term time and return home for holidays. She attended this school for seven years, and while still boarding there spent two years in mainstream classes at an intermediate school in this city. After this, she returned home and her secondary education was at the local high school.

Karen remembers pre-school as a very positive experience. It was close to her home and she attended with children who lived near her. She felt as if she fitted in and was accepted, 'it didn't really matter that I was different'. Going away from her family at 5 years of age was still remembered as a traumatic experience:

> I think to start with I was very lonely and withdrew into myself, as I was a shy child anyway, I think this made me more shy and withdrawn.

At the residential school there was a mixture of students; some were visually impaired, others totally blind. Karen made friends relatively quickly but said that she and her friends would have liked the chance to meet and interact with sighted students. On occasions, classes from a nearby school would visit the school for the blind, or Karen and her fellow students would visit the local school:

> But it was not enough, though it was fun, but you did not make any lasting friendships and we did not even have regular kids coming in at playtime or after school. It was very cut off from society.

In addition to these visits to and from neighbouring schools, a Brownie and Girl Guide pack was based at the school. Brownies and Girl Guide groups from around the city would visit the school for the blind on a regular basis to 'come to do the "be a friend to the blind" badge . . . it was sort of like being in a zoo'.

At the school there were a number of day pupils whose families already lived in the area or who had been able to move there so that their child could attend the school. Karen would sometimes spend time with these students at their homes, and she would meet their sighted friends. Mostly, however, her peer group were all students at the school who were blind themselves. At home, during school holidays, Karen missed these contacts. She had lost touch with those friends she had from pre-school, and did not know others of her age in her community. Consequently she often felt lonely and missed peer contact.

After her primary education in the special school, Karen, along with eight other blind students of her age, attended an intermediate school near the residential school. Although the intermediate had a resource room for blind students, they were all placed full-time in regular classes. While out-of-class times were spent mainly with other blind students, 'as this was the easiest thing to do', some of their sighted friends also congregated in the resource room at lunch and other recess times.

Academically, Karen enjoyed her early years at the residential school. She remembered the classes as being small, and that there was a good deal of individual attention available to students. In addition to the academic focus of her classes, she received instruction in the use of Braille, typing, and orientation and mobility. As the primary school years passed, however, the initial attraction of the small number of students in each of these classes began to pall:

> I think we were happy with it until we got a bit older, but by the time we got to 10 years, we got bored that there were only nine kids in the class and we were getting a bit bored with each other and wanted to extend.

At this time Karen's parents began to push for her to return to her home town for her secondary education:

They really pushed for it and had to push hard, they were not encouraged about [me] going to my local high school . . . My family had never wanted me to go away in the first place, but they did not have an option at that stage. Back in the mid-seventies although there were blind children at high school, I do not think there was any totally blind kids who had gone to normal primary schools.

Karen remembered that when she began at her local high school, 'my family and I were really excited about going'. She maintains that it 'was no big deal as I had learnt Braille by then and I could get around independently, could type'. Although the residential school that Karen attended had the responsibility of providing Braille transcriptions and related services for students around the country, she reported feeling that her decision to go home and attend her local high school 'was a hassle for them'.

In general, Karen was very positive about her secondary school experience. There were the probably inevitable difficulties in settling into a new social situation, of making friends and of adjusting to the demands of secondary education:

it was harder for me going in at the third form level, most of the other kids in my class knew at least one other person as they had been at intermediate together. I think that to start I was a bit of a novelty, everyone wanted to be my friend so that they could learn how to Braille or to have a go with my cane or whatever. Although I would not have done it any other way, it was really neat and the teachers were very supportive, some of them actually learnt Braille and wanted to do all they could to assist me. I was still not just one of the other students. I was still visible and obvious.

Karen explained that although the staff at the school were anxious to ensure that her needs were met, the strategies they used often served to single her out and created difficulties with other students.

Some [students] complained that they were not getting their work done as much as they should as they were having to read stuff out from the board to me. They tried to put in place a buddy system, when everyone in the class had to take turns at sitting with me and I hated that. Like all these people did not want to be there and were being made to be there to read stuff off the board. Once the novelty wore off I knew that some people were going to find it a hassle.

The efforts that some teachers went to also affected Karen's performance in class to the extent that she felt that she was under a great deal of pressure to do well:

Because people were going to so much trouble for it to be a success I felt that I had to try all the time, I could not be an anonymous student. I could never be a bit invisible. If I did not do well in a subject there would be a meeting [about] why this was happening . . . I felt I had to perform. This just does not happen with other kids.

While Karen said that it was important for her teachers to ensure that she could participate in all curriculum areas and in the class programme, she felt that it should have been possible for assistance to be provided in a way that was not so intrusive, or did not single her out from her peers to the extent that she often felt very different:

> I really enjoyed the classes where I just went in and was treated like anyone else, and if I had not done my homework I would get told off as well. The teacher would not single me out, they would say, 'What do you think Karen?' I always felt visible, as walking round the school I had my cane and I had my Brailler and everyone would have known me in the school, if not to speak to then by sight. I always felt that I was very obvious, and it was nice when I could be one of the crowd, just be a student.
>
> I did need extra support and organization but I think that they should do it in an unobtrusive way, and try to integrate students as fully as possible while making sure that they do reach their full potential. I think it is particularly difficult with visual impairment students as there are some subject areas where, if it is a very visual subject and a lot has to be done on the board, then you do need to have extra tuition, if not, then the other students have the burden placed on them ... Later on when I was doing chemistry and biology as well I used a teacher's aide. This worked well as she fitted in and would be there to do my part of the experiment, but in a group situation. Where I could do it myself she would keep out, but she was there. I would rather have the aide there and participate than just sit there when the class did something I could not do.

Although she experienced difficulties in being a focus of attention, Karen enjoyed secondary school:

> Yes, I liked high school. I had a lot of the same experiences as other kids have. I mean no one really loves high school. I did enjoy going to school and I enjoyed most of the stuff. I felt a bit out of it socially but I think it was because like most kids in their teenage years you want to be part of the popular group and I wasn't, and there was nothing I could have done about that. It was just the way it was. I did not fit into the sporty group either, because I could not play team sports and I did not want to fit into the really academic group because they were nerdy and I did not have a niche. I had a few close friends but I did not really fit into a group. That is not specifically for disabled students, other students have the same problem.

Karen went from school to university. This was initially a difficult time. The campus, so much bigger than a secondary school, was daunting, and the numbers of people she had to interact with were so much greater than at school. Although Karen found her way to where she had to attend lectures, she did not know what else was available on campus or how to get there. As had happened when she first began at secondary school, she found herself socially isolated, although she noted that the experience of loneliness at university is not something that affects only disabled people.

Karen said that the impact of disability on people's lives depends very much on the individual. There are those who 'fall by the wayside' because disability is such a negative experience for them. There are some who Karen said 'take it too seriously', emphasizing their disability in personal and political advocacy. Karen's view was that she preferred to get on with other things in life. However, she acknowledged that the presence of disability in a person's life requires them to be organized, to respond to the pressure that disability imposes, and to do well: 'I felt I had to do better than other people and I had to prove myself.' Karen thought that people with disabilities are vulnerable and that the feeling of being 'the odd one out never leaves you, feeling isolated always stays with you'. She said that many of the support agencies, including schools, can reinforce these feelings of isolation:

> They forget that the experience of disability can be really disempowering, and then not being able to do things in a classroom that everybody else is expected to do just reinforces that. Your self-esteem goes down . . . You always have to make the extra effort, you always have to feel grateful.

Karen's experience of both regular and special education has left her in no doubt that it is not acceptable to exclude children from their local school on the grounds of their learning needs. She is adamant that wherever a student lives, they should have access to the supports necessary to ensure that they are not disadvantaged. She also said, however, that there were some classes and subject areas where inclusion is perhaps not in the best interests of the blind student:

> In maths for instance, it is such a visual subject. I would have to have somebody sitting beside me to tell me what was happening on the board and then I had to try to visualize it so I could understand. I just fell behind . . . so I had individual instruction in the third and fourth form and then again in the sixth and seventh form. It made a huge difference.

In other curricular areas there also needs to be change:

> In PE the curriculum needs to change. Whenever there were team sports I had to miss out. Oh they would say, go and do some weights or something, but all that does is reinforce what you can't do. When you're that age too, you are so self-conscious, when you can't see what others are doing, if you're learning about a dance or something you just don't want to do it. Even if they used audible equipment or just changed the games it would make things better.

To this end, Karen feels that teachers are inadequately trained to meet the needs of people who are different. In her own time in the education system Karen felt that many of her teachers were scared and that they did not know where to go, or what to do, to get assistance. She felt that this was unfair, that teachers should have the information they needed, and that this should be a part of initial teacher training. Also, resources, such as the transcription service, are not adequately funded, creating delays and limiting access to material that is essential to students and teachers. While the inclusion of students who are blind or visually impaired into their local schools is something Karen strongly supports, she said that because resources are limited, children are missing out:

I am glad that I wasn't coming into the education system 15 years later. Kids in schools need orientation and mobility instruction and they need to learn Braille from qualified people and not from teacher's aides who are learning at the same time. If they get something wrong, they teach it to their students and it's very hard to undo those mistakes. There are blind children in schools now who are barely literate.

Karen feels very strongly that people with impairments are disabled by a society that sees impairment as a negative attribute. The result of this is that the community at large has the perception that people who are blind are less able to contribute, and this results in fewer opportunities for people to participate. She is equally adamant that there are barriers placed in front of people with impairments that ensure they cannot participate with their non-disabled peers:

I don't expect people to anticipate my needs all of the time, but they need to be prepared to listen and to consult and then to do the things that they can without barriers. Part of education is about learning to live in a sighted world and that's OK, but it's hard to know just how much you need to compromise when you're constantly faced with people who just don't want to help. The bolshy [disabled] ones are the ones who get somewhere because they are prepared to be disliked to get what they want.

The need to act as a self-advocate is an important one for Karen:

You have to be an expert on your own needs . . . but it is so much more difficult to advocate for yourself than for another person because there is so much more at stake.

Inclusion and Exclusion: Personal and Political

These accounts show some of the effects on people's lives of disabling environments. To be disabled is to need to advocate for access to education and other culturally valued resources that are available as of right to your fellow citizens. Disability is being grateful for support while lacking the power to be secure that your school or society will continue to meet your needs. It is to be at risk of labelling that can exclude you from learning opportunities and segregate you from your friends and community. To be segregated can mean that you are treated as less than human (Blatt, 1987).

In addition to illustrating the material and political origins of disability, these accounts provide positive information about inclusion in education, with ideas on supportive teacher and peer strategies that acknowledge the needs created by particular impairments and environments (Crow, 1996). This suggests the importance of disabled people bringing their direct experience in these areas to advising and educating disabled students and education professionals (Oliver, 1988).

For each of our participants their lives at school and beyond speak of the sustaining value of friends. In suggesting that the role of friendship is a key understanding that we might take from these accounts, we locate emotion as important in the study and practice of inclusion in education. Friendship does not exist without respect and care in knowing another person and, like inclusion, emphasizes equality and reciprocity in relationships. This challenges the inequality and pressures towards assimilation generated within disablist and exclusionary structures (Brown and Smith, 1992).

Research is also about caring, in this case caring, sometimes passionately, to know about people and things (Polanyi, 1958). In this endeavour some researchers value the emotions of detachment that derive from a belief in objectivity. Others, including ourselves, work with the emotions of engagement necessary for collaborative research, wanting to understand the possibly diverse meanings people assign to their lives and to resist the 'dogmatism of a single tale' (Grumet, 1991, p. 72). Research as democratic dialogue with students, teachers and others, need not restrict the critical, questioning analysis that is central to interrogating existing ideas and practices, generating understanding and creating theory. Rather, including others in such endeavours requires us to communicate ideas so that they are open to scrutiny and comment from a wider community than just that of our academic peer reviewers. In such ways research on inclusion might become more inclusive research.

References

BLATT, B. (1987) *The Conquest of Mental Retardation*, Austin, TX: Pro-ed.

BROWN, H. and SMITH, H. (1992) 'Assertion not assimilation: A feminist perspective on the normalisation principle', in BROWN, H. and SMITH, H. (Eds) *Normalisation: A reader for the nineties*, London: Tavistock/Routledge, pp. 149–71.

CLANDININ, D.J. and CONNELLY, F.M. (1988) 'Studying teachers' knowledge of classrooms: Collaborative research, ethics and the negotiation of narrative', *The Journal of Educational Thought*, **22**, pp. 269–82.

CROW, L. (1996) 'Including all our lives: Renewing the social model of disability', in BARNES, C. and MERCER, E. (Eds) *Exploring the Divide: Illness and Disability*, Leeds: The Disability Press, pp. 55–73.

GOODLEY, D. (1996) 'Tales of hidden lives: A critical examination of life history research with people who have learning difficulties', *Disability and Society*, **11**, 3, pp. 333–48.

GRUMET, M.R. (1991) 'The politics of personal knowledge', in WITHERELL, C. and NODDINGS, N. (Eds) *Stories Lives Tell: Narrative and Dialogue in Education*, New York: Teachers College Press, pp. 67–77.

LATHER, P. (1986) 'Research as praxis', *Harvard Educational Review*, **56**, 3, pp. 257–77.

LIMERICK, B., BURGESS-LIMERICK, T. and GRACE, M. (1996) 'The politics of interviewing: Power relations and accepting the gift', *Qualitative Studies in Education*, **9**, 4, pp. 449–60.

LINCOLN, Y.S. and DENZIN, N.K. (1994) 'The fifth moment', in DENZIN, N.K. and LINCOLN, Y.S. (Eds) *Handbook of Qualitative Research*, Thousand Oaks: Sage, pp. 575–86.

LLEWELLYN, A. (1995) 'The abuse of children with physical disabilities in mainstream schooling', *Developmental Medicine and Child Neurology*, **37**, pp. 740–43.

OLIVER, M. (1988) 'The social and political context of educational policy: The case of special needs', in BARTON, L. (Ed.) *The Politics of Special Educational Needs*, London: Falmer Press, pp. 13–31.

POLANYI, M. (1958) *Personal Knowledge: Towards a Post Critical Philosophy*, London: Routledge & Kegan Paul.

SCHEURICH, J.J. (1995) 'A postmodernist critique of research interviewing', *Qualitative Studies in Education*, **8**, 3, pp. 239–52.

SCHÖN, D.A. (1991) 'Concluding comments', in SCHÖN, D.A. (Ed.) *The reflective turn: Case studies in and out of educational practice*, New York: Teachers College Press, pp. 343–59.

SOBSEY, D. (1994) *Violence and Abuse in the Lives of People who have Disabilities: The End of Silent Acceptance?* Baltimore: Paul H. Brookes.

TRIPP, D.H. (1983) 'Co-authorship and negotiation: The interview as act of creation', *Interchange*, **14**, 3, pp. 32–45.

WOLCOTT, H.J. (1990) 'On seeking — and rejecting — validity in qualitative research', in EISNER, E.W. and PESHKIN, A. (Eds) *Qualitative Inquiry in Education: The Continuing Debate*, New York: Teachers College Press, pp. 121–52.

Chapter 8

Three Voices from the First Generation of Integration Students in Norway

Kari Nes

From 1976 The Norwegian Education Act for Compulsory Education was extended to cover all children. This law is sometimes called 'The Integration Act'. In the preliminary part of the law, integration is defined as belonging, participation and responsibility. It requires that every child, irrespective of race, culture, sex or disability, should be given equitable and suitably adapted education, preferably in the local school. A right to receive special education locally was also established by the law, and was seen as a natural part of adapted education. Even during the years preceding 1975, very few handicapped children were institutionalized, but it was not until the beginning of the 1990s that institutions and special schools were actually closed down. This meant that children with identified special educational needs born in the 1960s, who had their school years in the 1970s and 1980s, were, with few exceptions, 'integrated' in school in one way or another. Most students continued to live at home until the age of 18–20 years or more (Helgeland, 1992; Vislie, 1995).

After almost three decades of integration, the first 'generation of integration' students are now adults. How do they live today, and what do they have to say about their schooling? Were they really integrated in the sense that they belonged to the school and their community, took part in these and had responsibilities? Are they integrated now? And if we put on this decade's glasses of 'inclusion' (Ballard, 1995; Skrtic, 1991), how does it look then? One attempt at formulating what inclusion is about is found in the new Norwegian Core Curriculum: 'The teacher must make use of the variations in pupils' aptitudes, the diversity in the classroom, and the heterogeneity of the school as resources for all-round development as well as the development of all' (Ministry of Church, Education and Research, 1994, p. 19).

In order to throw some light on these matters I talked with three people, 'Eva', 'Laila' and 'Rolf', who are now in their early thirties. They belong to the first generation of students integrated into schools in this country, being born in the mid-1960s. Each was diagnosed as having mild intellectual disabilities. Rolf has a physical impairment as well. Their school careers were mixed as to the degree of formal integration. During pre-school and primary school they each lived with their families and went to mainstream classes in the catchment area where they belonged. However, none of them started school until the age of 8, when in Norway entry to school was at 7 years of age (and from 1997 school began at age 6 years). From the seventh grade their schooling varied, but, for each person, involved regular as well as more or less special types of education. All three participants now live on their own in small apartments in ordinary residential areas, supported by invalid benefits. Two work in sheltered working places, and one, Laila, does not work. They all still live within 30 kilometres from where their families lived when they were young.

The Research Procedures

I first met Eva, Laila and Rolf when they were teenagers. My professional work with them as pedagogical/psychological adviser lasted across three years or more at the time. When asked, they all agreed to be interviewed about their school experiences. I had previously recounted Laila's story until age 17 (Mordal, 1982) and she agreed to participate once again in my research. Eva said, even if she hardly could find time for the interviews, that she had been thinking that well-functioning people with intellectual disabilities — like herself — would have some interesting information to report on integration.

The interviews were undertaken during 1996 with three to four meetings per person taking place at home in their own apartments. The interviews were semi-structured using a conversational approach in which we constructed together the account presented here (Kvale, 1996). After having explained my intentions, I started by asking an open question about school days. If the information I was seeking did not occur spontaneously, I added questions about withdrawal programmes, recess, and friends. Sometimes I drew attention to certain events from my earlier contact with them.

Most of the talks with Rolf and Laila were taped, but Eva refused this. Transcripts of the interviews, along with a written explanation about their possible use, were offered to them. I played or read aloud to each of them most of their previous interview with me, to get any additional comments they might wish to make. My interpretations were in part also presented to the participants and discussed with colleagues.

I faced several ethical problems in this work. I was taking advantage of my knowledge of the client situation of these three people; 'their pain is our gain'. As a matter of principle I wanted them to give their informed consent to let me use the information they submitted. One way of meeting the dilemma of asymmetry in relation to persons defined as intellectually disabled, was to recommend to them that they show material on informed consent to a local professional whom they trusted. Eva and Rolf chose to do this. Also, protection of the participants includes using fictitious names in this account, and omitting identifying details.

Another ethical dilemma had to do with Laila. I met her in what seemed to be a rather critical time in her life after she had experienced losses of people close to her. My questions may have underlined her growing feeling of being alone and not having achieved much in life. There I was, being concerned and listening, arriving from far away after 15 years' absence, and then a short while later moving out of her life again, when I had got what I wanted. It was also the case that her reflections on her unfortunate career made her particularly interesting to talk to, which caused me still worse feelings.

Meeting Laila gave me more than I had expected. Not only Laila, however. The three participants were all interesting to talk to, I felt. My feeling of surprise revealed my own prejudices about the capability of people categorized as intellectually disabled. Me prejudiced, in a field where I have been working and analysing for a long time and where I ought to have had all the correct understandings and attitudes?

After introducing Eva, Laila and Rolf, the results of the interviews will be presented according to my identification of key themes. Are their stories accounts of belonging, participating and responsibility? Some of the issues arising will be discussed, and some are left to speak for themselves.

Eva

When you meet Eva, she does not say much if you do not start the conversation, but then she reveals her interest and her good memory of when we last met. She even has a cautious smile to offer.

Eva grew up in a rural area with her parents and siblings in a working-class family. After part-time attendance at kindergarten, her parents were advised to postpone Eva's schooling for a year due to 'immaturity'. From the age of 8 she joined a mainstream class in the small local primary school, a five-minute walk from home. She had remedial lessons out of class. Due to suspected organic disease she spent one year when she was 13 in a hospital far away. There she had to join the hospital school. At this time she received a medical diagnosis, which was also believed to explain her learning problems.

For lower as well as upper secondary school Eva joined a special school as a non-resident. She was now 20, and after this she had two years in a special class in a regular upper secondary school. By that time she had moved from home into a 'boarding house' with special care in the community centre. Since then she has been helped by welfare agencies to buy her own flat, where she receives practical help a couple of times each week.

For nearly 10 years now she has had a combination of protected work and adult education in an activity centre for the handicapped in her local community. She walks or bikes to work. This career was interrupted by two years at a remote 'folk high school', a setting that offers a stimulating year, without examinations, to any young person. At the activity centre she serves guests in the café which is also open to the public. She has a busy social life in the evenings, and has a boyfriend (a lot older than she) who works in the same activity centre.

Laila

Laila is always alone when you see her, strolling on the quays or riding her moped. She starts a conversation by telling a joke or something odd, and you are not quite certain whether she really means what she is saying or not.

She was born the youngest in a fisherman's big family. There was no kindergarten or pre-school in her small village. We do not know much about her first years, but there are no indications of worries in her family that something was wrong with the little girl. However, she was found 'immature' when she started school, so after a few weeks she was recommended to leave — which she did — and come back as a first-grader a year later when she was 8 years old. Laila remembers having a few remedial lessons on her own in her first school years, otherwise she stayed in class. After grade 4 she moved to a big town with her mother, as her parents had split up. Her sisters and brothers had left school and were working by then. In town, Laila and her mother lived in a small flat and had to rely on social security. Laila did not have her own room. She hardly saw her father after this.

At the new school she was found not to adapt, and she got more support lessons and was sent for further medical and psychological/pedagogical examinations. An organic anomaly was diagnosed along with minor learning disabilities. In lower secondary school she continued in the mainstream class with some support lessons. Her shirking of lessons increased, and alternative solutions for schooling were suggested. But she refused to stay in a special class at the neighbouring school and would not attend a residential special school. In eighth grade she left school altogether (compulsory schooling was nine years then, extended to 10 years from 1997) but continued to attend some working days in a shop that had been part of her alternative weekly programme.

In upper secondary school Laila joined a special class in a regular school for two years. At the age of 19 she was found unable to work and was granted an invalid benefit. No alternative occupation was offered. She continued to live with her mother and partly with the mother's boyfriend as well. Some years ago her mother died, and recently Laila's boyfriend (25 years older than she) with whom she was living then, died too. So now she is renting a small flat on her own with no work and no public support apart from the benefit cheque every month.

Rolf

Rolf greets you cheerfully, clearly wanting a chat when you meet him in his electric wheelchair on the public scene — which is where he likes to be — in the shopping centre on Saturday morning for instance.

He was born into a rural, lower-middle-class family as one of three children. He has cerebral palsy, affecting his legs and his intellectual capacity. While growing up he has had many operations in his legs and numerous training programmes. He too started school at 8 years of age after being in part-time pre-school for a while. In the local primary school he had quite a few remedial lessons. Taxi or mini-bus took him to school.

Lower secondary schooling took place in a non-residential special school. From age 18 to 20 he stayed in a residential, upper secondary special school, not far from home. When he returned to the local community after a following year in the 'folk high school' some 10 years ago, he was helped to get an electric wheelchair and a flat on his own in the community centre, with assistance believed to be necessary in activities of daily living.

When he is not working in the joiner's workshop in the Day Centre or attending adult education, much of his spare time is filled with religious activity, since he has been 'converted' into a charismatic congregation. He does not have much contact with his family. Some time ago a wish to spend a year studying at a Bible School arose, and this year he is going there.

Local School

'I had lessons alone — that was not fair . . .' (Rolf)

What comes to mind when asked an open question about the local school? Rolf mentions his withdrawal programme several times, and 'no remedial lessons alone' is his quick answer when asked what changes he would have made in school. Adding to his frustrations is that he felt his reading never became very good, in spite of the withdrawal programme in reading and spelling the mother tongue.

> I liked it there, in primary school. We were 14 in class. That was better, to be in class. When the others were doing English, I had lessons alone — that was not fair, I was not allowed to come . . . So I am a little angry. The teacher I had, she, she . . .

'Greek mythology is Greek to me.' (Laila)

Whatever school was about, it did not seem relevant to Laila after she had learnt what she conceived to be the basics:

> I learnt reading and writing and arithmetic in the first four years. After that in a way it didn't have anything to do with me, I didn't see the point. Greek mythology is Greek to me . . . I didn't understand what they were doing . . . I was sitting there in class, did not say a word. Others were talking all the time and *they* were noticed by the teacher.

'. . . But then they *did not understand* me*!'* (Laila)

Laila did not see the point in school activities, but she also admits often not to understanding what was going on. However, her experiences of not *being* understood, not being taken seriously as a student, are clear: 'I didn't understand, but then *they* did not understand *me*!' Her learning potential was not really identified, at least she was not challenged to achieve. One illustration of this is her typewriter, which is frequently used. She bought it when she left school. During the interview she showed me a story that she had once had published in a newspaper. She said that she had that eagerness to write all the time at school too, but did not think that the teachers knew:

> They were not used to me being able to do it. They thought that when you were going to choose subjects yourself, then I ought to knit, to exercise my fingers and all that. I'd rather have had typewriting, that would have been much more fun.
> [Did you tell them?]
> Yes. They made me have those knitting lessons, but I didn't knit, I did nothing. They thought they could do anything with me! But if I'd had a typewriter, I might have written the one story after the other. But maybe I didn't have the fantasy then.

Laila seems to have been the victim of stereotypes about the preferences of students with special educational needs, girls especially: 'When they can choose, they never prefer writing to knitting.' Another example of not being taken seriously is shown in her description of the support lessons.

> I had remedial lessons, but I did not know why, I did not ask . . . We didn't do a thing in those support lessons, not a thing! Just talk! [What for?] I don't know, I think it was to get to know each other, I don't think it was to learn something, I think it was to pass time, simply — that is what I suspect . . . I was more talkative in those lessons, I thought it was fun to tell jokes and talk nonsense; in class I didn't say anything.

I asked if she remembered an incident from the support lessons in English, when the teacher told her to stop fooling around and do some work. Young Laila had got angry, but finally wrote what she was asked. The teacher had then been very surprised about her good English spelling. Laila interrupted me while I was recalling this and said 'Of course I can, when you get down to it, if you get started.' And then she explained to me her technique of recalling the spelling of English words like 'thought'.

In dropping out from school Laila's feelings of not being seen or valued are even more obvious. She told me at the time that it did not matter if she was there or not because they forgot about her at school.

> Did I say that? I don't remember [saying it], but I did think so, that I didn't mean anything to them — there were so many others.

'I learnt to write and do sums.' (Eva)

School was nice and useful, at least to start with — those seem to be Eva's feelings about it.

> I liked it at the primary school. There were 27 in class, I didn't dare to say much there. I had some remedial lessons every day, me and some others sometimes in a small room. I needed those lessons to learn, I think. I learnt to write and do sums.

Special and Other Schools

'Join the ordinary school!' (Eva)

The three participants in this study have been to different schools, mainstream as well as special. Which is the better? Nobody was too enthusiastic about the special school. Eva's attitude was clear. When asked what she would do if she had a child, she said:

> Then she would have been brought up quite differently! I would have let her decide for herself whether to go to a special school or a regular school. She would have been much more free. If she had the choice between special school and mainstream secondary school . . . *I* for my part would have been in the regular secondary if I had been able to manage, if I had had the choice . . . If I had managed the lessons. Probably I would have had to have support lessons there as well . . . Join the ordinary school, even in upper secondary! You might be in a small class and have some of the hours out working.

'There were so many lunatics.' (Laila)

How are the special school experiences viewed more specifically by our group? Laila:

> Once they sent me to a special school, but I didn't see the point. I was so scared, there were so many lunatics. I didn't have anything to do at that place.
> [Why did they send you there?]
> Because I was difficult, I went to town, not to the lessons, you know. I shirked school a lot, I didn't like it there. There was a bloke, an old man . . . but I didn't go with him — I didn't do anything wrong, but my mom didn't know that.

Eva:

> I liked it at the lower secondary special school, but not at the hospital school. At the special upper secondary there were what I would call conduct disorders — and at that time I was more anxious.

When looking at the part the special school played in their development, Eva and Rolf have positive as well as negative comments, whereas Laila totally rejected it and ran away after a fortnight. She was judged to have minor learning problems, but was eventually categorized as having major behaviour problems, with shirking as the most serious symptom. Her teachers and other professionals were seriously alarmed about her shirking, but the attempted efforts (special school, residential setting) were probably motivated not so much by the need to find better conditions for academic and social learning as by the need for behaviour control. Fear of promiscuity caused prompt action, a common response in order to control feminine sexuality.

'They gave me a good self-image.' (Eva)

Eva used to be extremely shy, but is not any more. So what has happened?

> I think the folk high school will be surprised if they see me now, that I am so social and talk so much. Because there I was afraid at first, until I got friends. They gave me in a way a good self-image. I worked with myself, and talked a lot to the psychologist and the befriender. The folk high school is the best school I've been to! They support people on their ideas. I wrote some poems about it, I don't remember where they are, but some of it is: 'You must go beyond your limits, dare to be yourself.'

Friends

'There were some who fancied me if there was nobody else.' (Laila)

Laila has not had friends of her own age, except when she was picked as last choice sometimes. She would rather not have them, she says, as they might be drinking or unpleasant in other ways: she has a way of maintaining her self-esteem in the absence of friends. What *is* a friend anyway? Someone you know the name and address of? Rolf says he has friends from his school days. He knows where they live, but he does not see them. Laila:

> After school hours we were out [the first years before moving] doing nothing particular, sleighing in the snow and . . . After we moved I did not have friends. I was not harassed in the way they talk about it now, just teased because of my dialect and things. There were some who fancied me if there was nobody else to go with. I was biking on my own and sometimes talking to grown-up people, that was just as good as having friends. It doesn't matter that much after all, having friends, they might have become boozers and junkies or maybe real snob, general manager and the like.
> [How were the breaks in lower secondary?]
> I just was going about there on my own.

'The befriender, she has written to me.' (Eva)

Is a friend someone who is paid for friendship? When Eva talks about people she knows, it is often about professionals of some sort. In her network the various professionals or employees — the work leader, the home helper, the befriender (a person employed to support leisure and social activities a few hours each week) and so on, almost exclusively female — have always played important parts. Eva actively expresses the importance of these people in her life. I think Eva means a lot in the life of the helping professions too, as she is articulate and supportive of *their* self-esteem. She has even adopted parts of their language, like 'integration' or 'quality of life' (and her curtains and furniture style match those of the home helpers).

In the breaks I was in the school yard. The others looked after me, especially one, she came to see me at home too — a real friend she was.

[Did you have friends at the folk high school?]

Yes, many, and the befriender I had there, she has written to me . . . I sometimes wish I had a usual friend, like you, not disabled, I mean.

Body

'I felt pushed to practise, practise, practise . . .' (Rolf)

The area of 'body' was not in my interview guide, but emerged with great power from Rolf:

All those doctors, they disappointed me. I had 14 operations. They have not made me any worse, but . . . I felt pushed to practise, practise, practise [at walking]! I couldn't remember all those practising hours. So I quit practising, and I am no worse! I'd rather use the crutches now and then [rather than all the practising].

Not being able to see substantial effects — he still can only walk a few steps — the surgery as well as the physiotherapy were regarded as causing pain and hindrance to Rolf's well-being, not the opposite, as was the intention. The possible subtle and long-term effects of the efforts are not as obvious. Besides, the message communicated easily may be: You are not good enough as you are.

If there was too much focus on the physical disability in Rolf's case, there was an under-estimation as to physical obstacles to learning in Laila's. She has a small hearing deficiency which was not known to her teachers, but which is clearly noticeable in my conversation with her now. Perhaps what teachers and others referred to as a lack of ability was rather a question of hearing loss? Laila is also quite short-sighted, yet for many years she went without glasses at school. She has some hereditary problems with her back, but across her school years was told that she made up things to have excuses for not attending school.

Life Today

In the mornings Eva works in the café of the activity centre, except for Wednesdays when she goes to pottery class along with some of the other disabled persons in the centre. For three afternoons a week a home helper provides assistance with her budgeting and with other personal needs. Eva is regularly involved in a choir or in club activities in the evenings. One night each week her befriender takes her out. In between she sees her boyfriend and her family. Eva's busy life takes place almost exclusively in special settings — even the choir and the club and her holiday trips are for disabled people, although she does work for a couple of hours each week in a regular shop.

Rolf's week is similar to that of Eva, except that religious meetings replace some of the evening events, and he rarely sees his family.

Laila has no regular activities at all, except for the appointments with the psychologist every fortnight. But she is not socially isolated — she has someone to talk to in the neighbourhood or on the phone, which she does a lot. Otherwise she spends her time going about on her moped or by foot with no clear purpose. At home she looks after the cat, writes stories on her typewriter and listens to pop music. She rarely sees her family.

Future

'I wish I could rewind . . .' (Laila)

Laila seems quite resigned to things as they are, and feels everything is too late. The idea of adult education or any other hints concerning rehabilitation are rejected. She looks upon herself as a loner, almost as a village idiot — she used the equivalent of that expression. 'I'm well trained for idleness', as she ironically put it. But in this there are glimpses of self-esteem when she presents herself as reliable and willing to help with babysitting and care-giving, and not to forget that she is one who does not taste alcohol, even if all the other unemployed do — and those are the ones she knows. While listening to music on her tape recorder she comments:

> I wish I could rewind [my life] . . . Maybe I had a 'hidden talent of being smart' (referring to the refrain of the song played) . . . I wouldn't have been on social security then. If I had been a boy, I'd have a job on the coastal steamer now.

Eva wants to extend her amount of ordinary work, but is concerned that the open labour market will not have room for her. Apart from that, she expresses no wish to change her way of living. Rolf, on the other hand, looks upon the future as open; he has not quite decided where to settle or what to do, being on the move as he is at the moment.

Inclusion/Exclusion?

Are Eva, Laila and Rolf included, or rather is the society in which they live inclusive? Were they included in the school years, and what connection is there between the extent of inclusiveness then at school, and now in their communities? Was — and is — for instance, the differentness and individuality of these three people really appreciated by professionals who worked with them (Ballard, 1995)? Did — or do — they feel as valuable as anybody else?

Traditional cues to evaluate the relation between society and disabled people are found in instruments made for assessing normalization, through terms such as living standards, quality of life and social role valorization (Wolfensberger and Thomas, 1983; Stangvik and Simonsen, 1993). Normalization ratings may throw useful light on *integration* criteria like participation, but are they adequate to evaluate central aspects of inclusion? From this background some aspects of the participants' experiences will be commented on.

Eva's feelings are that she has become increasingly social, competent and independent as a result of help from her schools and other supporting agents. 'I even dare to have a boyfriend now', she said. She feels that her quality of life is heightened — she uses those words herself. Besides, she considers herself as well-functioning in the disabled group; maybe her self-esteem is nurtured in a better way here than out in the open in the wider community? In many ways Rolf, too, seems to feel that he has improved his quality of life, when, for instance, he is standing up against the pressure to practise walking, and when he is able to pursue his wish to go to Bible School.

You may ask to what extent Eva and Rolf are included, however active, having many of their work and pastime relations in special settings. They have a parallel and separate world, although it is visible to everyone, and not behind the walls of institutions. This is in contrast to the official policy that people with special needs should have these met by the general public system, not by separate services. There is obviously a gap between the formulation of our ideas and policy about inclusion and the realization of inclusive goals (Lundgren, 1982; Haug, 1997).

'Gesellschaft' qualities, as Tönnies originally described them more than a hundred years ago, imply physical and emotional closeness, continuity, solidarity, care and social control (Bø, 1989). Despite all the efforts made to establish helping services, we still seem to believe that if we simply arrange for disabled people and others to live near each other, then primary group qualities will automatically rise (Gustavsson, 1997). Yet in this study we see that Laila has few social contacts. Rolf and Eva have social involvement at work and in leisure activities, but predominantly with other disabled people. Is this by choice? Would an inclusive society value the choice of a distinctive identity and of separate social networks that are supportive of this? In Denmark, for instance, people with intellectual disabilities increasingly organize on their own and with their own cultural expressions (Holm, Holst, Olsen and Perlt, 1997). If Eva's evening activities (and her curtains) were less centred upon the professionals in her life, and more her own, would not that represent an acceptance of difference needed in an inclusive society? Likewise, if Laila were encouraged in her writing to describe some of her unique experiences, might not that mean a chance for her own empowerment (Antikainen, Houtsonen, Huotelin and Kauppila, 1996)?

'Normalization' mainly concerns system-level issues such as legal and socio-economic arrangements. The term has an individual aspect too. The 'normal' and expected formula of normalization on the personal level is: low degree of disability = high degree of normalization, and the reverse also applies (Stangvik and Simonsen, 1993). That is, if the impairment is substantial, the chance of a life similar to average people's lives will be smaller than if the impairment is minor. In our group of three people the situation is not so, as Laila with the apparently lesser disability is the less favoured when you look at, for instance, work and organized leisure activities, since she has nothing resembling normal experiences in these areas, and never has had.

When it comes to school there are strong indications of Laila not being taken seriously as a student. Teachers did not expect her to attain anything much; her under-achievement is probably vast. Even if she was there physically with the other students, she did not take part. So in her case the integration criteria of belonging, participation and responsibility hardly can be said to have been properly met in school. Neither are basic aspects of inclusion: *Equity* is one part of inclusion, concerning 'togetherness' — and *excellence*, which has to do with developing one's potential, is another (Skrtic, 1991). Laila's ways were not appreciated as valuable parts of human diversity in school. To some extent the adult Laila deliberately seems to avoid basic parts of 'normalized life'; she prefers to go on being idle and to stroll on her own. She is able to withdraw from society's discipline of employment and conformity in other areas, but at the probable expense of achieving personal equity and excellence (Kristiansen, 1996).

One premise for being exposed to services meant to increase levels of normalization and to improve quality of life is being perceived as 'abnormal'. To attain a higher degree of normalization, one has to have been pointed out as being short of 'normality' in the first place. An inclusive society, on the other hand, implies that diversity is normal and that nobody is defined as abnormal. In our records we saw that the community professionals all the way along have been referring Eva and Rolf to the web of services for people with special needs, but Laila has not so easily been found to fit in. She was too good, or maybe too puzzling, for the diagnostic system, even if she had a medical label. So what happens when the regular system does not fit and you slip through (or avoid) the screening? Tordis in Marit Strømstad's story in this book also slipped through, but she and her mother fought the system and Tordis is inside. Laila definitely is an outsider. The inclusive power of society is not impressive when the need to fit into the diagnostic system — or to have someone to fight the system for you — still seems decisive in terms of what happens to you. We may ask with the Norwegian researcher Peder Haug whether the good intentions of 'integration' in this country have led to an absence of critical reflection and the necessary analysis that might lead to more significant and enduring changes in education and in society (Haug, 1995).

References

ANTIKAINEN, A., HOUTSONEN, J., HUOTELIN, H. and KAUPPILA, J. (1996) *Living in a Learning Society: Life-histories, Identities and Education*, London/Washington DC: Falmer Press.

BALLARD, K. (1995) 'Inclusion, paradigms, power and participation', in CLARK, D., DYSON, A. and MILLWARD, A. (Eds) *Towards Inclusive Schools?*, London: David Fulton Publishers, pp. 1–14.

Bø, I. (1989) *Barnet og de Andre*, Oslo: TANO.

GUSTAVSSON, A. (1997) 'Inanfor utanförskapet', in TÖSSEBRO, J. (Ed.) *Den Vanskelige Integreringen*, Oslo: Universitetsforlaget, pp. 100–128.

HAUG, P. (1995) *Spesialpedagogiske Utfordringer*, Oslo: Universitetsforlaget.

HAUG, P. (1997) 'Formulering og realisering av norsk politikk om spesialundervisning etter 1975', paper presented at the Congress of Nordic Society for Educational Research in Gothenburg, 6–9 March.

HELGELAND, I. (1992) 'Special education in Norway', *European Journal of Special Needs Education*, 7, pp. 169–83.

HOLM, P., HOLST, J., OLSEN, S.B. and PERLT, B. (1997) 'Efter normaliseringen', in TÖSSEBRO, J. (Ed.) *Den vanskelige integreringen*, Oslo: Universitetsforlaget, pp. 129–57.

KRISTIANSEN, S. (1996) 'Normaliseringens eftersleb', *Special Paedagogik*, 2, pp. 129–39.

KVALE, S. (1996) *InterViews: An Introduction to Qualitative Research Interviewing*, London: Sage Publications.

LUNDGREN, U.P. (1982) 'Between schooling and education. Notes on curriculum change within the second generation of school reforms in Sweden', *Educational Research Information Centre*, Washington.

MINISTRY OF CHURCH, EDUCATION AND RESEARCH (1994) *Core Curriculum for Primary, Secondary and Adult Education in Norway*, Oslo.

MORDAL, K.N. (1982) 'Daem glaemme mae . . . Unge jenters selvaktelse i hjem, skole og lokalsamfunn', Hovedoppgave. Institutt for samfunnsvitenskap, Universitetet i Tromsö.

SKRTIC, T.M. (1991) 'The special education paradox: Equity as the way to excellence', *Harvard Educational Review*, 61, 2, pp. 148–205.

STANGVIK, G. and SIMONSEN, O. (1993) *A Municipality for All Citizens*, Summary and Perspectives from the Project 'Municipal Competence for the Improvement of Quality of Life for Handicapped Persons' in Finnmark, Norway, ALH-rapport no. 7, Alta Laererhögskole.

VISLIE, L. (1995) 'Integration policies, school reforms and the organisations of schooling for handicapped pupils in western societies', in CLARK, C., DYSON, A. and MILLWARD, A. (Eds) *Towards Inclusive Schools?*, London: David Fulton Publishers, pp. 42–53.

WOLFENSBERGER, W. and THOMAS, S. (1983) *Program Analysis of Service Systems' Implementation of Normalization Goals, Normalization and Ratings Manual*, 2nd edn, Toronto: National Institute of Mental Retardation.

Chapter 9

Tordis? She is just Tordis!

Marit Strømstad

This chapter is about Tordis, a woman of 40 years of age at the time of this project. Tordis has lived all of her life in the town in which I grew up in Norway. Although she is the focus of this account, others are also involved. Olave is Tordis's mother, and she participated in this study, talking with me and, together with Tordis, commenting on the draft of this chapter. My own mother is here also. Tordis went to the local school where my mother was the sole teacher, and her comments describe Tordis in the rural school and community setting.

Me

What I intended when I started to write down my conversations with these people was to be an anonymous person in the background whose pen gave voices primarily to Tordis and her mother. But as the writing proceeded there emerged a confused and shameful me who insisted on being included in the story. As an experienced lecturer on special education and a person of liberal political views, I thought that I was accepting in my attitudes towards individual differences and towards people of different socio-economic backgrounds. The reader will see my discovery that I have problems with both.

I soon realized that my initial position was a naive one. The moment that I wanted to write about Tordis, I became part of the story. Nevertheless, when I knew that I had to read what I had written about them to Tordis and her mother, I struggled against the idea that I was part of this account. I did not want to expose myself and confess how difficult I found it to reach their point of acceptance. I did not want to admit that the way they talked about being different sounded objectionable and blunt to me. I tried to write my own reactions out of the story, but omitting my own part in it felt like cheating and not being honest either to them or to potential readers. The only possible solution was to tell Olave and Tordis about my anxieties, a procedure that I dreaded, but it turned out very well.

The Reading

Tordis and Olave came to my house for the reading of the first draft. I had told Olave about my problems on the phone and she greeted me with a broad smile.

129

'You must feel free, Marit', she said, and revealed that she understood my agony. 'Of course', she said, 'this is more natural to us than it is to you.'

I asked, 'Did you realize how difficult it was for me to talk to you about Tordis when she was present?'

'I wondered why it took you so long to come to the point', said Olave.

'At last I had to ask you what you wanted to know', Tordis added. 'Now I look forward very much to hear you reading.'

'I am not used to the way you talk', I said. 'It has something to do with my background too.'

'There are differences', replied Olave.

There was no need to say much more. I started to read.

The Voices

'It was a great party', my mother said, putting her coffee cup down on the table. 'I was so pleased when Tordis asked me to join the celebration of her 40th birthday.'

'Wasn't that to be expected? You have known her all her life and you were her first teacher.'

'Yes . . . but you know I was the one who stirred up the whole family when Tordis was 7 and due to start school. What I did then was hard — especially on the mother I think.'

'But they still invited you.'

'Yes, and I really enjoyed it. They had rented the entertaining rooms at the local community centre for the evening. Tordis often gives a helping hand at functions held there, but this time she was the whole show. We had excellent food, speeches were given, and people were dancing. Olave told me that Tordis had made all the arrangements herself. There were more than 30 guests, her family of course and many of the neighbours from the past. I met people I had not seen for many years. It was quite pleasant to talk to them again. Several of Tordis's fellow workers from the old people's home were invited too. The manageress gave a speech and praised Tordis for her reliability and trustworthiness. I don't think she exaggerated. Olave has always been a hard worker and Tordis takes after her mother.'

'If you think 40 years back, mother, what kind of life did you expect Tordis to live? Are you surprised to see how she gets along?'

My mother looked thoughtfully at me and gave no answer.

'You must remember all the strange things people said when she was born', I continued. 'Nobody knew anything for sure, but we all talked about that deviant child and wondered what would become of her.'

'Of course we talked', my mother reluctantly admitted. 'It was such a small rural society where we all knew each other and took great interest in other people's lives. But I think nobody ever breathed a word to Olave.'

'Nobody dared I presume. I was just a kid of 10', I said, 'and I had enormous respect for her. In fact she scared me. She was always so sinister-looking and rather rough in her ways.'

'Her life was probably not always easy', responded my mother. 'She had five children and money was scarce. Tordis was the youngest one. Olave was 38 years old when she gave birth to her. She never invited anybody to comment on the child and thus stopped us from expressing whatever thoughts we had about her. In my opinion the mother regarded Tordis as just like any of her other four children.'

'But she must have seen the difference?'

'Maybe she closed her eyes to it. I think I was the one who forced Olave to see it when she brought Tordis to school. It has bothered me ever since. Did I do the right thing? You remember the little schoolhouse, don't you? There was one single classroom where the first-graders came for Monday, Wednesday and Friday while the second-graders came the other three days. There were no spare rooms for groups, and no other teacher than me. The room was packed with children. How could I possibly manage a child like Tordis in the middle of the flock?'

'Was it impossible to get any help from the outside?'

'There was a single school psychologist, but he had the whole community to take care of. He came and took some tests.'

'Did he arrive at any diagnosis?'

'He was not sure, but he commented on her slanting eyes and we discussed the possibility of her having Down's syndrome. We knew so little about those things back in the sixties. People with mental retardation either were institutionalized when they were quite young, or they were brought up inside their homes as a shameful secret never to be talked about. Olave chose to do it in a different way. Tordis was never hidden or shielded. As far as I remember she got no diagnosis apart from being a slow learner. Together the school psychologist and I made up our minds to talk to Olave about sending her to a special school. It was an extremely difficult decision to take.'

'But all went well. Look at Tordis today!'

'Yes, look at Tordis today.'

So I made up my mind to look at Tordis today.

'Yes', Olave said on the phone, without any signs of hesitance or reluctance towards my proposition to write a paper on her daughter. 'Of course you are welcome to do that, Marit. Your mother was her first teacher, and she always was very good to Tordis.'

'There are some questions I would like to . . .'

'Come whenever you want.'

'But what will Tordis say?'

'Oh, she surely will have nothing against it. I will ask her before you come.'

'Will Tuesday be OK?'

'Fine. You are welcome.'

On the day agreed upon for my visit, I was rather embarrassed at finding not only Olave but Tordis as well, seated comfortably and full of expectations at the coffee table in their speckless little flat built connecting with the new house of Tordis's elder brother. Maybe Olave had not understood that I wanted to talk about Tordis? Or maybe she was due to leave after some small talk about the old days?

Waiting for her departure I ventured on the small talk and several cups of very good coffee. After two hours we had been through all our neighbours of the past, who had died, and who was married to the son and daughter of people we knew. I had admired photos of Olave's several grandchildren — they were all very nice. But Tordis still showed no signs of leaving. The possibility of discussing her in her presence never entered my head until she looked right into my eyes and said, 'It is thrilling that you want to write a book about me, Marit. Not all people with learning disabilities have succeeded the way I have.'

'So now you have to start asking questions', Olave said.

I think I saw a faint twinkle in her eyes, and it was then I realized that I was in for the lesson of my life concerning inclusion, normalization and acceptance of difference.

'I'm not quite sure how to start', I said awkwardly, looking at the walls. My professional training had not prepared me for a situation like this. 'Maybe you can tell me something from Tordis's childhood, Olave?'

'When I first got her in my arms I realized there was something wrong with her', said the mother. 'Though nobody at the hospital said anything about her looks, I saw at once that it was something wrong with her.' I stifled a groan at her bluntness and looked anxiously at Tordis, who calmly nodded her agreement: Yes, there had been something wrong with her.

'But you know I sort of closed my eyes to it and denied that something might be badly wrong', Olave continued. 'I never asked any doctor what was wrong with her and nobody volunteered any information. After seven days the baby came home with me and we raised her like any other child.'

'So she never had a diagnosis?'

'Telling exactly what was wrong you mean? No, but she is probably a mongo . . . monglo . . . ?'

'Mongoloid', I said, looking shyly at Tordis's slanting eyes. 'Something to do with chromosomes.'

'Yes, there must be something wrong with her chromosomes, people have said. My other daughter has a son and there is something wrong with his chromosomes too. Some of them were crushed at the moment of conception, but he is not a Mongoloid. He does not look like Tordis at all.'

'But you did not ask anyone exactly what it was?' I said, returning to Tordis.

'No, I did not. I wanted her to be like other children. After a week I took her home and raised her like the others. We never talked about her being different. Once when her father was ill, there came a doctor to see him and he stopped by Tordis, looking at her and fondling her head. I could see that he was worried but I did not invite him to talk about her.'

'And she grew up like norm- . . . as other children?'

'Yes, and a good child she was. Her brother and her sister spoiled her because she was the youngest one, and her father loved her. She used to take her nap after dinner with him.'

'What about other people? Did they say anything?'

'I don't think so.'

'Really?' I said. Even though this happened 40 years ago I had a vivid recollection of what had been on the agenda in the small neighbourhood.

'Oh maybe they talked', Olave said, reluctantly prepared to admit that gossiping is human nature.

'Like we do', Tordis unexpectedly joined in. 'Don't you remember, mother, when Karin gave birth to that strange child some months ago? We talked a lot about what was wrong with it.'

'Talking is not necessarily malign', I said, trying to keep my face under control. In a small society like ours where everybody knew each other, people naturally took interest in other people's lives. Where is the harm?

'And besides', Tordis continued, 'there is nothing shameful about being different. I was born like this. It is not my fault, so why should I feel ashamed of who I am?'

'True', I said. Looking into her candid eyes I felt strongly that the shame fell upon me. I was the one having problems in a situation that to them seemed perfectly natural. 'Are there things you want to tell me from your childhood, Tordis?'

'But it was not always easy', Olave interrupted. I could see that she was going back in her memory to those days when she fought for her daughter's right to be a child like other children. I remember my own mother saying bluntly that Tordis was an ugly child.

Olave said, 'Her uncle implored me to realize she was an idiot. But that was not true. Tordis is quite clever in many ways. Some days ago there was a man visiting from the local authorities to help us fill in some forms. He watched Tordis writing her name and said she has such nice handwriting. Then Tordis looked in his face and said that she was no idiot. You should have seen the expression on his face!'

Tordis smiled in pleasant memories of his shocked countenance and fortunately overlooked mine.

'No, I'm not', she stated calmly.

'I never got any help', Olave continued. 'I had nothing apart from the ordinary children's allowance. Others got much more help. But we managed. When you get a child like Tordis you have to take care of it. Perhaps you love it more than your other children.'

'I can't imagine how you managed', I said, remembering the small house of the cowhand. Five children in that tiny house.

'With no bathroom, no plumbing and only two bedrooms', Olave continued, smiling mischievously at me. I had a certain feeling she too recollected the difference to the house I lived in during those same years.

'Yes', I said sheepishly, regretting that I had brought in the topic of houses.

'We were used to it. As you know, my husband was a cowhand, and the farmer owned the house we lived in. Most of the people we knew lived in similar houses. But I remember very well when I got my first washing machine. It must have been in the late sixties. Till then I had to boil all the clothes for the whole family in the cellar, and drag them to the river to rinse them. Even in the winter I had to do that. It was hard work. But Tordis was no problem. She was toilet trained at normal age if that is what you are thinking about.'

'Do you remember any of this, Tordis?'

'No', said Tordis, 'but I remember spending much time with my father up at the farm. He took me with him to his work.'

'In that way I too was able to earn some money', Olave explained. 'There was plenty of work in the seasons. The children worked too. They weeded during summer and picked potatoes in the autumn. So did I. Besides I was always asked to help people with spring cleaning or slaughtering in the autumn. Of course Tordis never did that kind of work but she never was a nuisance. The relationship between her and her father was extraordinarily good. He died when she was 8. After that she cried when she saw her uncle. He had much the same appearance as his brother.'

'And then she reached school age?'

'Yes, I took her to school when she was 7.'

'I remember it very well', said my mother. 'Olave brought the child. Honestly I had dreaded that day because I knew them so well and was well aware of Olave's attitude towards her child. She wanted Tordis so strongly to be like other children, and I have always held Olave in great respect. Because of her I intended to manage Tordis in the classroom, but after a few days I realized that it was impossible. She was running about, never settling down to any work, always talking and disturbing the other children. She was good at practical work though, but letters and numbers just were not for her. What could I do, the physical conditions taken into consideration? As you know, I have always been of the opinion that children should go to the school they normally belong to, but at that time there were no local provisions. Children were just sent away from home. It tortured me to point out to Olave that Tordis was too diverging for the ordinary school. It would have been different today, of course.'

'How did Olave take it?'

'I think she was both disappointed and rather cross with me and the school psychologist. She never said anything to me, but I sensed her feelings.'

'Well, yes, I was cross with both of them — even your mother', Olave admitted. 'In a way they interfered. I felt like they had the right to do whatever they wanted to me and my child. Especially the psychologist', she added. 'Your mother was different. I believed her when she said she wanted to do what was best for Tordis. Besides, I knew her as a neighbour. It was easier to be cross with the psychologist.'

'Tordis?', said the now retired school psychologist when I phoned him and asked if he remembered her. 'Yes, I remember her faintly, but all details are gone from my memory. I seem to recollect taking some tests and finding her below average in all achievements. Your mother was rather disconsolate about it. She was a friend of the mother, wasn't she? By the way, I met Tordis at some dancing only a few years ago. She came there with her boyfriend. Much older than her, isn't he? But she was a surprisingly good dancer. I danced with her and it was a great pleasure. Sorry I can't help you. But in my opinion we did the right thing when we got her into the special school.'

'When I look back, I think we did the right thing', said my mother thoughtfully. 'Luckily we had that new special school quite close so she could still live with her family.'

'I hated it at first', Olave said. 'But considering her later development I think we did the right thing. Before she started there, I had taught her to read. We sat for hours by the kitchen table and worked together. At Skramstad (the special school) her reading improved. She learned to write and even mathematics. She is capable of taking care of her own money now. But I had never consented to sending her away at a boarding school. Not at the age of 8!'

'As far as I remember', I said, 'you got on very well with the teachers at the special school? Didn't I hear rumours about cakes baked for the parents' meeting and sometimes for all the pupils as well?'

Olave smiled. 'It was a very good school for Tordis', she stated. 'The teachers did all that could possibly be done for their students. They got personally involved in their pupils and really cared about them. I appreciated that.'

'I remember Skramstad well', Tordis contributed with a smile. 'I never thought it shameful to go to a special school. A school is a school, and it was natural for me to go to Skramstad. We had much fun on the school bus.'

'We never made any secret of her going there', her mother added.

'Why should we? After Skramstad I went to a boarding school at Gjøvik', said Tordis.

'That really was hard', said Olave. 'On the first day her eldest brother drove us the 60 kilometres to the school. She was only 12 years old. None of her siblings left home till they were 14. But Tordis neither cried nor complained about it.'

'It was fun at Hund', said Tordis. 'I came home every weekend. Then I took both the ferry and the bus on my own. After two years I moved to a small flat in town with one of the other students. We were taught to look after our own things, keep the house clean, and wear proper clothes and things like that. I did a link course for two years, working at an old people's home. We were allowed to draw a certain amount of money from our bank account every week. If we used too much money we had to go straight back to the boarding house. We never knew when the inspector would come to check on our housekeeping. Once she took us totally by surprise and we had to hide the dirty dishes in a kitchen cabinet so she should not see them.'

'It was a good thing she spent those years there', said Olave. 'I had never dared to let her live so independently. She learned to look after herself during those years. When she finished school she got a statement recommending her as a good worker. The teachers at Hund also helped her get a job afterwards. For 24 years now she has earned her living at the local home for old people.'

'I go there on my bicycle every day — even in the winter. It is 4–5 kilometres.'

'Do you like your work?'

'Certainly.'

'What do you do?'

'Wash floors, wash clothes, look after the old people.'

'The first years were not so pleasant', Olave interrupted. 'Tordis had to mow the lawn and collect eggs from the hencoop. None of the other girls had to do such work. But after the new manageress came, there have been no such problems. She often does the washing because she is the only one who knows how to handle the

135

washing machine. In a couple of years the old people's home is to be abandoned. The buildings are too old. But Tordis has been promised another job at the new home.'

'And now she lives with you, Olave?'

'Yes, this flat was built in connection with Arne, my son's house. He has promised to look after Tordis when I am gone. Not that she needs much looking after, but it is an assurance to know that she will always have someone to ask for help if necessary. Arne and Tordis have always got on well.'

'What do you say to that, Arne?'

'I thought it over and agreed to the arrangement when we built this house. In my opinion, Tordis should have moved to a flat of her own when she came back from the boarding school. That would have made her even more independent and capable of managing her own life. But as things turned out, she moved in with my mother. She will have a home here as long as she wants it or needs it. Tordis takes care of herself but she needs some support.'

'What has it been like to have a sister like Tordis?', I asked.

'Tordis? She is just Tordis. I was 13 when she was born and never thought about her as different. Honestly I do not remember much from her childhood. I had to move out and find work soon after she was born.'

'And you never talked about her with your parents or siblings?'

'In those days parents never discussed such matters with their children. Maybe my mother and father talked about it, but they never breathed a word to any of us. Perhaps I noticed that she was different, but it was kind of normal for her to be like she was. It was not till she was removed from the local school that I realized she was not totally like other children after all. But I never think of her as mentally retarded. The people who lived at the institution before it was abandoned were mentally retarded. Tordis never was like them.'

'What is the difference between her and those other people?'

'Perhaps only the fact that she was never sent to an institution.'

'Most people with mental retardation were institutionalized in those days.'

'But we never regarded her as mentally retarded. Like I said, she is just Tordis.'

'What do you do in your spare time, Tordis?'

'Run about', said Olave quickly, evidently pleased by the state of affairs. 'She is a very social and kind person. Our old neighbour gets a lot of help from her. Tordis does her shopping, collects her letters.'

'She is like a grandmother to me', said Tordis.

'And', said Olave, 'Tordis often gives a hand when the Pensioners' Club have functions or outings. Carrying luggage when we are travelling, or serving coffee at meetings. She is very popular with all the members.'

'It is nice to talk with them about old days', said Tordis. 'Besides, I often help at the local community centre. The manager needs someone to wait at tables or do the dishes after funerals or anniversaries.'

'But when he asked her to wait at a wedding I said definitively no', Olave interrupted.

Tordis looked annoyed at her mother. 'You gave in when he phoned you!', she reminded with a note of triumph.

'I did', said Olave. 'He told me that I had to trust my own daughter's competence. I imagined her pouring gravy down people's necks and that would be shameful. But yes, he persuaded me and all went well. She is doing these jobs spontaneously and is not paid for it. But thus she is engaged in her spare time and meets a lot of different people. Not to mention all the experience she gets through that kind of work.'

'Do you never do anything just for pleasure, Tordis?', I asked.

'Working is my pleasure!', said Tordis. 'It is boring to sit at home watching television. I have to get out and see other people. My friend and I often go out dancing. We both love traditional dancing. My friend is a great dancer. We have been close friends for more than 13 years now. Sometimes we go on different tours with the Pensioners' Club.'

'Does your sister never meet socially with people of her own age?' I asked her brother Arne. 'Both Olave and herself are always referring to social events in connection with people much older than Tordis. I can understand that Olave at her age is a member of the Pensioners' Club, but your sister is only 40.'

'I don't know her to have any friends of her own age', said Arne. 'She never went to school with the other children from here and does not know them. Their lives are different from hers and they do not have much in common. As long as she lives with my mother, she goes where she goes and finds her friends there. Of course it is mostly aged people. Her friend too is much older than her. Though she meets many people of her own age at the local community centre, I don't think she regards them as friends.'

'But they know and accept her.'

'Yes, in that way she is a natural part of the local society. By working there she is included in social life. She knows more people than I do.'

After the Reading

I put the papers down and looked expectantly at my visitors, Olave and Tordis.

'Exactly as it was!' Olave explained and sighed contentedly. 'You have got it down very well.'

Tordis said nothing. She was caressing my cat, who had not left her lap since she arrived.

'Did you like it, Tordis?'

'Yes.'

'Are you perhaps allergic to cats? You sound sniffly. Maybe you had better leave that cat alone.'

'No. She likes it.'

I turned to Olave. 'It was very surprising to realize that I was the one who had problems accepting Tordis', I said. 'I did not intend to write about myself, but . . .'

'It was not to be avoided', said Olave. 'I can understand that. To me Tordis never was different from other children.'

'And in a strange way your non-acceptance of her differences has led to the general acceptance of her as an independent person. It seems so natural to you. In a way it must be annoying that I want to write about her as something special?'

'It can be useful for people to read about it', said Olave. 'Even you admit that you have learnt something from us.'

'That is very true!'

After that we talked about other things.

Two days later Tordis told me, 'I am not allergic to cats, Marit. I was so deeply moved by your story about me that I was on the verge of tears, only I would not tell you.'

Me Again

The conversations with Tordis and Olave have made me reconsider my own attitudes concerning individual and social diversity. It is easy to preach acceptance and inclusion from a professional distance. I grew up with Tordis in my neighbourhood. Have I accepted her as a worthy member of society? Before I started to write this piece I would have said yes. Today I am not so sure. I regarded her as a person to talk and write about, not a person competent in her own right to share her experience of life with me.

Although we were the same age, I never played with her siblings because of class distinctions, which in those years set borders not to be crossed. Did I expect her family to be able to raise her to be a self-confident participating woman? Hardly. The truth is I am astonished to find her so conscious of her possibilities as well as her limits. Her success, which seems so natural and obvious to her mother and herself, is to me most surprising.

Tordis and her mother have succeeded with hardly any help at all. Olave's stubborn view of her daughter as a normal child excluded any professional assessment of her potential, except for that of the school psychologist. Having finished school, Tordis was never subject to any strategies to normalize her life, although she was taught some skills for independent living. Maybe she is so well adapted just because her mother refused to recognize her as a problem?

To a special educator that is a question to reflect on. Olave and Tordis have taught me that I still have much to learn. Thank you!

Chapter 10

Inclusion and Exclusion in Schools: Listening to Some Hidden Voices

Mel Ainscow, Tony Booth and Alan Dyson

When you're not in lessons it's like being at home 'cause you're with your mates, but not in lessons 'cause you have to work.

I can't do maths, me, 'cause teacher keeps talking through the lesson. You can't get on with it if he's stopping and starting you. He's good at maths but he can't teach it.

Sometimes lads get told off more 'cause they've got a reputation and have a really hard time put on them, but lassies just get told off and they leave it.

These are just a few of the comments we noted as we talked to students about their day-to-day experiences in an English secondary school. Their remarks suggest that they may be able to help us gain greater understanding of how school processes impact upon the capacity of students to participate in the opportunities for learning that are on offer. Indeed, the experience of listening to these young people leads us to argue in this chapter that students represent 'hidden voices' who, if listened to, may assist in making schools and classrooms more inclusive.

The school, which we call 'Richard Lovell', is on the outskirts of a large city and caters for students in the age range 11 to 19. In recent years it has developed something of a reputation for enrolling students with disabilities. Our involvement began in 1995 when we carried out a small investigation into processes of inclusion and exclusion in the school as part of an international comparative study (Booth, Ainscow and Dyson, 1998). We found our visits so productive that we persuaded colleagues in the school to allow us to continue visiting on a term basis in order to learn more about what goes on over time. This chapter presents an account of what we found during one of our visits, when most of our time was spent trying to listen to the hidden voices. Specifically it summarizes how the ideas of the students have thrown some further light on our understanding of the work of the school, particularly in respect to processes of inclusion and exclusion. As we will explain, however, their ideas also pointed to yet further questions and issues that we needed to address as we continued our work in the school. It also presented us with certain dilemmas regarding how we should present the findings of our investigations.

Methods

During previous visits to the school we had observed lessons, shadowed individual students, examined documents and carried out interviews with staff and parents. The decision to talk to students was taken, therefore, in order to add yet another set of perspectives to our developing account. In total, 62 students were interviewed, 48 in the age group 11 to 14, and 14 aged between 16 and 18. This sample was dictated by the ease of availability of these groups during the summer term and we planned to talk to students in the missing age group during subsequent visits.

In the case of the younger students, groups of four were interviewed together by one member of the team. The first four students on the register of a range of classes were selected, taking care to include a balance of girls and boys. In addition, three slightly larger groups of older students were interviewed, brought together simply because they had some free time available at a convenient moment.

Following a brief introduction by the team member during which our purposes were outlined, the students were asked to draw a picture that would illustrate their feelings about their school. Various possibilities were suggested, such as drawing cartoons, or walls of graffiti, and using words or phrases to highlight particular ideas. Then each student was asked to talk about his or her own drawing prior to more general group discussions. These were taped and the team member also kept notes of points of interest.

In general, the students seemed happy to talk about their experiences in the school, although the interactions were mostly between the team member and individual students. As always with group interviews, the atmosphere of support created by the presence of classmates has to be balanced against the tendency for comments to be swayed towards the views of particular participants. In some cases the agenda for discussion arose naturally from the drawings, although inevitably our developing ideas about the school led each of us to encourage the discussions to move in particular directions. In the main, we had the feeling that students did feel comfortable enough to express their views. For example, when one year nine student mentioned that they get less homework than students in a nearby school, his friend whispered, 'shhh'.

At the end of the round of group interviews, the members of the team reported their findings to one another and, through a process of debate, a number of themes emerged which seemed to encapsulate the main ideas that had occurred to us as we told the stories of our discussions with the students. This preliminary analysis was also discussed with a staff reference group, the members of which represented different subject departments. The main purpose here, apart from sharing our findings and reflections with interested colleagues, was to get some initial sense of how far the students' ideas had credibility with members of staff.

Although our analysis remains tentative, the reactions of the staff group led us to feel confident that at least the students had not used the meetings to mislead completely this team of middle-aged academics! On the other hand, we remain anxious that we may have listened to these student voices selectively and feel that there is much more that could be done within this particular school to gain insights from student perspectives. Consequently in what follows we provide what must be seen as a preliminary summary of our findings and interpretations, using the five themes that emerged, that is: views of the school; teaching and lessons; behaviour and control; help and support; and acceptance.

Views of the School

> It's a good school—it's just some of the teachers they badger you. You know what I mean?

Possibly the most surprising feature of all the interviews was that every student in the sample, including two who appeared to be on the edge of being excluded from the school because of their 'unacceptable' behaviour, talked of the school in generally positive ways. Typical comments were, 'Richard Lovell is great . . . ace . . . brill'; 'better than other schools'; and 'I am very happy at this school and I think it's a very good school to go to.'

When asked about the reasons for their positive attitudes, some students referred to particular subjects that they enjoyed. Here PE, technology and art were mentioned frequently. Younger students recalled their transfer from primary school and, in so doing, made many points about issues to do with size. Apart from commenting on the extent of the building, they also made reference to size in terms of range of opportunities, including after-school activities, length of PE lessons, choice of lunch options and, indeed, portions.

Possibly the most significant and frequently mentioned factor relating to these positive feelings, however, was not to do with the formal programme of the school but with the school as a source of social encounters. Once again size emerged as a relevant theme here. Put simply, school was seen as a place where there are many possibilities to make friends. As one of the older students noted, 'It just seems a lot easier to make friends here — it happens in lessons and free time.' Another student described how her move to the school at the age of 13 had changed her view of herself, giving her greater self-confidence. She commented, 'I did a lot better when I came to the high school.' Much of this she saw in terms of the chance to have so many new friends.

It seems, therefore, that for many of the students we talked to, school was first and foremost evaluated as a social experience and it was in this sense that Richard Lovell was seen as being 'ace'. Having said that, a small number of students also extended their emphasis on relationships to include certain members of staff. Here particular teachers were mentioned as having played a particular role in making their time in school more enjoyable. Most often mentioned in this respect were form tutors who had been significant. As we explain in the next section, relationships with staff were also seen as being central to the views of students about effective lessons.

Teaching and Lessons

> A good lesson is when it's all set out on the board and you can get it done in your own time rather than the teacher saying you've got 10 minutes to get this done.

Despite the emphasis placed by students on the social dimension of their life in school, it is also true to say that they did express strong views about more formal aspects of what they had experienced. Here, in particular, their views point to matters that we wished to pursue during later visits to the school.

Certainly the students tended to be clear about the importance of the purpose of coming to school. As one student put it, 'I'm here for a good education.' Indeed, this notion of a 'good education' was mentioned by a number of individuals, leading us to reflect on earlier comments from some of the teachers suggesting that there was a deep divide between certain sections of the local community and the school staff about the value of education. In general we found little evidence of such a divide. Rather, these students seemed committed to getting the best out of their time in the school and, in some cases, they also reported similar views among their parents.

In terms of the lessons themselves, there seemed to be mixed and, even, contradictory views. The older students tended to speak more positively about the teaching they had experienced as they looked back on their time in the school. Much of their comment tended to focus on the manner in which teachers conducted the lessons rather than the style or content. Good teachers were ones who get to know the members of the class, ones who you can 'have a bit of a laugh with'. On the other hand, certain members of staff were seen in a negative light because of their tendency to remain rather distanced from the students. Particular examples of this were reported, including when a teacher pushed his way through an entrance rather than taking turns to hold the door open for others to pass through. Such behaviour was characterized by one student as 'ignorant'.

Mention was made of where opportunities had been provided for students to pursue individual projects in some detail over an extended period of time. This approach was seen as being particularly valuable. Some also made reference to the value of group work, pointing to its capacity to facilitate their learning as well as enabling students to further widen their social contacts. When pressed, one of these older students suggested that there had been some group work in almost every lesson. (This rather shook us, since during our lesson observations we had witnessed very little of what we define as group work. A possible explanation of this apparent discrepancy may be to do with definitions as to what group work means.) These older students also noted something of a change of style as they had moved into the senior classes (known in England as the sixth form). As one student put it, 'In the sixth form the teachers talk with you; in the lower school they talk at you.'

This latter remark may explain, in part at least, the contrasting views of younger students about the teaching they experienced in the school. Certainly they did agree with their older colleagues about the importance of the teacher's manner and relationship with members of the class. Emphasis was also placed on the importance of teachers having 'respect' for the students.

Explanations were regarded as the most important feature of lessons. Effective teaching involved making the purpose of tasks clear and explaining how they should be carried out, whereas unsatisfactory teaching left students uncertain or even confused about what was required.

The emphasis placed on task completion during lessons relates to a broader theme that emerged from our discussions. A number of the students alluded to a certain pattern of activities that tended to be evident in many of their lessons. (For us this had a resonance with our own experiences of lessons in the school, where we had become aware of the existence of something of a 'house style'. Of course we would not wish to overstate this phenomenon, since we did see a range of teaching approaches in use. Nevertheless, during certain lessons we did experience a certain sense of *déjà vu*, as the pattern of activities followed those experienced during the previous lesson, albeit in a different subject.)

The student view of this pattern, or house style, was quite simply that it usually involved an initial presentation by the teacher, followed by individual tasks working from a textbook, a work sheet or from material written on the blackboard. It is in this context, perhaps, that the emphasis placed by students on the importance of explanations can be understood. Success in such a lesson is judged against the criterion of pace of task completion. Therefore, understanding what is required becomes a necessity. Difficulties are associated with 'not getting on' and, in some instances, may lead to conflict with the teacher. Where students get on well, thus completing the tasks ahead of their classmates, they may find themselves with nothing to do or, on some occasions, they may be required to do yet more of the same kind of task. Such students are sometimes defined by their colleagues as 'swots' or 'teacher's pets'.

Students had different perspectives on the place of homework. Some felt there was too much, although others seemed to do very little or even none. Certainly there seemed to be inconsistencies within the school as to when and how frequently homework was to be set. One student noted that they had much less homework to do than the students in another school locally. Others referred to distractions: 'When I get home me mates are round straight away and it's "are you coming out?"' For some, the difficulties this creates are overcome by various informal cooperative arrangements that are created in the classroom. So, for example, one student described how during the morning registration period he would find out which of his classmates had completed the maths homework and then ask to copy it.

From our previous visits to the school, we were aware of a concern among certain senior members of staff, including the head teacher, about what they describe as lack of differentiation in lessons. This idea of curriculum differentiation has become a matter of considerable debate in English schools since the introduction in recent years of a national curriculum, and there are widely differing interpretations of what it might involve. In the case of Richard Lovell High School it seems likely that the emphasis placed on task completion as an important criterion for judging student success and, therefore by implication, learning, leads some to see differentiation, at least in part, in terms of pace. This, in turn, provides some insight into the current argument in the school about the possible extension of student setting (streaming) arrangements, that is, teaching students in classes formed on the basis of attainment in the particular subject area.

Interestingly the students themselves tended to be generally positive about setting arrangements. They saw them as allowing individuals to work at their own pace and, where necessary, for those who needed it to get extra help. As one student put it, 'It's best in sets 'cos you're with people of your own ability.' Some were less happy, however, in that setting arrangements meant that they could not be with their friends in certain lessons. Students were generally clear about how the sets were formed and how they related to one another. One referred to being 'kicked out of' his set and being 'moved down'. Having said that, it was generally felt that the teachers treated the sets as being of equal importance.

Similarly, those younger students who are removed from certain lessons to receive individual help in small remedial groups, usually for reading, found this a positive experience. As one student put it, 'It means that nobody laughs if I make a mistake with a word.' It is also the case that some of the students value the withdrawal since this means that they miss certain unpopular subjects, particularly, we were told, French. Others recognize that their removal from certain lessons is one way of avoiding confrontations about behaviour.

Behaviour and Control

> The rules are daft. Like in technology, how can you stay in your place? Stupid really. . . . if you have a detention it doesn't get through to your head. So I don't take it seriously.

Many of our discussions with students seemed to find their way sooner or later to the agenda of behaviour, not least, perhaps, because we had become particularly interested in this aspect of the school. During the previous year the school had introduced a structured disciplinary system, called 'Positive Behaviour', that was intended to encourage more positive behaviour through the use of standardized procedures for allocating rewards and sanctions. This in itself appeared to generate many comments, reflecting a wide range of views.

Among the younger students there was considerable comment about the idea of teacher strictness. Having almost completed their first year in the school, these students seemed to feel that they had a good understanding of what goes on in this respect. Some described how they and their friends had fairly systematically tested out each teacher to see how far they would let things go before disciplinary action was taken. In this way teachers were graded on an informal scale related to their perceived degree of strictness. Students ofter preferred to be in lessons with teachers who were reasonably strict so that they could get on with their work. However, concern was expressed about the unfairness of some staff who punish the whole class because of the misbehaviour of individuals. One boy explained that a teacher who used this approach had told them that members of the class had to take responsibility for one another.

There was also some concern about the way that some teachers varied their treatment from pupil to pupil. As one student put it, 'People who get top marks are liked better than others . . . if they do something wrong they don't get into trouble.' Or, similarly, 'Those who work harder get treated better. The best ones get chosen to do everything, like the one who got picked to be on TV.' Another student described how Simon, who was a member of the school council, can 'get away with anything', whereas another boy, Ryan, who was on the verge of being formally excluded, gets into trouble because of his reputation.

Some students also reported that there was a fair amount of disturbance in some teachers' lessons. This was often seen as involving the approach taken by the teacher. For example, 'It's teachers, if they're not strict the kids run riot. In our German lessons, right, they have a bet on how many crosses you can get and the teacher goes along with it and shouts. That's exactly what they want him to do. . . . He's not really a bad teacher. The people in the class give him such a hard time he can't get it through. If people would listen to him he'd be all right but they just mess around.'

Some students suggested that most of the disruption was created by boys. One girl summed this up as follows: 'Boys are normally the ones that make trouble. Girls mature quicker, it's a proven fact. They have more sense, there's nothing you can do about it!'

On the other hand, one of the older students saw such difficulties as reflecting outside influences. He commented, 'It's their home background — they're not brought up to respect adults. They don't see the adults as being there to teach them.' However, some younger students said that their parents had chosen the school because of its reputation in the area for strictness.

Most of the students were well able to articulate the various procedures associated with the school's recently introduced disciplinary system, including the way the sanctions are used. They explained how misdemeanours led to students having their names written on the blackboard and that if this is followed by a certain number of crosses by their name during one lesson they can anticipate further actions. These include a detention organized by the faculty (referred to by students as 'getting a faculty') or, if things become more serious, students may be sent to a separate room to work alone in what is described as 'academic remove', a name derived from the traditions of the British private school system and an in-joke therefore for the teachers. It was striking how all the students referred to these various sanctions, using the rather strange terminology, in a matter-of-fact way, implying that they see them as an everyday part of their lives in school.

However, views about the value of the system varied considerably as the students moved up through the school. In the main, the younger ones felt it was satisfactory, although they recognized that a lot depended on the style and attitudes of each teacher. As one student put it, 'It's stupid that some teachers don't like some pupils and so they just put their names on the board and put about four crosses next to it just to get rid of them from classes.'

Older students tended to have more mixed views as to its value, for example 'it worked at first until we got used to it . . . we didn't really understand it at first.

Now things are a lot worse if you think about it. Before, how many people got suspended?' Those who still favoured the system tended to be somewhat reluctant to say so in front of their colleagues. Others described how they would 'play the system' as a form of distraction during some lessons. This might, for example, include going to the point where you are on the edge of being punished and then stepping back. Another form of in-class 'entertainment' was to find ways of getting a friend's name on the blackboard.

By the age of 14 or 15 many students saw the system as a 'joke'. They felt that removal from lessons was no real sanction, particularly for those who were persistent offenders. Some even saw it as a reasonable option to be sent to academic remove. As one student remarked, 'It's better than French!' Another student explained:

> People say that academic remove is a lot better than being in lessons. I didn't turn up for detentions so I got it. You just sit there and do whatever you want to from boxes. You don't get a proper break at dinner — you've got to go and get a sandwich and get straight back.

Having said that, it is also true that some students reported that their behaviour had changed as a result of experiencing the various sanctions, particularly when their parents had heard about it and applied further punishments. For example, one girl described how she had been 'grounded' for a month. In addition, students of different ages did place value on the commendation certificates issued for good behaviour or work. One girl explained how she pins these on her bedroom wall, and a young man in the sixth form remarked on his pleasure when a teacher had commended him for assisting another student.

Help and Support

> I'd prefer to have a teacher going round with me actually. It might calm my temper down. It would help me. I could have someone next to me all the time talking to me, not shouting at me.

Given what we heard about matters to do with classroom discipline, we found ourselves speculating about how the potential for escalation of disputes between staff and students in the school may be tempered by the overall atmosphere of help and support the students experience. The students explained, for example, that there is very little bullying in the school and where it does occur, they know where to turn for assistance. Furthermore they find that when incidents are reported they seem to be dealt with effectively.

Other evidence confirmed the existence of this overall supportive atmosphere. Students seemed to be surprisingly willing to admit to their own areas of difficulty and many reported that they felt that there was always someone you could turn to for help. There is a school council where students can take their grievances and those who had been involved in some way reported that this had led to real actions being taken.

The presence of additional adult helpers in some lessons seemed to be taken for granted as a normal part of school life and generally welcomed. One student commented about one such helper: 'We always have a laugh with her, she's good. She comes in and we say all right baby, because she's having a baby . . . she's always five minutes late so we say, come on, get her name on the board.'

It is interesting to speculate further as to what factors sustain the positive social atmosphere in the school. Certain individuals talked about the existence of a close and supportive climate within their home districts and it occurred to us that this may well be brought into the school by the students. It also seems likely that the presence in the school of a large team of support personnel there to support students said to have special needs may also have a wider impact on feelings of being supported. Finally there is the significant proportion of students with disabilities who, by their very presence, may impact on relationships and overall climate.

Acceptance

> Students with disabilities get away with everything. We were stood at the can machine the other day and there were three of them from the disability unit downstairs and they just came over and pushed us out of the way and they were only small. She pressed it, put her money in, and they were pressing all the buttons. . . . If we did that to them, like push them out of the way, we'd get done, but they didn't get done.

As we have explained, the students at Richard Lovell tend to focus on relationships when they talk about their experiences of school. This seems to be an enormous influence on what they find valuable there. Fortunately relationships in the school are generally positive and this seems to encourage the climate of support referred to above. This may also explain why the school seems to 'get away with' what we saw as a considerable range of exclusionary tactics, such as withdrawal from class, temporary suspensions and the creation of so-called 'bottom set' classes. In our experience such responses have tended to be met with negative student reactions in other schools. However, it is possible that it is not just relationships that are influential here. In addition, we were conscious of a strong sense of acceptance of differences among the students and, indeed, a concern with the rights of individuals that is generally rather unusual in English society. It carries with it echoes of debates that tend to be more apparent in other countries, for example in Australia, where it is common to hear that everyone has a right to a 'fair go'.

This sense of acceptance manifests itself in a variety of forms. It is noticeable, for example, in the relaxed relationships that seem to exist between girls and boys. Similarly we could find little or no evidence of racism among the students we met. But, given our professional backgrounds in special education, the most striking thing was the way in which students with disabilities are accepted as being just part of the 'normal' school community. Indeed this was similar to our experience of the reactions of young people in other schools where students with disabilities have been included over a period of time.

Students' disabilities, including category labels such as 'Down's', were frequently mentioned in a noticeably matter of fact manner during our discussions. For example, a blind student talked openly about her own disability and, indeed, referred to the disability of others in a 'taken for granted' tone. She explained how she travels to school by taxi with two other students, commenting, 'They're both special needs, Down's!' Similarly, in introducing one of her friends, Elaine, she remarked, 'She's special needs, not Down's!' (The distinctions made here are, in themselves, fascinating.) When one group was asked about students who experienced learning difficulties in their class, discussion focused on the reading difficulties of one of the individuals present. It was only much later in the conversation that the students drew attention to the fact that two members of their class have Down's syndrome.

Most of the students seemed very positive about the presence of students with disabilities in their classes. One student commented, 'I don't see why they shouldn't be in the school because they're just normal, just people same as all of us. They should all have the same chance as anyone else should have.' This theme of seeing people with disabilities as being part of what is normal was echoed by many of the students. For example, one student explained that 'we have a laugh with them, treat them as normal people', and another student commented, 'Sometimes they're teased but it's only normal joking. They don't do it seriously; they don't take offence.'

Some of the students were keen to promote the advantages that occur because of the presence of those with disabilities in the school. One argued:

> It's a good thing bringing them into the mainstream. It helps them cope a bit more. I've seen people who are at special school and they are so different to how the kids are here who are in the mainstream. I went to an athletics meeting with a special needs group. Ours were so well balanced but the kids from the special school had the same disabilities but were so different. Ours, because they've been with mainstream kids and are made to do things that they wouldn't do in a special school, it makes them realize that if they're asked to sit down they've got to sit down. Their kids were getting up and running all over the place and it was really dangerous.

One older student argued that all students had a right to attend their neighbourhood school. When pressed about those whose bizarre behaviour might disrupt classes, or those who might be a danger to others, he argued that at least they had 'a right to try!' In accepting the right of all students to be in their school, the students were also quick to point to the responsibilities that must go along with this. Here they were particularly critical of the fact that some of those with disabilities were at times given different treatment. For example, one person felt it was wrong that sometimes those with disabilities were allowed to get away with arriving late for lessons. Similarly, another student felt it was wrong that a blind classmate was allowed to swear in class. In a sense these feelings that everybody should have equal treatment can be seen as yet further evidence of the acceptance that everybody has a right to be present.

Many of the students talked about the occasional help they give to disabled classmates. One person talked about how he assisted a visually impaired student in his class. A clear look of joy was apparent in his face as he gave this account. Having said that, however, some still felt that sometimes too much adult assistance was provided for certain students, for example 'they could find their own way round school but they still get taken around'.

Including Ourselves

Our decision to listen to the views of a randomly selected group of students was part of an overall approach to understanding processes of inclusion and exclusion in schools (Booth and Ainscow, 1998). Traditionally such research focuses attention on the participation of students categorized as disabled or as being special because they are perceived as being 'abnormal' or difficult to control. It is thus located firmly within the traditional field of special education, however much the researchers wish to distance themselves from it. Our own view is that such an orientation is limiting in that it ignores the ways in which barriers to participation and learning arise in classrooms for many other students who are not categorized. Furthermore, we believe that attempts to treat the difficulties that arise for students in schools as if they can be resolved by addressing the education of a limited group of formally categorized students is counterproductive in that it deflects attention from possibilities for improving learning opportunities for all. Given our definition of inclusion as 'the process of increasing the participation of students in the mainstream', it makes no sense to restrict our concern only to the inclusion of some of those students vulnerable to exclusionary pressures.

As we listened to and then discussed our reactions to the ideas of the students at Richard Lovell school, we experienced a degree of uncertainty about how we should deal with the information we had collected. How were we to summarize and report their views? Indeed, what right did we have to do so, particularly if we imposed our own interpretations on their comments and, in so doing, directed those who subsequently read them to find the same range of meanings? In this way we were confronting issues raised by others who have attempted to explore the role of student voices in respect to understanding the experience of schooling (e.g. Rudduck, Chaplain and Wallace, 1995; Lincoln, 1995).

Within the recent literature on school improvement, the importance of involving students in the process of monitoring policies and practices is widely acknowledged and occasionally practised (Hopkins, Ainscow and West, 1994). However, others have argued for a more radical transformational approach, which seeks to go beyond simply treating students as producers of interesting data in order to explore how they might become partners in a dialogue that informs the life and development of their school community (Fielding, 1997). An example of what this might involve is provided in a study reported by Poplin and Weeres (1992). Called 'Voices from the Inside', the study was carried out by students, teachers, administrators and parents in four schools in the United States — two elementary, one middle and one high school. The aim was 'to create strategies that allowed everyone at the school site to speak and insured that everyone be heard' (p. 43). Thus the research allowed all participants to be both the researchers and, at the same time, the subjects of the research. Since the study began with the assumption that academics had already 'misnamed the problems of schooling', the roles of outsiders had to be rethought so that those on the inside could come to know and articulate the problems they experience.

As we debated these concerns, we revisited previous discussions we had had about our relationship with the school and about what our responsibilities and roles were in respect to the future direction of policies and practices. Put simply, were we just there to learn about the school for our own purposes or did we feel an obligation to make a direct contribution to the staff's improvement efforts? In this respect there were clear differences of emphasis between the three of us, although we all hoped that our involvement would be of some benefit to the school as a community. As we have reported, we elected to summarize some of the views of students to some of the teaching staff in the belief that this might facilitate their own reflections on how to move practice forward. There were, of course, potential ethical issues associated with this action and, as a result, we took care to keep our comments at a rather general level.

Certainly the opportunity to hear so many stories that emphasized the day-to-day support experienced by students at Richard Lovell High School brought to mind the various child-to-child support strategies, such as MAPS and Circles of Friends (Forest, Pearpoint and O'Brien, 1996), that are now frequently recommended as a means of including students with disabilities in mainstream schools (Ainscow, 1994). We felt that what the students had described to us was a school that seemed to be like one great circle of friends, albeit consisting of dozens of smaller circles that are created on an informal basis. It appeared that it was all of this that the students valued so much when they talked so positively about their school. However, it was also perhaps all of this that enabled the school to make welcome students who would be more usually excluded from secondary schools in England. In this sense the school seemed to manifest social support mechanisms similar to those described by Ballard and McDonald (1998) in their account of what they describe as 'an inclusive school' in New Zealand, although without the high degree of harmony of belief and purpose that they report.

It was also apparent, however, that the school employs responses that appear to marginalize some students on a regular basis, thus illustrating the many complexities faced by researchers as they try to understand processes of inclusion and exclusion. Perhaps surprisingly the students themselves tended not to see these responses as a problem. Indeed, as we have noted, they tended to accept them as part and parcel of normal school life. This suggests the possibility that it is not the responses in themselves that are the excluding mechanisms, but the intentions and perceptions of those involved. All of this further complicates the current debate about inclusion and exclusion. It raises the question, how do we know whether responses used within a school include or exclude? Certainly, the account reported in this paper provides strong evidence for the view that without listening to the often hidden voices of students it is impossible to understand fully the policies and practices of individual schools.

References

AINSCOW, M. (1994) *Special Needs in the Classroom*, London: Jessica Kingsley/UNESCO.

BALLARD, K. and MCDONALD, T. (1998) 'New Zealand: Inclusive school, inclusive philosophy', in BOOTH, T. and AINSCOW, M. (Eds) *From Them to Us: An International Study of Inclusion in Education*, London: Routledge, pp. 68–94.

BOOTH, T. and AINSCOW, M. (Eds) (1998) *From Them to Us: An International Study of Inclusion in Education*, London: Routledge.

BOOTH, T., AINSCOW, M. and DYSON, A. (1998) 'England: Inclusion and exclusion in a competitive system', in BOOTH, T. and AINSCOW, M. (Eds) *From Them to Us: An International Study of Inclusion in Education*, London: Routledge, pp. 193–225.

FIELDING, M. (1997) 'Beyond school effectiveness and school improvement: Lighting the slow fuse of possibility', *The Curriculum Journal*, **8**, 1, pp. 7–27.

FOREST, M., PEARPOINT, J. and O'BRIEN, J. (1996) 'MAPS, Circle of Friends & PATH: Powerful tools to help build communities', in STAINBACK, S. and STAINBACK, W. (Eds) *Inclusion: A Guide for Educators*, Baltimore: Brookes Publishing, pp. 67–86.

HOPKINS, D., AINSCOW, M. and WEST, M. (1994) *School Improvement in an Era of Change*, London: Cassell.

LINCOLN, Y.S. (1995) 'In search of student voices', *Theory into Practice*, **34**, 2, pp. 88–93.

POPLIN, M. and WEERES, J. (1992) *Voices from the Inside: A Report on Schooling From Inside the Classroom*, Claremont, CA: Institute for Education in Transformation.

RUDDUCK, J., CHAPLAIN, R. and WALLACE, G. (Eds) (1995) *School Improvement: What Can Pupils Tell Us?*, London: Fulton.

Chapter 11

Falling Down the Interfaces: From Inclusive Schools to an Exclusive Society

Alan Dyson and Alan Millward

This chapter is concerned with the notion of 'voice' (Gitlin, Bringhurst, Burns, Cooley, Myers, Price, Russell and Tiess, 1992; Gitlin and Russell, 1994) as it pertains to issues in inclusive schooling. We intend here to present the findings from a piece of research in which a number of voices can — however distantly — be heard: voices of professional service providers, of the Health Authority which commissioned the research and of the disabled people who participated as interviewees in that research. However, we make no pretence that the dominant voices in this particular contribution are other than those of the two liberal-minded but, alas, middle-aged English academics who are its authors. It is through us that the other voices have been elicited, interpreted and reported. Other contributors may well follow Keith Ballard's (1994) important lead in supporting parents of disabled children and disabled adults themselves in presenting their own accounts. That is not our intention here. Rather, our concern is with the impact of those other voices on our own thinking about inclusion. Such a venture is, we hope, more than mere self-indulgence; it is the voices of 'people like us' — comfortably positioned academics and professionals from the world of special education — that have dominated thinking about inclusive schooling. Such dominance has not always been entirely beneficial in its impact since, as we shall attempt to show, it has led to a narrowing of focus that threatens to undermine the seriousness and effectiveness of the inclusive schools movement. It may therefore to be appropriate to begin by saying something about ourselves.

Our professional backgrounds both as teachers and researchers have been in education and, in particular, in the peculiarly British phenomenon of special needs education in mainstream schools. We have, in other words, been concerned with that large minority of students whose relative lack of academic success in British schools is attributed to their having 'special needs'. This minority includes students with physical, sensory and intellectual impairments, but it is by no means restricted to them, comprising for the most part students who would not be regarded as disabled in the ordinary sense of the word.

Such backgrounds have made the focus of our professional and academic work a concern that students in this group receive something of a raw deal within British education systems and that they could in some way be educated 'better'. In particular we — together, no doubt, with many others from similar backgrounds — are dissatisfied with the apparent failure of many mainstream schools to accept, value and properly educate such students and are dismayed by their continuing displacement into separate systems, or, indeed, their removal from schooling entirely. We therefore find the basic tenets of the inclusive schools movement (insofar as it is a 'movement') easy to accept. We see no reason in principle why it should not be the task of mainstream schools to educate *all* students, why they should not do so appropriately and effectively, and why they should not do so through processes that enable all students to participate in the 'cultures and curricula' (Booth, 1996, p. 89) of those schools. Moreover, although we acknowledge the practical difficulties of such a project, we also believe that the solutions to many of those difficulties are already to hand and that examples of more inclusive practice abound.

At the same time, having worked for many years as teachers in more inclusive settings and having managed and advocated inclusion projects, we are also acutely aware that the notion of inclusion may not be as simple as it seems. As we have argued elsewhere (Dyson and Millward, 1997; Clark, Dyson, Millward and Skidmore, 1997), inclusion is a slippery concept that means different things to different people. Except in very general terms, there seems to be little agreement (and perhaps little discussion) about what level of participation, in what activities, in what sort of curriculum, with what degree of variation between individuals, is to 'count' as inclusion. We find ourselves, therefore, uncertain as to whether the principle of inclusion subsumes or overrides or conflicts with other educational and social principles — the principles of individually appropriate education or the maximization of life-chances, for instance. Above all, we are uneasy with the extent to which the unexceptionable moral values of inclusion and their powerful advocacy by certain groups and individuals make genuinely critical debate and analysis in this area difficult to sustain; inclusion is so self-evidently 'right' that to voice any doubts or caveats brands the critic as self-evidently 'wrong'.

We find ourselves, therefore, welcoming any opportunity that allows us to view the notion of inclusion from a different perspective. Such an opportunity has been provided by a project which we have recently completed, and which required us to step outside our accustomed frame of reference. Over the past year we have been working on a study commissioned by a Health Authority in the North of England and managed by a multi-agency steering group with strong representation from local disability groups. The project required us to investigate the service needs of young adults with 'physical and complex disability' within one local authority area in order to inform the strategic planning of service providers. The focus of the study was on people in the 16 to 30 age range who experience physical impairments together with other disabilities. This group was of particular interest to the commissioning Health Authority because individuals within it were likely to need multiple and complex services while at the same time not falling within the purview of the relatively coherent provision for children or elderly people. The selection of this group for study is one of a series of issues which this project raised but which, for reasons of space, cannot be dealt with fully here. More detailed discussion is found in the project's final report (Dyson, Millward and Robson, 1996).

The project had two phases. In the first phase we were to access data held by the statutory and voluntary agencies in order to map the demography of the target population and to identify the current pattern of service take-up. This would result in the production of a (anonymized) database which could be used for planning purposes. In the second phase, we were to carry out semi-structured interviews with members of this group in order to elicit their views on those services and on the services which they felt they wished to receive. The focus of the project thus fell beyond our more usual concerns with education and, in particular, with schooling. Moreover, despite the ambiguities that result from the priorities imposed by the commissioning Health Authority and, indeed, by our own academic concerns and preconceptions, the project gave us an opportunity to listen to the 'voices' of disabled people speaking about their lives and the efforts of professionals to intervene in those lives. The project therefore afforded an ideal opportunity for us to view our accustomed concerns and preconceptions from a somewhat different perspective.

The Project's Findings

Phase 1

Although the outcome of the first phase of the project (a database of individuals in the target population) has limited significance for the issues with which this chapter is concerned, the process of establishing that database does, we believe, tell us something of importance about the nature of service provision and service providers. Our attempt to create a database was a less than total success. Although the necessary data existed in various locations, it proved extremely difficult for the research team to access and collate. There appear to have been two principal reasons for this:

1. Service providers tended to collect and maintain data in ways that met their own immediate needs, but which did not allow for the exchange and collation of data for longer-term strategic planning purposes. Within each agency, data tended to be collected at the point of contact between the individual service user and the service provider; only those data were collected that were necessary at that point; and data were stored in forms that were difficult for other levels of the agency to access. Hence, schools, GPs, hospital consultants and field social workers held a mass of data on the individuals with whom they worked, but often this would not include data that was necessary for strategic planning at the centre of the agency and in any case it would be held in hand-written form and stored in filing cabinets that even the individual practitioners themselves found difficult to access. There were few, if any, means of collating data centrally so that the agency could plan strategically, and inevitably, therefore, no means whereby the different agencies could share data in order to plan coordinated services.

2. Senior managers within the agencies did not control the data which the agencies held, and were thus unable to secure access to data for the research team (or, indeed, for any other legitimate purpose). Despite the best intentions of those senior managers, access to data was effectively controlled by a whole range of middle

managers and field-workers who showed widely varying degrees of willingness and ability to make data available. Some of these individuals were genuinely concerned about the ethical issues raised by the collation of a centralized database (despite multiple safeguards — principally its anonymization — offered by the research team and the willing compliance of their colleagues elsewhere in the same agency). Others were reluctant to spend time on the task. Others were prevented from complying by their own line-managers as part of an intra-agency dispute. Others again could not access information within their own databases because they were held in impenetrable paper form. Whatever the reasons, the reality was that no agency had agreed policies and procedures for either giving or withholding access to the data held at its various levels and in its various sub-units. As a result, the agencies themselves were unable to access their own data for strategic planning purposes.

We are concerned here less with the (intriguing and important) issues surrounding data collection and collation in service-providing agencies than with what these issues tell us about the nature of those agencies. Far from the popular picture of highly centralized, monolithic agencies, what we encountered were fragmented and loosely coupled (Weick, 1976) organizations that found difficulty with even the preparatory work for strategic planning — let alone inter-agency collaboration and the development of coordinated multi-service provision. Two factors may account for this. The first is a series of recent reforms particularly in Education and Health, which have deliberately sought to weaken the control exercised by the centres of agencies (the 'old style' Education and Health Authorities) and to devolve power, resources and responsibility to the operating units of the agencies — to schools, GPs, hospitals and so on. The second is a more long-standing orientation of agencies to meeting the presenting needs of individual clients rather than to coordinating strategic preventive action on a wider scale. Put simply, GPs, consultants, teachers and social workers are resourced and organized to work with the individuals in front of them rather than to address issues such as the creation of a 'learning society' or a 'healthy society' or a 'caring society'. This is a theme to which we shall return in due course.

Phase 2

The second phase of the project was a good deal more successful — from the researchers' point of view, at least — though the issues it raises tend to confirm those arising from phase 1. In order to determine service users' views of the services they received or would like to receive, interviews were undertaken with some 65 young adults and their carers, in a variety of individual and group settings. Such interviews, of course, raise significant questions about the asymmetrical power relations between disabled interviewees and non-disabled interviewers, which are part of a much wider range of issues raised by research into disability (Clough and Barton, 1995; Oliver, 1992). Suffice it to say at this point that the research team instituted a range of safeguards that included structuring the interview loosely in terms of areas of 'universal social opportunities' derived from the United Nations Standard Rules on the Equalization of Opportunities for Persons with Disabilities (United Nations, 1993). What this effectively achieved was to base the interviews on the premise that service provision should be viewed less as a matter of responding to immediate need than as a means of facilitating access by disabled people to the same social opportunities as are available to all other people. The implications of this assumption will, we hope, become clear below.

The detail of what interviewees told us was, of course, of considerable significance to the service providers who commissioned the research, and in our report to them (Dyson, Millward and Robson, 1996) we included detailed interview analysis, direct quotation and extended summaries in order to inform their policy debates. For the purposes of this exercise, however, we shall take the risk of summarizing the complex views of interviewees.

Interviewees identified some examples of service provision which they perceived as both appropriate and effective. Young adults and/or their carers frequently expressed their appreciation of services such as respite care, home care, or the provision of technical aids in educational establishments. However, there was substantial evidence in interviewees' comments that many needs currently went unmet and that many services were seen as less than adequate. Young adults with physical and complex disabilities could not travel about the area freely; they did not receive adequate information about the benefits and services to which they were entitled; their opportunities for leisure and employment were limited; they were not fully involved in decisions about their futures and neither were they offered a wide range of choices about those futures. Moreover, where services were particularly good, it often appeared that this was because a well-informed, energetic and assertive service user, carer or professional had galvanized agencies into action through their own initiative rather than because high-quality provision was the norm for all service users.

When examples of service provision were analysed a little further, it became clear that the outcomes for young adults with physical and complex disabilities might be dependent on the actual combination of the disabilities. For example, those young adults with a significant learning disability in addition to their physical disability seemed to have access to a greater range of services. This appeared to be the result of historical patterns of provision rather than of any conscious policy decision. The result, however, was that those young adults viewed as having predominantly a physical disability were more likely to be faced by a service provision which we characterized as *reactive, ameliorative* and *fragmented.*

Provision was *reactive* in that it had a tendency to respond to presenting problems and demands rather than to some more fully worked out notion of need or entitlement. Agencies appeared to depend on a combination of apathy on the part of clients and a holding back of information on their own part in order to maintain levels of provision compatible with their tightly constrained budgets. Clients and their carers who were prepared to ask (or demand) often had their demands met. However, when clients or their carers had atypical need that called for services outside the 'standard' range, or were unaware of the services that were available, their needs often went unmet. At its most positive (and it did have its positive aspects), this reactive stance meant that determined professionals and carers in consultation with individuals and groups could release an impressive array of services. However, there was a large area of merely 'good-enough' provision, which responded to the most obvious needs and demands but went little further than it was compelled to go.

Provision was *ameliorative* in that, in reacting to the most obvious needs and demands, it seemed to have the implicit aim of ameliorating difficulties rather than achieving a degree of social participation equivalent to that of the non-disabled population. Disabled young adults and their carers were certainly not completely confined to their homes, not left without useful occupation, not allowed to become destitute, nor entirely excluded from social activity — and these are not inconsiderable social achievements. However, they could not move around the area freely; their 'useful occupations' might be part-time, unpaid or dead-end; the level of their benefits restricted their freedom of action and standard of living; and their leisure activities depended on the good offices (and — to a young adult — irksome presence) of able-bodied carers. Many (if not all) of their non-disabled peers would expect much more as of right.

Provision was *fragmented* in that there appeared to be no mechanism for coordinating services either at the strategic, whole-population level or at the level of the individual. The most obvious example of this was in the transitional arrangements that operate (or fail to operate) as young adults move out of the school system. The predominantly reactive mode of all three statutory agencies at this point meant that no single agency or individual professional took on responsibility for ensuring that the young adult's needs were known and responded to in a coordinated manner. As a result, young adults and carers were frequently left to pick their own way through a maze of agencies and organizations about which they might well have inadequate information and each of which took responsibility for only a fraction of the services that were needed. What an individual actually received, therefore, depended less on some notion of fully assessed need or entitlement than on the extent to which local branches of agencies were prepared to be proactive, the quality of local provision, and the ability of the individual to trigger agencies into action.

The picture of reactive, ameliorative and fragmented services that emerged from the interviews accords closely with the research team's own experiences in working with the agencies to set up a database. It is one with which disability activists and researchers into disability issues will no doubt be all too familiar. They will also no doubt have found themselves making the recommendations that we made to our commissioning Health Authority — for closer inter-agency collaboration, for the development of a strategic overview of service provision, for the establishment of 'one-stop shops' for agency contact, for a starting point based on rights and entitlements rather than currently available services and for the further involvement of disabled people and their carers in the planning process. Important as these issues are, however, we now wish to return to our original themes — how these findings impacted on our own thinking and what, if anything, they have to tell us about inclusive schooling.

Implications

The first point to make is that the local education authority within whose area this research was conducted has some claims to being regarded as one of the more inclusive LEAs in England. Although its policies have been developed without the fanfare of trumpets that has accompanied the sudden 'discovery' of inclusion elsewhere in recent years, the LEA has, in fact, been developing integrated provision since the 1970s. At the time of the research, although it retained a small infrastructure of special schools, it also had a wide range of satellite classes, resourced provisions and fully integrated settings that enabled pupils 'with special educational needs' to be educated alongside their peers in mainstream schools. A number of our interviewees, for instance, were attending a mainstream comprehensive school which for a number of years had included a significant number of students with physical difficulties both within the building and within mainstream classes. To this extent, therefore, their experience of schooling was one of inclusion.

However, regardless of how inclusive their schools may have been, it is evident that their experience of finding their way in the adult world was very different. Children with physical and complex disabilities in this authority might expect to find themselves provided, as of right, with a range of resources and services within the context of the mainstream school and classroom. As they became adults, however, services became more reactive and patchy. Increasingly, they had to find out for themselves what was available and pursue those services assertively, if not aggressively. Moreover, as the focus of their lives moved from school to work and an adult notion of leisure, so they found themselves more obviously disadvantaged and marginalized: paid employment was elusive; leisure opportunities were limited; mobility was restricted — and so on. There was, in other words, a mismatch between the inclusion that was available in schools and the exclusion that to a greater or lesser extent characterized the adult world. For us as educators, committed to the principle of inclusion and convinced of the significance of our work in this area, this raises some serious questions. What is the relationship between inclusion in schools and exclusion in the adult world? Does inclusive schooling do anything to address these wider issues of exclusion? If so, what exactly does it achieve and how does it do this? If not, is inclusive schooling anything more than a temporary respite from the somewhat brutal realities to follow?

Certainly, it is difficult to find much in the inclusive schooling literature that addresses these questions. There are, to be sure, many writers who see inclusion and exclusion in the education system as part of a wider pattern of social inclusion and exclusion — Keith Ballard's own linking of educational exclusion with the issue of the relationship between dominant and minority ethnic and cultural groups is one obvious example of this (Ballard, 1994, 1995, 1996). However, this is not quite the same as the identification and articulation of the processes whereby inclusive schooling might or might not have a wider impact on processes of social exclusion. The best we have at the moment tends to consist of bland statements and pious hopes such as these:

> There is an emerging consensus that children and youth with special educational needs should be included in the educational arrangements made for the majority of children. This has led to the concept of the inclusive school . . . The merit of such schools is not only that they are capable of providing quality education to all children; their establishment is a crucial step in helping to change discriminatory attitudes, in creating welcoming communities and in developing an inclusive society. (UNESCO, 1994; Framework par. 3)

Much as one may hope that this is the case, the mechanism whereby inclusive schools produce inclusive societies or, alternatively, the overarching political strategy of which inclusive schooling is a part, are far from clear. Certainly, the other empirical claim in this passage — that inclusive schools provide quality education to all children — can be, and has been, vigorously challenged (Reynolds, 1995).

In the short term, for instance, it is clear that there is a role that schools could usefully play, but that does not necessarily happen simply because a school becomes 'inclusive'. If service provision in the adult world is a maze, then schools could usefully prepare their students for finding their way through that maze, in terms both of understanding the services that are available and of developing the capacity to demand the services they need. There is, it seems, relatively little point in providing children with an impressive array of resources and services in school if those services suddenly disappear in the transition to adulthood. This is, of course, by no means a new idea. Nonetheless, it was clear in our work that, despite the relatively high level of inclusion in the authority's schools, young people felt themselves to be ill-equipped to face the adult world. Significantly, the one serious attempt we came across to prepare school-age students to advocate on their own behalf and to pursue assertively the services they felt they needed was being undertaken not by an educator but by a physiotherapist.

In the longer term, the mismatch between educational inclusion and social exclusion also raises issues about the extent to which 'inclusion' should be reconceptualized as a life-long project involving a wide range of social agencies. If, in other words, we are concerned with a significant restructuring of the education service during the childhood years in order to promote inclusion, then should we also be looking at how other services throughout life can be coordinated around similar ends? Our reading of the inclusive schools movement in the UK and — very probably — in the USA is that it is preoccupied with schooling to the exclusion of everything else. Post-compulsory education in scarcely mentioned in the literature, let alone the implications for Health, Social Services and other social agencies. It seems that these areas remain the preserve of 'the great and the good' within the traditional field of special education and of writers in the field of social policy — neither of which groups is much concerned with inclusive schooling. These issues appear to be taken more seriously in other countries, where the divisions between the services may be less rigid and a more holistic view of provision is possible (Stangvik, 1995). It may be, however, that the dominance of the inclusion literature by academics such as ourselves, whose backgrounds are in schooling, actually serves to inhibit the emergence of this broader perspective — a theme to which we shall shortly return.

Beyond this, however, there are wider implications. Although we have so far used the term 'inclusion' to describe some desirable state or process for adults, we are somewhat uneasy in so doing. This is because we perceive a fundamental difference between education and the adult services into which our interviewees were progressing. Education is, in the UK as in many 'developed' countries, a universal service. All children receive it and, for the most part, do so in institutions that are approved by the state and, to a greater or lesser extent, resourced by the state. Where, then, as in the UK, there is a dominant form of education delivered in a dominant type of educational institution, the question as to whether particular individuals and groups are 'included' in those dominant forms becomes a highly pertinent one. Moreover, insofar as the education service is controlled and resourced by the state, it becomes a relatively simple matter for the state to manipulate the system so that inclusion in this sense is increased. In the scale of conceivable social policy reforms, therefore, inclusion, however desirable and important in its own right, is a relatively minor endeavour.

The adult world and adult services are, however, different. By and large, those services cease to be universal and instead become more targeted on some perceived social need: financial benefits go to those who are poor; health care services are provided to those who are ill; social work services are provided for those in social need — and so on. Although some groups access some services on a permanent basis and all individuals are likely to access some services at some times, there is no equivalent to the universal service of education with its dominant forms of provision. There is, therefore, nothing strictly speaking in which individuals and groups can be 'included' in quite the same way as they can be in schools.

Instead, we tend in Western democracies to think in terms of the participation of individuals in some 'normal' range of social activities, or of their access to certain 'basic' rights and entitlements. The UN Standard Rules which we used in our research are, for instance, based on this kind of thinking — on the notion that citizens should be able to move around their areas, access employment opportunities, avoid poverty, live free of discrimination and so on. Inclusion in schooling is certainly an important component in this kind of social participation; however, they are not synonyms, and the difference between them is not merely semantic. Unlike inclusion, social participation is neither fully achievable in state-controlled institutions, nor totally amenable to direct state intervention — at least within the typical parameters of state activity in Western democracies. To take some examples: employment opportunities (and therefore levels of income and poverty) tend to be determined more by the operation of a market economy than by direct state control; discrimination and social acceptance are influenced by legislation but, perhaps more strongly, are the manifestation of pervading social attitudes and structures; mobility is susceptible to state intervention by way of national and local transport policy, but is also a function of the social geography of the environment, which is much more difficult to control.

The ameliorative, reactive and fragmented nature of services which we saw in phase 2 of our research, and the difficulties with strategic planning which we noted in phase 1, are an almost inevitable outcome of their having to operate within such an uncontrollable environment. Within Western democracies as they are currently constituted, health, social services and post-compulsory education simply do not and cannot set out to guarantee in terms of social participation what compulsory education can (if it chooses) guarantee in terms of inclusion. The essential markers of such participation are not in their control in the way that inclusion is in the control of the education service. Since, therefore, they cannot guarantee participation, the most they can set out to do is to lower some of the more obvious barriers to such participation. Agencies, therefore, tend to be oriented towards individual service provision at some point of obvious need — towards the treatment of individual patients by doctors, or the solution of individual problems by social workers rather than towards large-scale intervention in social structures and processes. Put crudely, if they cannot develop a coordinated strategy to make all citizens healthy, wealthy and happy, agencies can at least intervene in individual illness, poverty and misery as and when they arise.

All of this is not to belittle the central importance of state activity in maximizing social participation, nor is it to argue for the acceptance of what many may believe to be a patently unsatisfactory status quo. Rather, it is to highlight the difference between the relatively small-scale social reform that is inclusive schooling and the significant social restructuring that would be necessary to guarantee social participation. Such a guarantee would require the state to find means of controlling aspects of social life that have consistently eluded Western democracies. The delivery of full employment, or the elimination of poverty, or the ending of discrimination would entail a massive effort in lifting the quality of life of socially disadvantaged and marginalized people to the level of that of the majority. Moreover, unlike inclusion, such an effort could not be supported by shifting already committed state resources around the system. At the very least, it would require massive resource reallocation and resource generation, which in turn might require significant social and economic restructuring.

For this reason, the issue of social participation cannot be divorced from fundamental political and ethical questions concerning the sort of society we wish to live in, our notions of social justice, and our political and economic understanding of how such a society can be created and sustained. Simply coordinating existing services more closely — as we advocated in our report and again here — would do little to address the structural inequalities that characterize our society. It would make for more effective amelioration — but only for amelioration nonetheless. Anything more than this requires the development of a thoroughgoing analysis of those inequalities, of a model of a better set of social arrangements and of a plan of (political) action to bring that model into being.

Which brings us back to inclusive schools. Because the call for inclusion is concerned with the hermetically sealed world of education services, it has been possible to make that call with little if any reference to the sorts of analyses, models and plans referred to above. We have suggested previously (Clark, Dyson and Millward, 1995), that the inclusive schools literature tends to focus heavily on the articulation of the values of inclusivity and on the exploration of ways in which schools and classrooms can be made more inclusive in practice. Where a wider critical perspective is found in the literature, we added, it tends to be directed towards the assumptions and practices of segregated special education, and hence to be used as yet further justification for inclusion. These are entirely legitimate and significant concerns, of course, but they do mean that the inclusive schools literature is currently developing its programme with only the most marginal reference to wider issues of social participation and exclusion and to the social structures and processes that underlie them.

The reason for this is, perhaps, not difficult to seek, and relates directly to the theme of 'voice', which is central to this paper. The literature on inclusion is dominated largely by 'people like us' — that is by middle-aged academics on the radical wing of special education. Beyond these lie the practitioners, administrators, policy makers, parental groups and activists through whose efforts inclusive schools come into being and are sustained. All of us, we suggest, have a vested interest in maintaining a tight focus on schooling as such — some because that is our area of expertise, others because that is their field of professional practice, and others again because they see in schooling the possibility of carefully targeted and possibly successful political action. None of us, therefore, has the knowledge or inclination to develop the sorts of wider analyses to which we refer above. Indeed, it may just be that we fight a little shy of these issues in case the ethical certainties on which our position is built prove to be less unproblematic than we would like them to be.

This narrow focus, we suggest, impoverishes the inclusive schools movement in two important ways. First, it diminishes the accounts that can be produced of why schooling is exclusive and how it might become inclusive. Certainly, we have a well-established tradition of critical sociology in special education which Roger Slee (1997), along with the contributors to this volume, is currently developing most powerfully. This tradition is, as we suggested above, particularly illuminating in its critiques of special education and of the exclusionist assumptions and processes that underlie much policy and practice in this area. However, we find that these critiques tend to be much stronger on the deconstruction of those policies and practices than they are either on connecting them to wider social processes or on articulating any sort of political or conceptual programme as an alternative to them. In other words, the tradition of sociological analysis in special education falls foul of precisely the same dilemma as such analysis does elsewhere — that is the dilemma of how to link accounts at the macro-, meso- and micro-levels without either disconnecting the particular from wider phenomena or submerging it in 'grand theory' (Layder, 1993, 1994). It is not, perhaps, entirely unfair to suggest that underpinning many of the critiques in this field is a fundamentally Manichaean account of social processes, in which the forces of evil — a sort of free-floating malevolence on the part of professional educators and policy makers, which binds them unequivocally to their 'self-interest' — do battle with the forces of good — represented by 'people like us' and, in particular, by the similarly unproblematized 'voices' of disabled people.

This inevitably leads to the articulation of programmes of action in terms of 'contest' (Fulcher, 1993) and 'struggle' (Clough and Barton, 1995) in which the processes of 'struggling' and the programme towards which the struggle is striving are taken for granted. At the same time, other contributors to the field are busily developing more 'technicist' (by which we mean the use of a set of standard pedagogic approaches or techniques applicable to a wide range of teaching situations) accounts of how schools, classrooms and pedagogies might be restructured in order to become more inclusive (e.g. Ainscow, 1994; Rouse and Florian, 1996; Sapon-Shevin, 1996; Skrtic, 1991; Stainback and Stainback, 1992; Thousand, Villa and Nevin, 1994; Udvari-Solner, 1996; Villa and Thousand, 1995; Villa, Thousand, Stainback and Stainback, 1992; Wang and Reynolds, 1996 — and many more). There is, however, little connection between the critical analysis of exclusionary practices, the calls for 'struggle' and the technicist programmes for restructuring. The establishment of such connections would constitute a formidable task, which would require the inclusive schools movement to go beyond its traditional concerns and search more widely in the fields of sociology, politics and organizational analysis and development than it currently has been inclined to do. Without these connections, however, it is difficult to see how our accounts will ever be more than fragmentary.

The second implication of the narrow focus of the inclusive schools movement is that it makes it difficult or impossible to consider the contribution that might be made by some more inclusive form of schooling to social participation in the sense in which we have used the term above. We act, speak and write as though the maintenance of the presence of students with disabilities in mainstream schools and classrooms were enough. We thereby overlook questions of what children should be learning in those classrooms, what social purposes are to be served by the education system and how any proposed restructuring of education along more inclusive lines relates to a wider economic, political and social restructuring. We are prevented, therefore, from developing a more sophisticated and powerful notion of inclusion in the light of these questions. In this sense, our critics may have a case when they argue that we focus on the questions of 'place' to the exclusion of all else (Zigmond and Baker, 1995).

One specific example may serve to illustrate at least one of the directions in which the inclusive schools movement might profitably move. The understandable concern of that movement to distance itself from its historical roots in special education has, we believe, led it to overlook some of the valuable work that was undertaken when inclusion was unheard of and integration was still a fairly new idea. One of the basic tenets of that period — subscribed to, we believe, by at least one other 'person like us' in this book (Ainscow and Tweddle, 1979) — was that the segregated world of special education made it possible to develop an 'alternative' curriculum that would in some way be more 'appropriate' to students 'with special needs'. We are now all-too-familiar with the dangers of such assumptions, and too aware of the substandard nature of many 'special' curricula. Nonetheless, some of us tried (however naively) to develop alternative curricula that had a political orientation and a wider social awareness that is notably absent from the curricula in many inclusive schools (Dyson, 1981, 1985; Millward, 1987). We saw the mainstream 'academic' curriculum as being narrow in its scope, irrelevant to the life-long needs of very many students, and oppressive in its effect on students 'with special needs'.

163

Developing alternative curricula that would relate in some more direct way to the lives that students led and were going to lead was thus a means of enabling them to take control of those lives, challenging both the educational structures and the wider social structures which, we believed, so seriously disadvantaged them.

Unfortunately, in its preoccupation with 'place', the inclusive schools movement has substituted for this desire to develop a 'meaningful' curriculum a technicist concern with constructing a sophisticated pedagogy that allows all students to participate in the same curriculum — regardless of the quality, nature and purposes of that curriculum. It is, to be sure, difficult to argue for the inclusion of all students in the mainstream at the same time as arguing that the mainstream is fundamentally inappropriate. Nonetheless, one consequence is that, in the UK at least, the inclusive schools movement (including ourselves insofar as we are part of that movement) has almost entirely disengaged itself from questions of curriculum, and this at a time when the government has imposed on schools a heavily politicized National Curriculum that is, we suggest, inappropriate and irrelevant to the needs of many students — not least, those 'with special needs'. There is, then, an urgent need for us to re-open the curriculum debate, but to do so in the context of the wider social and political issues to which we have referred above.

The inclusive schools movement tends to present itself as a radical departure from the traditions of special education. We beg to differ. The history of special education in recent decades — at least in the UK — is one in which supposedly radical reformers have repeatedly sought ways of breaking down the barriers between special and mainstream education. However, because their focus has been too narrow and the scope of their actions too limited, all they have succeeded in doing is contorting special education into a variety of ever more sophisticated forms without generating the changes in its mainstream environment on which any real removal of barriers depends (Clark et al., 1997). Inclusive schooling as it is currently conceptualized is, we suggest, simply more of the same. The voices — among which we count our own — of liberal academics from within the field of special education are once again, and with the best intentions of the world, busily reconstructing their own sphere of influence and expertise. Such an endeavour is undoubtedly good. The question is — is it good enough?

We appreciate that many colleagues will wish to reject our critique of the inclusive schools movement, and will point to places in the literature or in practice where one or other of the issues we have raised is being dealt with more than adequately. However, we suggest that there is an acid test for inclusive schooling. It is this: could a young person leave a school which was, by common agreement, 'inclusive' and move into an adult world where he or she would experience discrimination, marginalization and disadvantage? If, as we suspect, the answer is 'yes', then there is a challenge for the practice of inclusive schooling. That challenge is to develop a form of inclusive schooling that enables that young person to survive in the short term, and is part of a coordinated attack on the sources of discrimination, marginalization and disadvantage in the longer term. There is also a challenge for 'people like us' — the academics who seek to support inclusive schooling. That challenge is to develop the sorts of powerful and fundamental social and political analyses to which we have referred in the final part of this paper. We freely admit that this is a renewed call for the development of a 'knowledge base' relating to inclusion — a call that we have made previously (Clark, Dyson and Millward 1998). We make it again because we do not believe that the inclusive schools movement has yet risen to this challenge.

References

AINSCOW, M. (1994) *Special Needs in the Classroom: A Teacher Education Guide*, London: Jessica Kingsley Publishers/UNESCO Publishing.

AINSCOW, M. and TWEDDLE, D.A. (1979) *Preventing Classroom Failure: An Objectives Approach*, Chichester: Wiley.

BALLARD, K. (1994) (Ed.) *Disability, Family, Whanau and Society*, Palmerston North, NZ: Dunmore Press.

BALLARD, K. (1995) 'Inclusion, paradigms, power and participation', in CLARK, C., DYSON, A. and MILLWARD, A. (Eds) *Towards Inclusive Schools?*, London: David Fulton, pp. 1–14.

BALLARD, K. (1996) 'Inclusive education in New Zealand', *Cambridge Journal of Education*, **26**, 1, pp. 33–45.

BOOTH, T. (1996) 'A perspective on inclusion from England', *Cambridge Journal of Education*, **26**, 1, pp. 87–99.

CLARK, C., DYSON, A. and MILLWARD, A. (1995) 'Towards inclusive schools: Mapping the field', in CLARK, C., DYSON, A. and MILLWARD, A. (Eds) *Towards Inclusive Schools?*, London: David Fulton, pp. 164–78.

CLARK, C., DYSON, A. and MILLWARD, A. (1998) (Eds) *Theorising Special Education*, London: Routledge.

CLARK, C., DYSON, A., MILLWARD, A. and SKIDMORE, D. (1997) *New Directions in Special Needs: Innovations in Mainstream Schools*, London: Cassell.

CLOUGH, P. and BARTON, L. (1995) (Eds) *Making Difficulties: Research and the Construction of SEN*, London: Paul Chapman Publishing.

DYSON, A. (1981) 'It's not what you do — it's the way that you do it: Setting up a curriculum for less-able high school pupils', *Remedial Education*, **16**, 3, pp. 120–3.

DYSON, A. (1985) 'A curriculum for the "educated man"?', *British Journal of Special Education*, **12**, 4, pp. 138–9.

DYSON, A. and MILLWARD, A. (1997) 'The reform of special education or the transformation of mainstream schools?', in PIJL, S.J., MEIJER, C. and HEGARTY, S. (Eds) *Inclusive Education: A Global Agenda*, London: Routledge, pp. 51–67.

DYSON, A., MILLWARD, A. and ROBSON, S. (1996) *Young Adults with Physical and Complex Disabilities*, Special Needs Research Centre, University of Newcastle.

FULCHER, G. (1993) 'Schools and contests: A reframing of the effective schools debate?', in SLEE, R. (Ed.) *Is There a Desk With My Name On It? The Politics of Integration*, London: Falmer Press, pp. 71–91.

GITLIN, A., BRINGHURST, K., BURNS, M., COOLEY, V., MYERS, B., PRICE, K., RUSSELL, R. and TIESS, P. (1992) *Teachers' Voices for School Change: An Introduction to Educative Research*, London: Routledge.

GITLIN, A. and RUSSELL, R. (1994) 'Alternative methodologies and the research context', in GITLIN, A. (Ed.) *Power and Method*, London: Routledge, pp. 24–39.

LAYDER, D. (1993) *New Strategies in Social Research*, Cambridge: Polity Press.

LAYDER, D. (1994) *Understanding Social Theory*, London: Sage.

MILLWARD, A. (1987) 'Old wine in discredited bottles? Curriculum development for the low attainer', *Oxford Review of Education*, **13**, 3, pp. 297–306.

OLIVER, M. (1992) 'Changing the social relations of research production?', *Disability, Handicap and Society*, **7**, 2, pp. 101–14.

REYNOLDS, D. (1995) 'Using school effectiveness knowledge for children with special needs — the problems and possibilities', in CLARK, C., DYSON, A. and MILLWARD, A. (Eds) *Towards Inclusive Schools?*, London: David Fulton, pp. 109–26.

ROUSE, M. and FLORIAN, L. (1996) 'Effective inclusive schools: A study in two countries', *Cambridge Journal of Education*, **26**, 1, pp. 71–85.

SAPON-SHEVIN, M. (1996) 'Full inclusion as disclosing tablet: Revealing the flaws in our present system', *Theory into practice*, **35**, 1, pp. 35–41.

SKRTIC, T.M. (1991) *Behind Special Education: A Critical Analysis of Professional Culture and School Organization*, Denver: Love.

SLEE, R. (1997) 'Imported or important theory? Sociological interrogations of disablement and special education', *British Journal of Sociology of Education*, **18**, 3, pp. 407–19.

STAINBACK, S. and STAINBACK, W. (1992) (Eds) *Curriculum Considerations in Inclusive Classrooms: Facilitating Learning for All Students*, Baltimore: Paul H. Brookes.

STANGVIK, G. (1995) 'Decentralizing special education in Norway: Developing a follow-up project', paper presented to the New Zealand Association for Educational Research Annual Conference, Massey University, Palmerston North, 7–10 December.

THOUSAND, J.S., VILLA, R.A. and NEVIN, A.I. (1994) *Creativity and Collaborative Learning: A Practical Guide for Empowering Students and Teachers*, Baltimore: Paul H. Brookes.

UDVARI-SOLNER, A. (1996) 'Theoretical influences on the establishment of inclusive practices', *Cambridge Journal of Education*, **26**, 1, pp. 101–19.

UNESCO (1994) *The Salamanca Statement and Framework on Special Needs Education*, Paris: UNESCO.

UNITED NATIONS (1993) *United Nations Standard Rules on the Equalization of Opportunities for Persons with Disabilities* (A/C.3/48/L.3, 1 October 1993), New York: United Nations.

VILLA, R. and THOUSAND, J.S. (1995) (Eds) *Creating an Inclusive School*, Alexandria, VA: Association for Supervision and Curriculum Development.

VILLA, R.A., THOUSAND, J.S., STAINBACK, W. and STAINBACK, S. (1992) (Eds) *Restructuring for Caring and Effective Education: An Administrative Guide to Creating Heterogeneous Schools*, Baltimore: Paul H. Brookes.

WANG, M.C. and REYNOLDS, M.C. (1996) 'Progressive inclusion: Meeting new challenges in special education', *Theory into Practice*, **35**, 1, pp. 20–5.

WEICK, K.E. (1976) 'Educational organizations as loosely coupled systems', *Administrative Science Quarterly*, **21**, pp. 1–19.

ZIGMOND, N. and BAKER, J.M. (1995) 'Concluding comments: Current and future practices in inclusive schooling', *Journal of Special Education*, **29**, 2, pp. 234–50.

Chapter 12

Concluding Thoughts

Keith Ballard

In these concluding remarks it is not my intention to present a summary of the studies. Rather, I want to suggest some ideas about inclusion and exclusion, and about research on inclusive education, that participation in this international project has raised for me. These are not views that are necessarily shared by my research colleagues, although in various forms the issues have been discussed when we have met together to formulate this work. They address in particular the wider contexts within which inclusion is practised, researched and interpreted. I set them down here to include the reader in an ongoing debate.

Special Education, Effective Education and Inclusion

In many of the chapters in this book there is reference to the student who has 'special' needs that are met by the strategies of 'special' education. Often this terminology is part of legislated and organizational arrangements in the education system being described. This categorical discourse maintains the idea that there are two kinds of student and two kinds of education, one special and the other typical, ordinary, not special. Within this dualist conceptualization inclusion can be thought of as a problem of adjustment, a 'technical problem' (Slee, 1997, p. 412) of policy analysis, resource management and teacher training to be resolved by the further development of existing mainstream and special education. Slee (1997), however, rejects this approach, seeing it as an attempt by special education to assimilate disabled students into schools that, while they may strive to cater for all, have not addressed the 'deep culture of exclusion' that pervades their societies (p. 412). This is a culture within which the disabled are defined as 'special', not like us, and where, as Slee (1995) says, teachers can still ask 'what about the twenty nine others . . . with little sense of shame' (pp. 37–8).

While such criticism of special education features in the literature on inclusion, it has been seen as equally important that a critical appraisal be undertaken of the assumptions and possible limitations of inclusive education (Clark, Dyson and Millward, 1995, p. 176). Particular attention in this regard has been given to evidence that increasing the diversity of the student intake may make it more difficult for a school to score well on the comparative league table tests that are claimed to indicate its academic and social performance (Reynolds, 1995). The implication is that, using such measures, inclusive schools will be shown not to be 'effective' schools. This lowered effectiveness seems likely to be exacerbated in systems that devolve responsibility for performance to each school, reduce state spending on education and create a commercial model in which the idea of a common education for all is replaced with a 'hierarchy of unequally funded schools which perpetuate class, gender and ethnic divisions' (Smyth, 1993, p. 8). These education systems increase existing inequalities. In this context disabled and other minority children, who are often overrepresented in schools in poorer socio-economic areas, seem likely to be further disadvantaged (Barton, 1997; Reynolds, 1995), especially where a government sees differential outcomes from schools as part of a natural order of inequalities in society that it is not their wish to change (Walford, 1993).

The tests of effectiveness usually referred to in this debate have become a central component of market theory applied to education. They provide data intended for use by parents when choosing one school over another and by governments for holding teachers accountable for children's learning. Those who do not support a market model of education see such tests as having more to do with the surveillance of teachers and control of the school curriculum than with assessing meaningful goals for education in a democracy (Codd, 1993; Smyth, 1993). Whatever the case, the literature in this area signals that within a market model schools may confront significant challenges to how they operate and how they might assess their per-formance should they move to become more inclusive. There is tension between achieving 'excellence', as defined by government prescribed measures, and equity. Competition among schools leads them to reject disabled and other students who may not enhance their market reputation (Brown and Riddell, 1994). This might be seen as a limitation of inclusion. On the other hand, it may be asked if the difficulties schools experience in a competitive environment should override the equity goal of removing barriers to participation and learning for students. Making explicit the assumptions behind different positions on this and related issues might encourage a debate around underlying concepts and ideologies, and support analysis of the frames of reference that guide policy and practice (Skrtic, 1995b). For example, Cook and Slee (1994/95, p. 12) note that improving education for girls and women has not come about as a result of 'diagnosing individual levels of femaleness' to identify these students' 'special needs', but through challenging gender discrimination in the curriculum and in teaching. The knowledge base for this transformation has been ideological, located in feminist thought and political action opposing patriarchy. As this example indicates, inclusion is not, and never has been, just about 'place', achieving a presence in existing classrooms. Its origins and ongoing challenge involve the politics of identity and difference, a struggle over fundamental beliefs about disability and about education.

Inclusion and School Reform

Listening to voices from inside our education systems as we worked on this book revealed the extent to which students are excluded in present arrangements. Teachers embedded in a sociocultural context that sees disabled and failing students as the responsibility of a medical, curative model of special education may remove students from class, as in the Netherlands study. Even where students remain in the mainstream, our research shows that their particular sensory (Chapter 7), intellectual (Chapter 4) or health-related needs (Chapter 6) may not be met. This evidence for exclusionary pressures might lend support to the idea that, rather than an adjustment to existing practices, inclusive education should be conceived of as a transformation that moves away from thought and actions maintaining segregation and towards creating new, non-discriminatory approaches to the tasks of education.

There now seems general agreement from both those who support and those who oppose inclusion that there is nothing about 'special' education that is not already part of practice in regular classrooms (Audette and Algozzine 1997; Skrtic, 1995a). Rather, special education is supported as a political strategy for ensuring that some students, those who fit predetermined categories, receive additional resources and are not ignored or neglected (Abberley, 1987; Skrtic, 1995a). Restructuring schools from this position seems likely to maintain segregationist thinking through medical model labelling of disabled children as pathologically different (Ainscow, 1997). As Fulcher (1995) suggests, the term 'special educational needs' establishes a categorical status signifying deficit and failure in students, directing attention away from problems in teaching and school organization and constructing a discourse around resources and 'needs' rather than student preferences and rights. An alternative approach is to design schools that respond to student diversity without creating differently valued categories of students. This would seem to require teachers who do not discriminate against 'them' as opposed to 'us' but who, nevertheless, acknowledge and respect the differences of impairment, culture and other experiences that shape the individual (Booth and Ainscow, 1998). These teachers 'discriminate' in the sense that they attend to the particular requirements of individual students, but they do this in the context of accepting responsibility for the education of all children and young people in their community.

Skrtic (1995a) proposes that such thinking is the basis for making better schools. At present, says Skrtic, most schools cope with diversity by eliminating it, moving the disabled and other problematic minorities into 'special' settings or allowing them to be lost through failure, truancy and expulsion. This is because the school is designed to achieve particular goals in highly determined ways from a chosen range of students. In contrast, schools that value diversity emphasize the need to include all students in the culturally valued activities and goals of education. They organize to achieve this through collaborative problem solving, using the uncertainty of diverse demands as a challenge that engenders creativity and flexibility.

Skrtic's proposal is for schools to be redesigned as 'adhocratic' organizations. These respond to student needs by reflective, collaborative, ad hoc problem solving within the school community. The emphasis is on bottom up, rather than top down, management and innovation, focusing on the importance of interactions at the level of teachers and students. These interactions are also the focus of most of the case studies in this book. There is an interesting contrast here with proposals from the literature on effective schools. The goal is similar to that of Skrtic, to create schools in which all children can learn, but in the effective schools model this is to be achieved through identifying a positivist scientific knowledge base that applies across schools and would prescribe good practice to be followed by teachers (Reynolds, 1995). A similar emphasis on conformity to prescribed practice is central to the related proposal that schools might be designed to operate like the 'Highly Reliable Organization', such as air traffic control, that cannot be allowed to fail (Reynolds, 1995). In these organizations teaching would be specified 'in fine detail' and there would be a 'hierarchical form of leadership' to ensure that procedures are adhered to (Reynolds, 1995, p. 125).

Some of the case studies in the present volume might contribute to a knowledge base that could, for example, suggest how professionals and parents might work together (Chapters 3 and 4), what to include in teacher training on disability and difference (Chapters 8 and 9), and the role of students in maintaining a culture of inclusion in a school (Chapter 10). On the other hand, I think that what these case studies also communicate is the individuality of disabled students and the complex determinants of teachers' and other people's responses to them. Julie Allan's study (Chapter 5), for example, showed how in environments with apparently similar pressures for exclusion and inclusion some students resisted while others embraced being identified as disabled, different, special. Such complex knowledge, insight and understanding might be difficult to capture in a prescription for practice, but as part of a teacher's personal knowledge (Donmoyer, 1990; Elbaz, 1991; Polanyi, 1958) might usefully contribute to a 'reflective discourse within a community of interests' which is central to Skrtic's (1995a) adhocratic practice and, he suggests, to democracy, which he sees as 'premised on the principle of innovation through voice, participation, and inclusion' (p. 265).

For Skrtic the reconstruction of schools around these ideas is a major project in which the aim is to educate the 'cultivated citizen', rather than continuing present trends to train students in particular skills believed to serve industry and the economy. He sees working collaboratively as a central goal of education, identified by Dewey as a move away from a 'possessive form of individualism . . . to a social form of individualism' more appropriate for a pluralistic, interdependent society (p. 253). For some of us in our work for this book, when we engaged with people who we thought of as different from us we discovered, and wondered at, our own prejudices and what these meant for our role in society. Such experiences might usefully contribute to discussions on what we mean by participation with others and by inclusion, and how to set out to achieve this. In Chapter 11 Alan Dyson and Alan Millward urge that such a dialogue be located in the wider social and policy contexts of our societies. This might include asking what we mean by citizenship? What do we mean by participation in societies that exclude people through unemployment, poverty and other structurally created discrimination? How does the curriculum and teaching in schools reflect our thoughts and decisions in these areas?

Research and Inclusion

As well as different views on inclusion, this collection also presents several approaches to the research task. The reader will feel more comfortable with some

studies than with others. This is an issue of feelings. Readers will respond emotionally in their support (the experience of pleasure and affirmation in finding ideas
similar to one's own), for example, of the objectivist beliefs of positivist studies
(which for them will represent 'proper' science). These same readers are likely to
reject (with feelings of annoyance or disdain) those research studies here that overtly
include subjectivity and emotion (which they will regard as improper, as not science).
Other readers will identify with (this 'feels right' in terms of their belief systems)
studies using interpretivist thought and research practice (which they see as a legitimate and well established model of science and scientific method). They may pay little
attention to (and will probably not enjoy reading) studies that make realist assumptions and objectivist claims.

For those who doubt that personal feelings and beliefs are deeply involved in
the choice of scientific paradigms, let them begin a discussion along these lines with
people of different persuasions. The politics of research method are as emotional as
any other deeply held convictions and are as much about power, influence and
social control — of researchers and of how the world is to be known and named
(Israelite, 1996; Clough and Barton, 1995) — as the politics of schooling. Research
and education are social activities embedded in historical and cultural contexts, and
both are sites of struggle over whose voice shall prevail and therefore whose ideas
will influence action.

Increasingly, education and social science researchers are aware that those
they study and the society within which they undertake their work will no longer
privilege them as the creators and arbiters of knowledge and meanings. In part this
involves recognition that the dominant positivist enterprise cannot achieve its goal
of providing general laws and information that are believable across cultures and
experiences and of use in particular school and community settings. Equally significant is the challenge to all researchers that their work has often misrepresented
minority groups, including disabled people, has harmed them through this mis-
representation and has failed to contribute to their empowerment and emancipation
(Wood, 1997). Research did not, and does not, 'discover' inclusive education, it
takes part in constructing the meanings of inclusion and creating the practices that
are said to be inclusive (Clough and Barton, 1995). Such work cannot avoid the
critical scrutiny of disability activists and other community groups, who may ask
different questions and have different agendas than those that apply in the peer
review process that we previously have relied on to confirm the acceptability of our
methods and to legitimate the use and development of our concepts and theories.

Disabled people have called for a literature of authentic accounts of their
experiences that will end their invisibility and challenge existing descriptions that
have failed to include them (Oliver, 1997; Morris, 1996). The voices of disabled
students and the recollections of disabled adults on schooling and related issues
may contribute to such work, while the voices of teachers and others involved in
their lives provides a context for analysing what happened to them and why. On the
other hand, interpretive case studies such as those in the present book might be
criticized as voyeuristic (Roman and Apple, 1990) exploitative, or as research as
intellectual tourism (Barnes and Mercer, 1997) with well paid academics adding to

their publication lists and career opportunities by reporting on people who will gain nothing from their involvement in such work (Oliver, 1997). These accounts may be seen as dangerous in maintaining a literature on disability that is not written by disabled people themselves, and that may not be accountable to them. Such work leaves the experience of disability open to readings that are against the realities and the wishes of disabled people and that may be used to further disempower them (Rae, 1997). Also, research that does not engage directly with disabled students, teachers, parents and their allies, in efforts to actually change oppressive practices, may be seen as having no value at best, or as helping to maintain disablist thought and actions.

Attending to such concerns and challenges seems to me to be important for developing inclusive education. In particular this is because much of the work on inclusion research is undertaken in academic and teacher education settings in which there are few, if any, disabled people. I agree that inclusion must refer to more than disability and has to address issues such as culture, poverty and places beyond the classroom and school. Yet I emphasize disability in these comments because, from working with parents of disabled children, I worry about losing a focus on what is clearly unfinished business. Inclusive education developed from the movement for integration through mainstreaming, and this was about disabled students. This movement was originated by parents who sought justice for their children, and its work and achievements owe only a little to academic theorizing, and even less to help from the substantial funding and other resources controlled by researchers. In a similar way, the theorizing of disability as social oppression and challenges to disablism came from disabled people themselves, not from mainstream social and other researchers (Barnes and Mercer, 1996). As can be seen from the present studies, disabled students in our various countries continue to experience prejudice and exclusion. Their struggle is ongoing. Their struggle has helped us to realize that an agenda for inclusion involves confronting educational practices that harm people who differ in other ways too, such as in their beliefs, sexuality and economic circumstances. The struggle by disabled people may be helped by challenges to other forms of discrimination, and may not succeed without these also being addressed, but caution may be needed to see that it is not submerged and diminished in the wider movement.

In the following paragraphs, therefore, I present some ideas on research, disability and education. That is not meant to ignore or diminish other minorities, or to disengage from the interconnected experiences of all those affected by exclusion and the interdependencies of thought and strategies that are needed to create inclusion. To the extent that any of the people referred to here find them of interest, and to the extent that it is appropriate for me as an outsider to the minority experiences named here to present these ideas, I suggest some research strategies that may have relevance for people in subjugated positions.

For research on disability and education, then, one response would be for an emancipatory research agenda over which disabled (or other minority) people have control (Oliver, 1997). The inclusion of previously excluded voices presenting their realities and constructs could engender a radical revision of thought and practice. Morris (1993), for example, says that the personal experiences of prejudice, rejection, and oppression of disabled women, which is not represented in feminist theory, would transform thinking in that area.

This might not be easy to achieve, in part because there are issues to address that are especially challenging, and in part because research communities are as resistant to change and threat to their prevailing positions of power as any other group. Disabled people have seen their own knowledge 'frequently derided as emotional and therefore lacking validity' (Crow, 1996, p. 64), and have been told that their demand for a voice is a threat to the 'independence' of researchers (Barnes and Mercer, 1996, p. 2). Addressing these issues is essential, although this need not mean excluding some people from a research field in order to include others. Inclusion would seem to imply making space for all, anticipating that disablist and other harmful ideologies might then be exposed for scrutiny and challenge (Brantlinger, 1997). In any case, research needs to be sensitive to issues that may not receive attention from those committed to particular goals at particular times, and to the possible missing voices when advocacy is focused on particular people and concerns. For example, some disability activists have been criticized for maintaining a social model of disability that does not acknowledge the effects of impairment (Crow, 1996) or take account of the experiences and needs of those with a chronic illness (Williams, 1996). For such reasons, Shakespeare (1996) suggests, some researchers may take on the responsibility of pursuing an 'independent line', although they should not confuse this with 'being neutral or objective' (p. 117).

One strategy that could bring the experience of disability (or of people who are unemployed, gay, lesbian, or of children — who are also often unheard and unheeded) into researching and theorizing inclusive education would involve offering funding and resources to interested disability (or other) groups. Inviting disabled people to be consultants or participants in research undertaken by predominantly non-disabled people is not the same and, as Maori in New Zealand have found, can result in the minority view being heard but then ignored (Bishop, 1996). People with no knowledge of the lived reality of a culture or experience then dominate the research process and subsequent report. For this reason Maori have called for what they term 'parallel development' (Walker, 1987, p. 156), a situation where the funding available to Pakeha (European) institutions is available in equitable proportion to their own organizations. The integrity of Maori procedures and knowledge are then maintained, approaches to research from within their own culture are developed (Bishop, 1996), and their research findings may also be made available to the wider community. Coming together in a sense of identity to write their own history and analyse their own contemporary subjugated experience has been seen as important by feminists (Brown and Smith, 1992) and by linguistic and cultural minority groups such as the deaf (Lane, 1992). An apparently exclusionary practice allows for inclusion in the wider society from a position of collective strength that can challenge the ideas, practices and power structures developed within the self-referencing dominant groups of that society.

I suggest this as but one possible strategy. Others, such as people working collaboratively as allies, may also be valued by minority groups. Nevertheless, it may seem odd that, at the end of a book on inclusion, I suggest that people might separate off and work among themselves, for a while at least. Yet this seems to me to be worthy of consideration at this stage in the history of the countries and cultures represented in this book. Each chapter contains evidence that mainstream school and society often know little about disability and, despite some valuable instances of inclusion, continue to exclude disabled people from experiences available to other citizens. Separate development that is chosen and enacted by a minority group asserts their wish for self-determination while retaining the right to participation in mainstream settings and agendas. This is not the same as forced segregation that denies people opportunities legitimately available to others (Ferguson and Asch, 1989). Withdrawal may be for specific tasks and until such time as the balance of power shifts to allow minorities to have an effective say in control of their lives. It would confirm that inclusion is neither an assimilationist practice nor a simple process that will be easily understood or achieved, and that it therefore warrants the strength that comes from diverse thought and effort.

Can Research Make a Difference?

Cautiously, Fulcher (1995) suggests that research that acknowledges the political nature of the issues in disability and education might help people to 'suspend the analysis' they currently use and 'reframe' the ideas that organize their interactions in these areas (p. 20). Shakespeare (1996) says that action, rather than research, will lead to change. Nevertheless, he sees a role for studies that offer evidence for a social problem and for analysis that alters people's consciousness, helping them to advance disability rights more forcefully. Noddings and Witherell (1991) see stories and narrative as research that may motivate us to action because they present us with 'real people in real situations struggling with real problems' (p. 280) and this challenges us to think how we might respond to their needs and wishes.

The reader's role is central in terms of generalization and action from studies such as those in the present collection. An agricultural model of sampling strategies and statistical probability does not apply here (Maling and Keepes, 1985). But in any case it is always the users of research who generalize a study, who ask themselves if they believe what they have read and, if so, how it might apply to situations they work in and how to assess critically and ethically the validity and usefulness of their decision. Even where people and settings are dissimilar from one's own, involving different cultures, for example, a reading that influences us becomes part of our personal knowledge, and so part of the experience that we bring to solving problems in our own work and lives (Donmoyer, 1990; Polanyi, 1958). This personal knowledge might include, but is more than, what some describe as the 'scientific knowledge base' for their work. A study that speaks strongly to us might be experienced as almost real, as if we had taken part (Donmoyer, 1990, p. 192), so that, for example, I have the sense that I have met Tordis, and that I have watched those students in the school that Mel Ainscow, Tony Booth and Alan Dyson introduced us to. They are people who now influence how I think and what I consider doing. It is the users of research who make complex, often intuitive judgements, translating what they have read and expanding their imagination of how things are and how they might be different (Donmoyer, 1990).

There are different ways of researching the world just as there are different ways by which people may be moved to action. The studies in this book have been shaped by the idea that there is value in an understanding of personal experiences and meanings, those of participants and of researchers. Personal accounts can make the abstractions available in samples and statistics, principles and theory, alive and real, perhaps causing us to care about what happens to another person (Noddings and Witherell, 1991). The emotion of caring may move us to action, and it is our individual selves, as teachers and citizens, who are 'the ultimate source of organisation and change in any social setting' (Ferguson and Ferguson, 1995, p. 107). This is not to individualize issues as the medical model does, it is not the reductionism of positivist thought, nor is it the individual gaze of educational psychology (Olssen, 1993), all of which have contributed to locating disability and other oppressed experiences in the person and not in their environments. What I suggest here is concern for the individual in political, cultural and material context, and for action, individual and collective, focused on changing those contexts to meet people's rights and needs, not fitting people into modified but still problematic regimes. This attention to the individual reflects, I think, what Skrtic (1995a, after Dewey) refers to as social individualism, sensitive to the 'interdependent community of interests' of an inclusive democracy (p. 253).

Exclusion and Inclusion

In his critical history of IQ testing, Stephen Jay Gould (1981) showed how these fundamentally flawed psychometric instruments are linked to a culture of exclusion given life through racism, eugenics and the incarceration of those deemed intellectually inferior. Gould ended his book with an epilogue reporting on Doris Buck, a women sterilized without her consent under an American law that from 1924 to 1977 sanctioned these operations for people 'considered feeble minded and antisocial' (p. 335). Her story is one profound instance of pain and loss that gives the reader a direct, personal link to the implications of a powerful exclusionary ideology and its meaning in people's lives.

Ideas similar to those challenged by Gould a decade ago have recently returned to prominence through Hernstein and Murray's (1994) book *The Bell Curve*, in which they propose that IQ, ethnic origin and poverty are genetically linked; that a growing and intellectually inferior underclass is a threat to the well-being and order of society; and that an end to affirmative action and welfare payments would encourage the poor into work and discourage them from breeding. Hernstein and Murray envisage that an economically privileged 'cognitive elite' (p. 91) will increasingly be segregated from people who are poor because they 'are not very smart' (p. 142). The success of this book and its 'anachronistic social Darwinism', says Gould (1995), would seem to 'reflect the depressing temper of our time — a historical moment of unprecedented ungenerosity' (p. 4).

In my collection of New Zealand newspaper cuttings I have an article under the headline 'Poor are poor because they are stupid' (Johnson, 1996, p. C6) and another in which one of our senior politicians (Roger Douglas, minister of finance in the 1984–90 Labour government) is reported saying that a growing and dangerous underclass in New Zealand will eventually have to be 'fenced off' in some parts of the country (Clifton, 1996, p. C1). These ideas, supported in Hernstein and Murray's book and in related sources (Murray, 1984; Olasky, 1992), derive from the claim that some people are biologically and morally inferior to others. They contest, or ignore, the effects of New Right libertarian economic and social policies that have deliberately created increased levels of unemployment and poverty in New Zealand (Kelsey, 1993) as elsewhere (Galbraith, 1992; Saul, 1997). Whatever the readers' politics or their position on individual versus systemic explanations for poverty, Hernstein and Murray's ideas would seem clearly to involve pressures for exclusion rather than inclusion. Challenging these ideological pressures in our respective societies will be part of developing schools and communities that value inclusion.

In the second of our research group's projects, Tony Booth and Mel Ainscow (1998) urged that we attend to exclusion as well as inclusion, and I will close this book repeating that idea. I will also close acknowledging that some readers (and probably some of my research colleagues) might have sought a framework, structure or model that would organize the research undertaken and presented in this volume in a more integrated way than does the notion of insider voices. It is probably true that such a task was beyond my conceptual powers, but it is also true that from the beginning of the project I have worked with the idea that listening to people on their own terms is important and that, while there is a place for common parameters and coordinating theory, it might not always be necessary to tell the reader how to think in this way. In any case, I like John Ralston Saul's (1997, p. 195) proposal that 'The virtue of uncertainty is not a comfortable idea, but then a citizen-based democracy is built on participation, which is the very expression of permanent discomfort.'

We cannot be certain about what inclusive education is at this, or perhaps any later time. We can engage with people and ideas to work on what it might be, reducing barriers to participation and learning as we go.

References

ABBERLEY, P. (1987) 'The concept of oppression and the development of a social theory of disability', *Disability, Handicap and Society*, **2**, pp. 5–19.

AINSCOW, M. (1997) 'Towards inclusive schooling', *British Journal of Special Education*, **24**, 1, pp. 3–6.

AUDETTE, B. and ALGOZZINE, B. (1997) 'Re-inventing government? Let's re-invent special education', *Journal of Learning Disabilities*, **30**, 4, pp. 373–83.

BARNES, C. and MERCER, G. (1996) 'Introduction: Exploring the divide', in BARNES, C. and MERCER, G. (Eds) *Exploring the Divide: Illness and Disability*, Leeds: The Disability Press, pp. 1–16.

BARNES, C. and MERCER, G. (1997) 'Breaking the mould? An introduction to doing disability research', in BARNES, C. and MERCER, G. (Eds) *Doing Disability Research*, Leeds: The Disability Press, pp. 1–14.

BARTON, L. (1997) 'Inclusive education: Romantic, subversive or realistic?', *International Journal of Inclusive Education*, **1**, 3, pp. 231–42.

BISHOP, R. (1996) *Collaborative Research Stories: Whakawhanaungatanga*, Palmerston North, New Zealand: Dunmore Press.

BOOTH, T. and AINSCOW, M. (1998) 'From them to us: Setting up the study', in BOOTH, T. and AINSCOW, M. (Eds) *From Them to Us: An International Study of Inclusion in Education*, London: Routledge, pp. 1–20.

BRANTLINGER, E. (1997) 'Using ideology: Cases of nonrecognition of the politics of research and practice in special education', *Review of Educational Research*, **67**, pp. 425–59.

BROWN, S. and RIDDELL, S. (1994) 'The impact of policy on practice and thinking', in RIDDELL, S. and BROWN, S. (Eds) *Special Educational Needs Policy in the 1990s: Warnock in the Marketplace*, London: Routledge, pp. 214–35.

BROWN, H. and SMITH, H. (1992) 'Assertion, not assimilation: A feminist perspective on the normalisation principle', in BROWN, H. and SMITH, H. (Eds) *Normalisation: A Reader for the Nineties*, London: Tavistock, pp. 149–71.

CLARK, C., DYSON, A. and MILLWARD, A. (1995) 'Towards inclusive schools: Mapping the field', in CLARK, C., DYSON, A. and MILLWARD, A. (Eds) *Towards Inclusive Schools*, London: David Fulton, pp. 164–77.

CLIFTON, J. (1996) 'The artful Roger', *Sunday Star Times*, 3 March, p. C1.

CLOUGH, P. and BARTON, L. (1995) 'Introduction: Self and the research act', in CLOUGH, P. and BARTON, L. (Eds) *Making Difficulties: Research and the Construction of Special Educational Needs*, London: Paul Chapman, pp. 1–15.

CODD, J.A. (1993) 'Managerialism, market liberalism and the move to self managing schools in New Zealand', in SMYTH, J. (Ed.) *A Socially Critical View of the Self-managing School*, London: Falmer Press, pp. 153–70.

COOK, S. and SLEE, R. (1994/95) 'Schools, failure and disability', *Education Links*, **49**, Summer, pp. 11–13.

CROW, L. (1996) 'Including all our lives: Renewing the social model of disability', in BARNES, C. and MERCER, G. (Eds) *Exploring the Divide: Illness and Disability*, Leeds: The Disability Press, pp. 55–73.

DONMOYER, R. (1990) 'Generalizability and the single case study', in EISNER, E.W. and PESHKIN, A. (Eds) *Qualitative Inquiry in Education: The Continuing Debate*, New York: Teachers College Press, pp. 175–200.

ELBAZ, F. (1991) 'Research on teacher's knowledge: The evolution of a discourse', *Journal of Curriculum Studies*, **23**, 1, pp. 1–19.

FERGUSON, P. and ASCH, A. (1989) 'Lessons from life: Personal and parental perspectives on school, childhood and disability', in BIKLEN, D., FERGUSON, D. and FORD, A. (Eds) *Schooling and Disability*, Chicago: National Society for the Study of Education, pp. 108–40.

FERGUSON, P.M. and FERGUSON, D.L. (1995) 'The interpretivist view of special education and disability: The value of telling stories', in SKRTIC, T.M. (Ed.) *Disability and Democracy: Reconstructing (Special) Education for Postmodernity*, New York: Teachers College Press, pp. 104–21.

FULCHER, G. (1995) 'Excommunicating the severely disabled: Struggles, policy and research-ing', in CLOUGH, P. and BARTON, L. (Eds) *Making Difficulties: Research and the Con-struction of Special Educational Needs*, London: Paul Chapman, pp. 6–24.

GALBRAITH, J.K. (1992) *The Culture of Contentment*, Harmondsworth: Penguin Books.

GOULD, S.J. (1981) *The Mismeasure of Man*, Harmondsworth: Penguin Books.

GOULD, S.J. (1995) 'Mismeasure by any measure', in JACOBY, R. and GLAUBERMAN, N. (Eds) *The Bell Curve Debate: History, Documents, Opinions*, New York: Times Books, pp. 3–13.

HERNSTEIN, R.J. and MURRAY, C. (1994) *The Bell Curve: Intelligence and Class Structure in American Life*, New York: The Free Press.

ISRAELITE, N.K. (1996) 'On feeling right: A paradigmatic epiphany', in HESHUSIUS, L. and BALLARD, K. (Eds) *From Positivism to Interpretivism and Beyond: Tales of Transformation in Educational and Social Research (The Mind-body Connection)*, New York: Teachers College Press, pp. 56–60.

JOHNSON, P. (1996) 'Poor are poor because they are stupid', *Sunday Star Times*, 28 January, p. C6.

KELSEY, J. (1993) *Rolling Back the State: Privatisation of Power in Aotearoa/New Zealand*, Wellington: Bridget Williams Books.

LANE, H. (1992) *The Mask of Benevolence: Disabling the Deaf Community*, New York: A. A. Knopf.

MALING, J. and KEEPES, B. (1985) 'Educational research and evaluation', in EISNER, E. (Ed.) *Learning and Teaching the Ways of Knowing: Eighty-fourth Yearbook of the National Society for the Study of Education*, Chicago: NSSE, pp. 265–85.

MORRIS, J. (1993) 'Feminism and disability', *Feminist Review*, **43**, pp. 57–70.

MORRIS, J. (1996) 'Introduction', in MORRIS, J. (Ed.) *Encounters with Strangers: Feminism and Disability*, London: The Women's Press, pp. 1–16.

MURRAY, A. (1984) *Losing Ground: American Social Policy, 1950–1980*, New York: Basic Books.

NODDINGS, N. and WITHERELL, C. (1991) 'Epilogue: Themes remembered and foreseen', in WITHERELL, C. and NODDINGS, N. (Eds) *Stories Lives Tell: Narrative and Dialogue in Education*, New York: Teachers College Press, pp. 279–80.

OLASKY, M. (1992) *The Tragedy of American Compassion*, Washington, DC: Regnery.

OLIVER, M. (1997) 'Emancipatory research: Realistic goal or impossible dream?', in BARNES, C. and MERCER, G. (Eds) *Doing Disability Research*, Leeds: The Disability Press, pp. 15–31.

OLSSEN, M. (1993) 'Science and individualism in educational psychology: Problems for practice and points for departure', *Educational Psychology*, **13**, 2, pp. 155–72.

POLANYI, M. (1958) *Personal Knowledge: Towards a Post-critical Philosophy*, Chicago: University of Chicago Press.

RAE, A. (1997) Chair, British Council of Disabled People, personal communication, Leeds, 4 September.

REYNOLDS, D. (1995) 'Using school effectiveness knowledge for children with special needs — the problems and possibilities', in CLARK, C., DYSON, A. and MILLWARD, A. (Eds) *Towards Inclusive Schools*, London: David Fulton, pp. 109–26.

ROMAN, L.G. and APPLE, M.W. (1990) 'Is naturalism a move away from positivism? Materialist and feminist approaches to subjectivity in ethnographic research', in EISNER, E.W. and PESHKIN, A. (Eds) *Qualitative Inquiry in Education: The Continuing Debate*, New York: Teachers College Press, pp. 38–73.

SAUL, J.R. (1997) *The Unconscious Civilisation*, Harmondsworth: Penguin Books.

SHAKESPEARE, T. (1996) 'Rules of engagement: Doing disability research', *Disability and Society*, **11**, 1, pp. 115–19.

SKRTIC, T.M. (1995a) 'Deconstructing/reconstructing public education: Social reconstruction in the postmodern era', in SKRTIC, T.M. (Ed.) *Disability and Democracy: Reconstructing (Special) Education for Postmodernity*, New York: Teachers College Press, pp. 233–73.

SKRTIC, T.M. (1995b) 'Theory/practice and objectivism: The modern view of the professions', in SKRTIC, T.M. (Ed.) *Disability and Democracy: Reconstructing (Special) Education for Postmodernity*, New York: Teachers College Press, pp. 3–24.

SLEE, R. (1995) 'Inclusive education: From policy to school implementation', in CLARK, C., DYSON, A. and MILLWARD, A. (Eds) *Towards Inclusive Schools*, London: David Fulton, pp. 30–41.

SLEE, R. (1997) 'Imported or important theory? Sociological interrogations of disablement and special education', *British Journal of Sociology of Education*, **18**, 3, pp. 407–19.

SMYTH, J. (1993) 'Introduction', in SMYTH, J. (Ed.) *A Socially Critical View of the Self-managing School*, London: Falmer Press, pp. 1–9.

WALFORD, G. (1993) 'Self-managing schools, choice and equity', in SMYTH, J. (Ed.) *A Socially Critical View of the Self-managing School*, London: Falmer Press, pp. 229–44.

WALKER, R. (1987) *Nga tau Tohetohe: Years of Anger*, Auckland: Penguin Books.

WILLIAMS, G. (1996) 'Representing disability: Some questions of phenomenology and politics', in BARNES, C. and MERCER, G. (Eds) *Exploring the Divide: Illness and Disability*, Leeds: The Disability Press, pp. 194–212.

WOOD, R. (1997) 'Doing disability research: For the benefit of the few or the good of the many?', paper presented to the International Conference on Doing Disability Research, University of Leeds, 3–5 September.

Notes on Contributors

Mel Ainscow is Professor of Special Needs and Educational Psychology in the Faculty of Education at the University of Manchester. He is also Dean of the Research and Graduate School. His recent publications include *From Them to Us: An International Study of Inclusion in Education* (Routledge) and *Understanding the Development of Inclusive Schools* (Falmer). Currently he is involved in a series of studies looking at issues of inclusion and exclusion in classrooms, schools and educational systems.

Julie Allan is a Lecturer in Education at the University of Stirling, Scotland. She has been involved in a number of research projects on inclusion and is currently researching special schools in Scotland. Her book, *Actively Seeking Inclusion*, is also published by Falmer.

Jeff Bailey is Professor of Special Education, University of Western Sydney, Nepean, and Director, Children's Hospital Education Research Institute, Royal Alexandra Hospital for Children, Sydney, Australia. He has published widely on attitudes toward disability, computing in special education, and the role of psychology in special education. His current research is in the area of Attention Deficit Hyperactivity Disorder (ADHD), the reintegration of students with chronic illnesses into schools, and the assessment of educational outcomes for students with intellectual disabilities.

Keith Ballard is an Associate Professor in the Department of Education at the University of Otago, New Zealand. His research interests are inclusive education, action research with families of disabled children, and qualitative methodologies. With Lous Heshusius, York University, Ontario, he recently edited a collection of studies, *From Positivism to Interpretivism and Beyond: Tales of Transformation in Educational and Social Research (The Mind-Body Connection)*, Teachers College Press, New York, in which researchers examined their experiences of paradigm shift.

Belinda Barton is the Coordinator and Research Associate at the Children's Hospital Education Research Institute, Royal Alexandra Hospital for Children, Sydney, Australia. Her current research is on hospitalized students with chronic illnesses returning to school, and the social aspects of children and adolescents with Neurofibromatosis Type 1. She is also involved in the clinical assessment of children, and enjoys statistics.

Tony Booth is a Senior Lecturer in Education at the School of Education, Open University, UK. He has been researching and writing about processes of inclusion and exclusion within education policy and practice, in the UK and internationally, for the last twenty years.

Colleen Brown is a Senior Lecturer in Communication Studies at the Manukau Institute of Technology, New Zealand. She heads an advocacy group, the Coalition of Parents for Special Education, and is on the Board of the government's Specialist Education Service. Her present research is on advocacy for the parents and caregivers of disabled children.

Alan Dyson is Professor of Special Needs Education and Director of Research in the Department of Education, University of Newcastle upon Tyne, UK. He has published widely in the field of special needs education and is a member of the Advisory Group on Special Educational Needs which is working on the implementation of the recently published Green Paper in England. He has been at Newcastle University since 1988. Prior to that, he spent 13 years as a teacher in special and mainstream schools in Newcastle and elsewhere in the north-east of England.

Trevor McDonald is an Educational Consultant (Special Education), Community School District Two, New York. His background is in primary and special education. Prior to moving to New York in 1997 he taught at the Dunedin College of Education, New Zealand, and completed his doctoral thesis at the University of Otago on the communication experiences of people with severe disabilities. His present research interests include people with severe disabilities and support strategies for teachers in inclusive settings.

Alan Millward is a Senior Lecturer in Education and Co-director of the Special Needs Research Centre at the University of Newcastle upon Tyne. Before joining the University he worked as a teacher in both special and mainstream schools. He has worked extensively with teachers and schools in developing their responses to children with special educational needs. He has published and researched widely in the field of special educational needs, completing a number of funded research projects for the British government and other agencies.

Kari Nes is an Associate Professor in Teacher Education and Postgraduate Special Teacher Education at Hedmark College, Hamar, Norway. She has been a teacher and counsellor in special education, working primarily in mainstream settings. Her present research is in the areas of integration, the concept of 'one school for all', and in problem-based learning in teacher education.

Sip Jan Pijl is a Senior Researcher at the Groningen Institute for Education Research, University of Groningen, The Netherlands, and a staff member of the Interuniversity Centre for Educational Research (ICO). He works part-time for the European Agency for Development in Special Needs Education located in Denmark. He is involved in studies on the integration of students with special needs into regular education, and has conducted international comparative research on integration.

Ysbrand J. Pijl works as a Senior Researcher at the Groningen Institute for Education Research, and at the Institute for Social Psychiatry, at the University of Groningen, The Netherlands. He has published research on selection and decision making in both regular and special education. Articles on artefacts in educational research show his interest in statistical methods and research design.

Marit Strømstad is an Associate Professor in the Department of Teacher Education, Hedmark College, Hamar, Norway. She worked as a speech therapist in institutional settings until 1991 when she moved to her present position to pursue her interest in how to change schools and educate teachers for the inclusive school. Her research at present is on the role of collaboration and supportive group work in classrooms and on teacher education for inclusion.

Kees P. van den Bos is an Associate Professor of Learning Disabilities in the Special Education Section, Department of Education, University of Groningen, The Netherlands. He coordinates the special interest group on learning difficulties at the University. The emphasis in his research and teaching activities is on learning difficulties, and he has published several articles on reading problems.

Linda Ware is an Assistant Professor of Special Education at the Warner Graduate School, University of Rochester, New York. Her research interests include issues of identity and resistance among youth with disabilities, curriculum issues informed by parents, and the uses of narrative in qualitative research.

Index